The Garments of Court and Palace

Also by Philip Bobbitt

Tragic Choices (with Guido Calabresi)

Constitutional Fate: Theory of the Constitution

Democracy and Deterrence: The History and Future of Nuclear Strategy (with
Lawrence Freedman and Gregory Treverton)

United States Nuclear Strategy: A Reader

Constitutional Interpretation

The Shield of Achilles: War, Peace, and the Course of History

Terror and Consent: The Wars for the Twenty-First Century

The Garments of
Court and Palace

Machiavelli and the World That He Made

PHILIP BOBBITT

ATLANTIC BOOKS
London

Published in Great Britain in 2013 by Atlantic Books, an imprint of Atlantic Books Ltd.

10 9 8 7 6 5 4 3 2 1

A CIP catalogue record for this book is available from the British Library.
Hardback ISBN: 978 1843546849
E-book ISBN: 978 1782391425

Printed in Great Britain by
TJ International Ltd, Padstow, Cornwall

Atlantic Books
An imprint of Atlantic Books Ltd
Ormond House
26–27 Boswell Street
London
WC1N 3JZ

www.atlantic-books.co.uk

For Guido Calabresi

Il miglior fabbro

Italy at the End of the Fifteenth Century

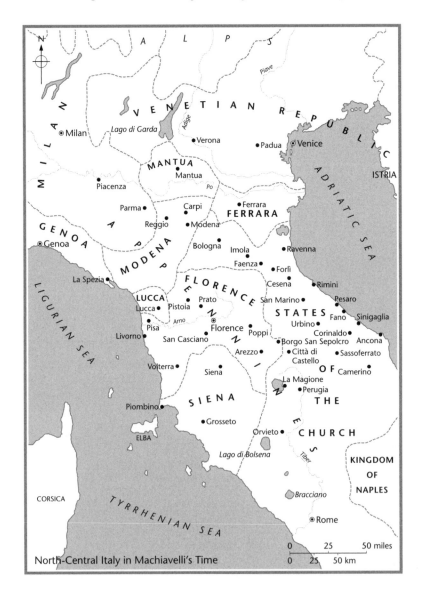

North-Central Italy in Machiavelli's Time

Contents

* Readers who are unfamiliar with Machiavelli's life and times may want to read this abbreviated biography first, though they run the risk that the main text will then seem repetitive. Other readers may prefer to consult this section occasionally to clarify the sequence of events, or skip it entirely.

Prologue

Arte dello Stato – The Machiavelli Paradox

THERE CONTINUES TO be enormous interest in Machiavelli and his works, but it is not entirely clear why this is so.[1] *The Prince* is often described as a great book that changed the world, yet while it is doubtless secure in its inclusion in a canon of such books, it has been so variously and contradictorily interpreted that any change in the world it may have brought about is likely to have been through a kind of horrible inadvertence that would have amused, though perhaps not surprised, Machiavelli.

Indeed, there remain a number of controverted questions about even the most basic of Machiavelli's views. Was he a forthright totalitarian or a human rights-respecting republican? Was he a Christian or a pagan? Did he give priority to the lawgiver or the war fighter? Was he essentially an ethical writer or an unabashed amoralist? Was he the first political scientist, attempting to do for statecraft what Galileo sought to do for cosmology, or was he a committed sceptic where prediction is concerned? Was he a Renaissance humanist or a neoclassical realist? Did he believe that the affairs of mankind were determined or that there was a decisive role for individual free will?

There are passages in Machiavelli's works that would appear to support each of these antinomies, and there are some writers who have concluded that his ideas were simply incoherent, while others have decided that they were written in the code of satire or of some gnosticism even more oblique. In the course of this book, my own views on each of these questions will become evident, and though

I have tried to marshal evidence for my interpretive conclusions, I would be surprised if many of the facts or passages to which I draw attention, while perhaps new to some general readers, were not familiar to the large collegium of Machiavelli scholars. I hope, rather, that my particular perspective – that of a constitutional lawyer and historian of diplomacy and strategy – has offered a means of putting these excerpts, events and surmises into a persuasive and sensible pattern; and that the concepts I have elaborated in previous books and introduce again here provide a structured and useful way to understand the complex and sometimes apparently contradictory body of Machiavelli's work.

My book is a commentary, which Harvey Mansfield – one of the most gifted scholars of Machiavelli – has trenchantly defined: 'A commentary,' he writes, 'attempts to bring forth and interpret the author's intent, and so supposes that he has one, that it is worth finding, and that it is not manifest on the surface.'[2] My principal objective is to empower the reader, so that she can read *The Prince* armed with analyses that I have provided, and come to the conclusions that she judges to be right as to Machiavelli's purposes. In that sense, this book shares with *The Prince* itself a desire to put aside many orthodoxies that appeal to persons interested in the affairs of state but which, if actually applied, would undermine their power to understand and practise statecraft – a power that Machiavelli tirelessly sought to enhance. I believe that once Machiavelli is read in the way that I suggest – as the clear-sighted prophet of a new constitutional order with its basis in the union of strategy and law – his works can be very helpful indeed to the diplomat and the statesman. Furthermore, because he saw something on the historical horizon – the emergence of the modern state and its fundamental ethical qualities – that is still relevant to us and will be so long as we have states, he will remain influential. Finally, because we are entering an era not unlike Machiavelli's own in which a new constitutional order is emerging, his work will become the subject of even greater contemporary interest.[3] The morphology of the state was first depicted by Machiavelli with his description of the princely state, a constitutional order that would evolve, successively, into the kingly states, territorial states, imperial state-nations, and eventually the industrial nation states within which we now live. This achievement is clearer now than it has ever been, just as it is now clearer that he was grievously misunderstood by his feudal contemporaries.

Five particular ideas have structured the understanding of *The Prince* since it was posthumously published in 1532, and it is these basic background assumptions that have given rise to those long-standing scholarly problems that remain so notably prominent in the study of Machiavelli's work and which are themselves artifacts of the Machiavelli Paradox.[4] That paradox is: how can a man's body of work mark him out as one of the most – perhaps *the* most – influential political philosophers since Aristotle when there is such profound disagreement over what he was actually saying?

The first of these background understandings is that *The Prince* is a 'mirror book' – that is, it is exemplary of a genre going back to classical times in which the writer advises a prince or official at court how to behave. Cicero's *De officiis* provides a model for this genre, but so too do a number of other influential examples.* *The Prince* is obviously a radical departure from books of this kind because it does not advise a ruler to adopt the classical virtues and indeed urges that, in some contexts, the ruler should depart from such a practice. The observation that *The Prince* is a kind of perverse mirror book is the

---

* Such as Baldassare Castiglione's *The Book of the Courtier* and Erasmus' *Institutio principis Christiani* ('Education of a Christian prince'), written as advice to King Charles of Spain (later the emperor Charles V); and John Skelton's *Speculum principis*, a work written for the future Henry VIII and presumed lost. A copy of this treatise, which may not be the one presented to Henry, is in the British Museum; see F. M. Salter, 'Skelton's Speculum Principis', *Speculum*, vol. 9 (1934): 25.

basis for the claim that a Machiavellian prince is one who disdains classical or Christian virtues – a claim that has provoked much controversy. But both the claim and the controversy, though derived from this background understanding, are not identical with it. Critics may differ as to whether Machiavelli is writing his mirror book to serve as a warning or as a guide, but they agree that it falls into the category of mirror books either way.

The second basic understanding is that *The Prince* is a work that seeks to serve autocracy and therefore appears to be incompatible with the republican ideas Machiavelli expressed in his *Discourses on the First Ten Books of Livy* (hereinafter the *Discourses*). This observation has given rise to the following questions: was Machiavelli lying about his true preferences when he wrote *The Prince*? Did his views change as he became older? Is the corpus of Machiavelli's work inconsistent, or is it perhaps coded in some way to hide his true preferences because they were likely to offend his political patrons?

The third fundamental notion is that *The Prince* represents Machiavelli's solution to the problem of destiny and fate. *The Prince* counterposes two ideas – *fortuna* and *virtù*. It answers the question whether or not a prince can control his fate by suggesting that he can, mainly through the sufficient exercise of *virtù*. The metaphor for this struggle between *fortuna* and *virtù* given by Machiavelli is that of a mighty river, the currents and tides of fortune, that is banked and directed by levies, the product of human ingenuity and enterprise. The principal example of a leader of such *virtù* in *The Prince* is the violent, Nietzschean figure of Cesare Borgia, of whom Machiavelli appears to be a star-struck fan. But this observation, too, has given rise to some difficult questions. Because Cesare Borgia ultimately fell and did not master so much as suffer his fate; because Machiavelli suggests with respect to other contemporary figures – Pope Julius II and the Florentine *gonfaloniere* Piero Soderini among them – that it is the temper and character of the times that determine success; and because he concludes that no man's nature is so flexible that it can invariably adapt to the change in the times – for these reasons it would appear that *virtù* is not sufficient to determine destiny. To account for this contradiction, it has often been suggested that perhaps Machiavelli came to the latter, more despairing view late in life when he found himself far from power and no longer able to influence events.

Fourth, it is well known that *The Prince* was originally dedicated to Giuliano de' Medici, ruler of Florence, and it has long been assumed – an assumption for which there is good evidence[5] – that it was prompted by the possibility that Giuliano, who was acquainted with Machiavelli and whom Machiavelli admired, might restore him to his role as secretary to the Florentine chancery. This is why some writers describe *The Prince* as an 'employment application'. But this interpretation raises the problem of the actual dedication to Giuliano's successor Lorenzo, who was not favourably disposed to Machiavelli and of whom there is no evidence that he in fact ever read the work or even received it. Moreover, Machiavelli's grandiloquent conclusion to *The Prince*, his exhortation to liberate Italy, seems absurdly out of place when proffered to the incompetent and syphilitic Lorenzo.

Finally, it is often claimed that in *The Prince* Machiavelli separates politics from ethics. For many humanists, it is suggested, the correct political choice is the proper ethical choice; the good is the true and vice versa. For Machiavelli, by contrast, the prince must sometimes make choices that do violence to the very values that Machiavelli accepts as virtuous – values that differ little from those of Renaissance humanists. This raises the following questions (among others): is *The Prince* the beginning of political science, because it separates fact from value? Is Machiavelli 'a teacher of evil', who initiates the modern era's detachment of political activity from any governing moral rules?

It is my view that each of these fundamental, structuring ideas about *The Prince* is mistaken, and thus that the problems they create for scholarship are largely pseudo-problems, or at least greatly exaggerated ones. By this argument I mean to resolve the Machiavelli Paradox with a single, consistent and comprehensive reading. I realize this is a radical and even hubristic conclusion by one who is not a Renaissance scholar, much less a specialist in the secondary literature of Machiavelli scholarship. How will I sustain such bold claims?

I will argue that the missing element in our reading of *The Prince* and its companion masterpiece, the *Discourses*, is their constitutionalism. Machiavelli stood at the cusp of a change in the constitutional order from a feudal order to that of the first modern state, the princely state of the sixteenth century. He was almost alone in recognizing this, and his writings must be read accordingly. This can be confusing because sometimes the same word – *lo stato* ('the state'), for example – must be read in different ways, depending on whether Machiavelli is referring to the estate of the prince, his status, or the novel idea of a princely state – a new constitutional order; and doubtless this is in part responsible for the initial misunderstanding of his work by his contemporaries. Reading Machiavelli in the light of its constitutional purposes, and their relation to the developing strategic scene that emerged in Italy in the late fifteenth century, reframes each of these five background assumptions.

In the present book, I will take up Machiavelli's ethics and morality; his ideas of how a state should, as a practical matter, be governed; his understanding of the historical processes of state formation; and his own personal experiences as these reflected the changing constitutional order. I will claim that *The Prince* is not principally a mirror book at all but basically a constitutional tract, with consequences for his moral precepts that were widely misrepresented; that Machiavelli is, and always was, committed to the constitution of republican government endorsed in the *Discourses*, which the precepts of *The Prince* do not repudiate or contradict; that his theories of *fortuna* and *virtù* can only be reconciled by understanding them within this constitutional context and in light of his extensive diplomatic and strategic experience, which continued until almost the end of his life; and that the writing of *The Prince*, like other crucial initiatives in Machiavelli's life, and indeed the structure of the book itself and its puzzling consummation, were consequences of the strategic opportunities offered to Italian rulers when this change in the constitutional order from feudalism to the princely state presented itself to them – opportunities that Machiavelli saw at first hand and desperately tried to illuminate for the political leaders of his day.

This is the Machiavelli of constitutional and strategic studies, whose great treatise on these subjects and their relation to each other has been unappreciated as such. This Machiavelli is the true source of his importance, and so my criticism and commentary will be directed at him, and neither at the necromancer of evil portrayed by some of his critics, nor at the benign liberal humanist depicted by others. It is not that the conventional scholarship is plainly wrong – it is not – but that, without this constitutional dimension, it is radically incomplete and therefore misleading.

What follows this Prologue, therefore, is that understanding of Machiavelli's great works which finds resonances and harmonies in my studies of the relationship between history, strategy and law. This is my Machiavelli, the constitutionalist. I hope that I will be pardoned for this personal perspective; as Isaiah Berlin once observed with respect to Machiavelli's critics, 'where more than twenty interpretations hold the field, the addition of one more cannot be deemed an impertinence.'

The Unholy Necromancer and his Koran for Courtiers

Thomas MORE: Master Rich is newly converted to the doctrines of
  Machiavelli.
Richard RICH: Oh no.
Duke of NORFOLK: Oh, the Italian. Nasty book, from what I hear.
More's daughter, MARGARET: Very practical, Your Grace.

Robert Bolt, *A Man for All Seasons*, Act 1

'THE END JUSTIFIES the means' is perhaps the most famous
statement Machiavelli never made. As a number of scholars
have pointed out, this phrase is actually 'a gross mistranslation' of a
key passage in *The Prince*:[1] *e nelle azioni di tutti li uomini, e massime de'
principi, dove non è iudizio da reclamare, si guarda al fine.** The much-
quoted fragment – *si guarda al fine* – can be translated as 'one must
consider the outcome', but in context it really refers to the consequences of his acts for the stature of the prince – that is, to the blame
or praise he earns – not to the relationship between means and ends
generally.[2]

It should not surprise us that readers often prefer to take their
learning from another person's critique of a classic, which will marshal many sources besides the one under consideration and thus

---

* Bondanella translates the passage: 'in the actions of all men, and especially of
princes, where there is no impartial arbiter, one must consider the final result.'
Bondanella and Musa, *The Portable Machiavelli* (Penguin, 1971), p. 21.

provide the reader with the makings of a plausible erudition, while saving him the chore of studying the text unaided. There is an unfortunate history of books that bowdlerize Machiavelli's words, beginning not long after the initial publication of the *Discourses* in 1531 and *The Prince* in 1532. In 1576 a Huguenot essayist, Innocent Gentillet,[3] published a book in French, *Discours sur les moyens de bien gouverner et maintenir en bonne paix un royaume ou autre principauté: Contre Nicolas Machiavel florentin*, in which he offered fifty maxims allegedly derived from the *Discourses* and *The Prince,* each maxim followed by an acerbic discussion. These ripostes attacked what Gentillet apparently believed to be Machiavelli's position on the use of courtiers (three maxims); the role of religion in establishing a state (ten maxims); and the appropriate rules for a prince in governing (thirty-seven maxims). Gentillet savaged as odious and pernicious the maxims he himself had translated. He appears to have believed that a Florentine love of deceit, added to a lust for violence, had entered French life with the person of Catherine de' Medici – the daughter of the Medici duke to whom *The Prince* is dedicated and the persecutor of the Protestant Huguenots – who had instructed her court in the ways of Italian politics by indoctrinating them with Machiavelli's ideas. Thus began the poisonous portrait – the embodiment of state treachery, evil and violence – whose legacy we have inherited. Gentillet's maxims do constitute a sort of mirror book, as they strip Machiavelli's work of its constitutional elements entirely.

The next year, 1577, Gentillet's book was translated into Latin, *Commentariorum de regno aut quovis principatu recte & tranquille administrando, libri tres: Adversus Nicolaum Machiavellum Florentinum,* by another Huguenot refugee, with an accompanying preface warning the English against Machiavellian ideas, which he claimed had been responsible for the oppression of Protestants in France, including the notorious St Bartholomew's Day massacre. Then, in 1602, the first English edition of Gentillet appeared, *A Discourse upon the Meanes of Wel Governing and Maintaining in Good Peace, a Kingdome, or*

Other Principalitie: Against Nicholas Machiavell the Florentine, which was actually a translation of the Latin version.*

Although the *Discourses* and *The Prince*, Machiavelli's two principal works, were not published in English until 1636 and 1640 respectively, it has been decisively shown to be a mistake to assume, as was once generally the case, that Machiavelli was unknown to Elizabethans except through Gentillet. There were various editions in Italian, French and Latin in English libraries, though these were relatively rare. We have, for example, the memorandum of the Lord Chancellor of England, Stephen Gardiner, who in 1553–5 advised Philip II of Spain, Queen Mary's husband, how to manage the English. Gardiner's manuscript simply adopts large passages from the *Discourses* and *The Prince* (some 3,000 words). Because he does so without attribution, we might infer that persons in the Renaissance English court were generally familiar with the original works.

We do know from letters and diaries that during this period people in England read Machiavelli, however, and we know that a reading knowledge of Italian was available to many people. Italian was widely taught at the Henrician court, Elizabeth I spoke it, and it was considered an essential accomplishment of an English courtier. The poet Thomas Wyatt was familiar, for example, with Luigi Alamanni's poetry and translated an epistolary satire of the Florentine poet (Alamanni was a close friend of Machiavelli and a member of the Orti Oricellari, and it was to him that Machiavelli had dedicated a short book). But for a similar reason – the court's ease with and access to French works – it would be a mistake to assume that because Patericke's English edition of Gentillet did not appear until 1602, Gentillet's damning portrait of Machiavelli was unknown to Elizabethan readers. Quite the contrary, we can see as early as

* This edition bore the date 1577, which has confused many scholars, who assume that its author Patericke delayed publication until 1602; it is now generally agreed that the 1577 date was simply copied from the Latin edition.

1578 the pervasive influence of Gentillet in England. The best example is the Cambridge scholar Gabriel Harvey,[4] 'who found the false version more fertile than the true one . . . who knew the original well and as a scholar should have respected it, yet who submerged the scholar in the pamphleteer and used Gentillet's text because of its more lurid possibilities in drama and invective'.[5]

That same year, John Stockwood delivered and published 'A Sermon preached at Paule's Crosse'. In it, Stockwood claimed to be horrified by

> the most wicked assertion of the vnpure Atheist Machiavel, who shameth not in most vngodly manner to teach that princes need make no accounte of godlynesse and true religion . . . This poyson and a greate deale more suche filth blusheth not this malaperte and pelting Town-clerk of Florence to spew out, teaching Princes not to make accounte of religion, or godlynesse: and yet must this vile beaste in many courtes of other nations be the only Court booke, nay the Alcoram and God of courtiers, whose diuellish precepts they put in dayly use, learning to be godlesse. The Lord graunte he take no place among our courtiers.

This last complaint – that Machiavelli had written a Koran for courtiers[6] – comes verbatim from Gentillet.[7]

Even scholars who had taken the trouble to acquaint themselves with Machiavelli's original text nevertheless have often found Gentillet's misrepresentations irresistible. As late as 1603, Sir Richard Barckley was still repeating the slur about a 'Courtier's Koran'.

There were notable exceptions, including the great figures of Alberico Gentili and Francis Bacon.[8] Lord Clarendon saw what was happening and wrote in the middle of the seventeenth century that 'Machiavel was in the right, with those who take what he says from the report of other men . . .'[9] Generally, however, it was Gentillet's distorted and maimed account that captured the imagination because his impressions offered the enduring mould of infamy.[10] Sometime around 1590, an actor stepped onto a London stage and delivered the prologue to Marlowe's *The Jew of Malta*. The actor invoked the spirit of Machiavelli, who claims not to have died in 1527 but to have possessed the soul of the French Catholic leader, the Duc de Guise, who had brutally suppressed Protestants in the recent French wars of religion and, following his death by assassination, has now flown to England:

> Albeit the world think Machiavel is dead,
> Yet was his soul but flown beyond the Alps;
> And now the Guise is dead, is come from France
> To view this land, and frolic with his friends.
> To some perhaps my name is odious;
> But such as love me, guard me from their tongues,
> And let them know that I am Machiavel.[11]

Soon, in *Henry VI, Part 1*, Shakespeare was referring to 'that notorious Machiavel', and in *Henry VI, Part 3* he has Gloucester claim:*

> I can add colours to the chameleon,
> Change shapes with Proteus for advantages,
> And set the murderous Machiavel to school.[12]

This adoption of the image of Machiavelli's prince as a glamorous embodiment of evil reaches its apogee in Milton's portrait of Satan in *Paradise Lost*.[13] The Prince of Darkness is a riveting portrayal of what Milton believes is flawed in *The Prince* – *virtù* without Christian

---

* Indeed, this play provides a nice example of princes who failed because they did not heed the advice in *The Prince*. For purely personal reasons, Edward IV neglects to make a dynastic marriage, proving that he is unfit to be a prince, and his followers desert him. Only the unscrupulous Gloucester is depicted as understanding the arts of a ruler; as Clifford says in Act 2, Scene 6: 'And, Henry, hadst thou sway'd as kings should do, Or as thy father and his father did, Giving no ground . . .' I am indebted to Paul Woodruff for this observation.

virtue – while at the same time presenting Hell as a lawless principality dependent on the whim of a single leader, an idea that actually resonates with Machiavelli's claims in the *Discourses* that republics are to be favoured because of their stability and moderation. Still, it is the diabolical depiction that has given us the notion 'Machiavellian' for manoeuvres that reflect a Mephistophelean preference for guile and cruelty.*

While there are passages in *The Prince* that, standing alone, apparently advocate a ruthless perspective towards politics, we shall see in the ensuing chapters that to be properly understood these passages must be integrated into the whole of Machiavelli's work and related to his diplomatic experiences, the constitutional context within which he was writing, and the historic strategic events that occurred in Italy during his lifetime.

Still, this insistent question remains: what was it about Machiavelli that brought him to the attention of the world in such a diabolical light – a light that has continued to play upon his enigmatic features and doubtless accounts, in part, for his fascination?† They say the devil always has the best lines, and there is much epigrammatic writing in Machiavelli that would ensure his fame, especially if his thoughts were unsettling and provocative. But there are other factors besides clever wordplay that account for the shock and discomfort produced by Machiavelli's work.

Each of the following elements set the stage for a shattering

---

* That is no doubt why the violence-prone rap artist Tupac Shakur decided to adopt the pseudonym 'Makaveli', why Mussolini described *The Prince* as 'the statesman's supreme guide', why Hitler kept a copy by his bedside, and perhaps why one was found in Napoleon's abandoned coach at Waterloo. There is even a lyric expressing the Machiavellian posture against conventional virtue in the Broadway musical *Camelot*, 'The Seven Deadly Virtues'.

† Indeed, Mansfield chides Maurizio Viroli for sanitizing Machiavelli and, in the process, making him less compelling. Harvey C. Mansfield, review of Viroli's *Machiavelli*, *American Political Science Review*, vol. 93, issue 4 (1999): 964.

reversal of the expectations of Machiavelli's readers. As we shall see, there was a profound change in the constitutional order of Europe as feudalism gave way to the first princely states, the nature of which change Machiavelli was the most prescient observer and the most skilled analyst but which very few others appreciated. Moreover, the wholesomely didactic genre into which Gentillet's amputations appeared to fit – the mirror book for feudal princes – is outrageously upended by the content of *The Prince*, which advocates a wholesale rejection of the advice given to princes in this genre at least as far back as Cicero, and indeed even of the purposes of advice itself. Furthermore, it must be conceded that standing alone – stripped of its companion volume on republics, the *Discourses* – *The Prince* invites misunderstanding and exaggeration, partly because of its brevity and curtailed scope. Finally, Machiavelli's struggle to reconcile men's fates with their talents and their luck led him to a unique resolution that rejected both the humanist and the Christian assumptions of the period, and while this foreshadowed by centuries the notion of the collective virtuosity of groups, it mystified his contemporaries.* In the present book, I will take up each of these striking reversals of expectation. Each aggressively challenged the assumptions of Machiavelli's day and perhaps even disabled his initial readers from seeing him rightly. The awful pity is that some readers today still suffer from those original misimpressions. I hope to show how he ought to be remembered – as one of the great constitutional theorists.

Niccolò Machiavelli was, like his most important precursor

---

* 'The essential function of Machiavelli's republic is to organize men's natural efforts at satisfying their desires in such a way that they collectively generate far more glory, dominion and wealth than they could have attained individually.' Kenneth Austin, reviewing Markus Fischer's 'Well-Ordered License: On the Unity of Machiavelli's Thought', *Sixteenth Century Journal*, vol. 33, issue 2 (2002): 539, 540.

Thucydides, a philosophically inclined writer who drew on human experience as he had known it in the service of the state in order to understand and help others understand the nature of political action. Thucydides, who had served the Athenian city state as a leading general, was interested in the classical state as a collective historical entity – its mores, its illusions and its sustaining self-concepts. Correspondingly, Machiavelli, who had served extensively as a Florentine diplomat and senior bureaucrat, was interested in the ethical consequences of the newly emerging neoclassical state – principally, the requirements of a new ethos of individual action when a person acts on behalf of the state.

Thucydides gave us the intellectual discipline of historical studies; it is from him we have inherited those elements of dispassion, the marshalling of evidence, and the refusal to accept supernatural intervention as the decisive factor of human affairs that characterize the historian. There is a remarkably similar legacy in Machiavelli's work that counsels us to avoid wishful thinking, free ourselves of hypocrisy when we assess our own acts, and realistically appreciate the varieties of qualities essential to successful statesmanship. But unlike Thucydides' bequest, Machiavelli's has not given us a unified discipline. It has instead brought forth a Rorschach kaleidoscope of conflicting interpretations that is of dubious practical value. This is the paradox of Machiavelli.

Machiavelli was in fact the poet-philosopher of the princely state, the author of the very idea and requisites of the neoclassical modern state. This is his most important legacy, not the means and manoeuvres which he futilely recommended to his uncomprehending contemporaries that they might achieve the establishment of such a state. He was a Christian adversary of the Renaissance Church, it is true, but he is neither an ecclesiastical reformer with theological motives like Luther nor a prophet unarmed like Savonarola. He was the most significant figure since Thucydides to recognize and illustrate the fundamental, mutually affecting relationship between law and war that determines the character of the state. He anticipated by five centuries the description of political argument as requiring, inevitably and irreducibly, the recursion to the human conscience* to resolve political disputes. Though he did not describe it as such, he was an advocate of the 'duty of consequentialism' that arises from the responsibility of a leader to a democratic republic. Finally, there is in *The Prince* and in the *Discourses* – which works taken together we might simply call *The State* – an implicit assertion of the condition of social scarcity, the idea that we can never serve all our values to the fullest at the same time.[14] The recognition of this fact of social and political life led Machiavelli to his concept of the cycling of policies and personalities he describes in his works, as we struggle over time to preserve the values we have undermined and are forced to abandon the values we have served.

* See Philip Bobbitt, *Constitutional Interpretation* (Blackwells, 1991), pp. 163 *et seq.*

Book I

Ordini – The Important Structure of *The Prince*

T HE OVERALL ARCHITECTURE of *The Prince* belies the assumption that it is merely a mirror book, and instead conclusively establishes that it is principally a treatise on the constitutional order. But what difference does this make? Why is it so important whether *The Prince* is simply a mirror book? Because it was the misunderstanding of his purpose that permitted – no, forcefully invited – contemporary reaction to Machiavelli as a fiend. Expecting a mirror book, his readers were given a mirror instead.

Chapter 1

The Emergence of the Modern State

THE MOST SIGNIFICANT terms the student of *The Prince* must master are *virtù* and *fortuna*; chapter 7 of the present work is devoted to an analysis of these terms and their significance for Machiavelli's work. But there is another concept – *ordini* – that is also crucial, because it was the potential emergence of the *ordini* of the modern state that provoked Machiavelli's visionary insights.[1] Because the notions of *virtù* and *fortuna* dominate *The Prince*, while the idea of *ordini* is the most significant term in the *Discourses*, *ordini* has generally been neglected as a concept that is critical for our understanding of *The Prince*.[2]

Ordini refers to the institutional and constitutional structures and ethical assumptions associated with, but not limited to, the basic laws of the state.[3] Perhaps its closest English equivalent is the term 'constitutional order'. Today, most of the states of the developed world are industrial nation states, the constitutional order that dominated the twentieth century and which arose in the late nineteenth century in the United States and Germany. But the first modern states, which arose in the early sixteenth century, were not nation states but princely states.

At the end of the fifteenth century, the constitutional order of medieval society was not divided into separate states, with each prince a sovereign within his own territory and no persons or territories remaining outside the domain of princes. Quite the contrary, a complex system of overlapping duties and entities prevailed. Vertical power was horizontally limited: for example, while a prince could demand military service from the feudal vassals who were obligated to him, and while some of these lesser lords owned land to which peasants were attached, the prince had no direct authority over his vassals' peasants. Moreover, medieval Christendom was regulated by the universal, overarching Church that spanned all societies and which by the fifteenth century had supreme jurisdiction over wills and marriages in all sectors. Finally, an urban stratum of medieval society comprising artisans, merchants and townspeople of various functions was in many aspects of life independent of both the clergy and the nobility. A great number of these townspeople were Jews, who, though often operating under severe civil restrictions, were largely autonomous. Some cities were self-governing; some were under princely patronage.

The princes of this constitutional order did not rule territorially, in the sense of having a fixed settlement and identification with that locality and its people. Nor were they the princes of states: rather, they governed scattered realms, each with a rudimentary household apparatus that was impermanent and fixed only to the person of the prince. As Adam Watson, a distinguished diplomat and international relations theorist, once observed: 'Medieval Christendom was not yet a society of politically distinct states. But first in Italy, and then throughout the area, the complex horizontal structure of feudal society crystallized into a vertical pattern of territorial states, each with increasing authority inside defined geographic borders.'[4]

Throughout the first half of the fifteenth century, Ottoman Turks threatened Christian Constantinople. This increasing peril drove a population of talented people westwards to Italy, many of them educated in the classical traditions of which Constantinople had been the repository. When the city finally fell in 1453, its defeat was engineered by the introduction of a military technology that also ultimately doomed the city realms of Italy and that would summon forth the modern state.

The huge iron cannon of the Ottoman commander Mehmet II that eventually battered into rubble the hitherto impregnable walls of Constantinople were too unwieldy for anything but lengthy, fixed sieges. But when French engineers used the techniques for founding church bells to make lighter-weight bronze cannon, they brought about a revolution in warfare. These were the cannon that Charles VIII brought with him when he invaded the Italian peninsula in 1494.

In 1498 the Venetian Senate declared that 'the wars of the present time are influenced more by the force of bombards than by men at arms'. Machiavelli, writing in 1519, reflected that after 1494 'the impetus of the artillery is such that there is no wall so thick that it will not collapse in a few days'.[5] Suddenly the high walls, turrets, towers, and moats that ringed the city centre were rendered obsolete. The wealthy but weak cities of Italy needed much greater revenues in order to tear down their now vulnerable high stone curtains and to replace them with lower walls, further out from their city centres, on which they could place their own artillery to keep besieging forces at bay. They needed larger and more reliable military forces than the hastily recruited and unreliable *condottieri* on whom they had depended. They needed alliances and treaties that would outlast the persons of their signatories, the perishability of which had been an unfortunate feature of medieval jurisprudence. They needed ambassadors who could stay for extended periods at foreign courts and manage alliance relations and report intelligence, and indeed the first permanent legations date from this period.[6] They needed an administrative apparatus that could raise and spend these revenues and that could maintain the complex logistics of peninsular warfare. In short, they needed states. Thus, the modern state originated in the transition from the rule of princes to that of princely states that necessity wrought on the Italian peninsula at the end of the fifteenth century.[7]

All the significant *legal* characteristics of the state in international law – embodied in formal terms such as legitimacy, personality, continuity, integrity and, most importantly, sovereignty – date from the moment at which these human traits, the constituents of human identity, were transposed to the state itself. This occurred when princes, to whom these legal characteristics had formerly been attached, required the service of a permanent bureaucracy in order to manage the demands of a suddenly more threatening strategic competition.[8]

Besides the immigration from Constantinople, there were several other factors that made Italy the birthplace of the new constitutional order that succeeded the feudal realms of Europe. The peninsula was dominated by five cities: Rome, Naples, Florence, Milan and Venice. These realms were well defined and contiguous, as opposed to the often disparate and contended dynastic inheritances of princes. Also, the cities were wealthy – Florence had an annual income greater than that of the king of England and the revenue of Venice and its *terra firma* at the middle of the fifteenth century was 60 per cent higher than that of France – in a world that had recently come to a money economy.[9] These cities could afford a bureaucracy and could profit by it. Moreover, the wealth of these cities was coveted by others – and by each other – yet their populations were too small to create effective forces, requiring them to rely for defence on mercenaries or foreign forces lent to them. From 1494 Italy became the prize for which Spain, France and the Holy Roman Empire contended. Spain had been consolidated with the marriage of Ferdinand and Isabella which united Castile and Aragon; France had been united after the defeat of the English and the Burgundians. Now, all eyes in Europe were focused on the security of these rich, fragile Italian city realms as they faced the new and menacing technology that would render vulnerable the sheltering walls and trenches that had protected them from predators. Men of letters and artists were urged to design countermeasures to the artillery that invaded Italy. Leonardo's notebooks of this period contain sketches for a machine gun, a primitive tank and a steam-powered cannon. Michelangelo repeatedly submitted drawings of fortifications that he thought would withstand bombardment by the new technologies of warfare.

Finally – and as we shall see, perhaps most importantly – excepting the Venetian Republic, the leadership in each of these cities faced a crisis of legitimacy.

The European medieval landscape had been roughly split into two parts. To the west were realms where dynastic power had devolved on princes who were hemmed in by customary law, the autonomy of their vassals and nobles, and the local rights of towns. These were domains where the principle of dynastic legitimacy was sound, but the power of the prince was circumscribed; once liberated by the constitutional innovations of the princely state, these realms would surpass that constitutional order and create a new one, the kingly state of the seventeenth century.

In the east and in central Europe, princes were subject to the dual universality of the pope and the Holy Roman Emperor, both elected rulers representing complex, competing interests. As cities in Italy and princely realms in the Netherlands and parts of Germany began to assert their independence and to accumulate wealth and power, they found themselves subject to assaults on their legitimacy because their assertions of independence were endorsed neither by the papacy nor by the Holy Roman Empire. As Adam Watson put it, 'The most conspicuous Italians, from the Medici, the Sforzas and the Borgias down to dozens of smaller rulers, had power without legitimacy. The Western kings had legitimacy without much power.'[10]

The defining characteristic of an *ordino*, of a constitutional order, is its basis for legitimacy. The constitutional order of the industrial nation state, within which we currently live, promised: give us power and we will improve the material well-being of the nation. The constitutional order of feudalism conferred legitimacy by dynastic descent: give us power, it proclaimed, because our father (or uncle) had it. But what would confer legitimacy on the novel constitutional order of princely states in Italy whose rulers were 'new' princes

– persons with attenuated dynastic claims (if any) who had come to power through recent events of their own making?[11]

Consider the situation of the leaders of the principal cities. In Milan the ruling dynastic line had ended in 1447. One candidate for the succession was Francesco Sforza, a *condottiere* and the husband of the last male heir's illegitimate daughter. The Holy Roman Emperor, Frederick III, claimed the duchy of Milan as forfeit to the empire, there being no rightful dynastic claimant; the kings of France and Spain also pressed dynastic claims to the duchy.

Florence was said to be a republic but was effectively ruled by the Medici. Cosimo de' Medici had returned from exile in triumph in 1434 to dominate the Signoria, an oligarchical governing body. Through his command of credit and capital, Cosimo was able to rule Florence without any dynastic claim to authority; indeed, much of his success depended upon his maintaining the fiction that he was but one citizen among many. But because the Medici rule thus depended upon ever fresh proofs of competence and patronage, it was always vulnerable to the disenchantment of the public.

In Rome the papacy was held by a Catalonian family, the Borgias. Pope Alexander VI behaved in every way like a Renaissance prince, delegating authority to his children and using the powers of the papacy – including excommunication and the interdict – in order to further the expansion of his family's power. Yet he did not have the dynastic imprimatur of a prince and could not assure the succession of his illegitimate progeny.

Naples was in the possession of the Spanish king after a century of disputed successions, recurrent revolutions, turmoil and anarchy. The city's location provided a base to Spain from which further adventures might be launched while its instability presented a temptation to France to assert its claims to the Neapolitan realm. It also provided an example to the other cities of Italy of what might happen to them if the great kings outside the peninsula were to invade.

To these problems of legitimacy Machiavelli proposed an answer.

This was the creation of the neoclassical* state itself, which would enable the Italian cities to reorganize themselves strategically and which would shore up the stature of the leaders that brought about this reorganization. As Machiavelli put it:

> It is hardly surprising that none have been able to do what it is hoped will be done by your illustrious House, nor that in so many revolutions in Italy and in so many manoeuvres of war it always appears that the faculty of military ability seems to have become extinct. Our previous methods of warfare have become outmoded and no one has yet been able to create new ones. Nothing could bring so much honour to a rising man as discovering such new laws and new orders.[12]

The 'new laws and new orders' he proposed amounted to a reification by which the princely state was objectified and separated from the person of the prince. This meant that, while the prince who successfully defended the state would achieve legitimacy for himself, the state itself would be immortal, guaranteeing a process of legitimacy for itself that was not dependent on any particular dynastic line.

These insights, however, led directly to a fatal misapprehension of Machiavelli's work. His counsel to new princes – the rules and methods he counselled them to employ – was misread by feudal commentators and Renaissance humanists alike as brutal and uncivilized advice to princes of the status quo. For the same reason, Machiavelli's separation of a prince's personal morality from his duty to protect the state baffled and horrified critics with its separation of Christian ethics from political action.

I will argue in the coming chapters that Machiavelli's practical advice for establishing, maintaining and defending a princely state, while often counterintuitive and refreshingly direct, was in fact novel

* 'Neoclassical' because it recapitulated the classical idea of the state as embodied in the Greek city states and the Roman Republic.

only to the extent that the constitutional order itself was novel; those aspects of Renaissance statecraft that appeared most sinister actually had ample historical precedents (and contemporary examples, for that matter). Machiavelli's statecraft does not constitute his original contribution to statesmanship; indeed, his preferred method is to give examples from his own diplomatic experiences and from antiquity, illustrating his advice. His originality lies in the constitutionalism his advice is meant to serve, and to sever the two – to focus on the craft while ignoring its purposes – leads to a number of misapprehensions.

Despite many claims to the contrary, Machiavelli did not separate ethics from political action, nor did he deride Christian virtues. As we shall see, his depiction of the two faces of princely leadership – the personal and the institutional – was essentially ethical in nature. Bifurcated and no longer coterminous, as had been the case with feudal leaders, these two faces turned towards different spheres of action and responsibility. When Machiavelli writes that he loves Florence more than he loves his own soul, he is not suggesting trading one for the other, but showing that – as was not the case with feudal princes – he could distinguish between governing and living.

The Prince is a profoundly constitutional book, foreshadowing the changing constitutional order in Europe and the emergence of the first modern states. That is why it is devoted to the situation of a 'new' prince who must find a source of legitimacy. While that fitted the situation of the Medici, Borgias, Sforzas and other leaders who did not have a dynastic claim to power, Machiavelli's solution – the princely state – was about much more than simply finding a source of legitimacy for any particular powerful family or city oligarchy. The princely state is, by definition, a 'new order of things'. The necessity for such a state is what links all parts of *The Prince* – the nature of various principalities, the crucial role of the army, the behaviour and tactics of the prince, and above all the creation of the new state of Italy itself – and links *The Prince* to the *Discourses*. 'Therefore,'

Machiavelli wrote, 'so that Italy may at last find its redeemer, this opportunity must not be permitted to pass by.'[13]

After 1494 Machiavelli devised the following proposals:

(1) Florence should rely on a conscripted militia instead of mercenaries; the love of gain would inevitably corrupt the *condottieri* who would avoid decisive battles to preserve their forces, betray their employers to a higher bidder, and seize power when it became advantageous.

(2) The 'new' prince must create institutions that would evoke loyalty from his subjects which in other countries was underwritten by the feudal structure of vassalage.

(3) Because legal and strategic organizations were interdependent, strong and dependable arms were needed to protect the integrity of the principality, especially its laws, and a strict adherence to law was required to ensure the loyalty of the 'new' prince's subjects.

(4) Permanent embassies and sophisticated sources of intelligence must be maintained in order to enable successful diplomacy.

(5) An enduring governmental structure must be created that would outlive the vagaries and temperament of any particular prince and on which the prince and his successors could rely.

All of these recommendations were impelled by one conclusion: rulers must cease to be merely princes and must develop princely states or be crushed by the more powerful realms of Spain, France and the Holy Roman Empire.

Alexander VI, his son Cesare Borgia, Julius II, Leo X and Clement VII did not appreciate this; they saw matters through feudal eyes, perceiving only the necessity to establish the legitimacy of their familial claims to power. Machiavelli, however, understood that this new order was needed by these very leaders above all, and that the emergence of the constitutional order of the princely state could lead to a future for Italy that would allow it to repel the predation of greater, but as yet unreformed, powers. For if a princely state could be created in the heart of Italy, linking Rome and the nominally papal vicarages of the Romagna to Florence and its possessions, a formidable strategic entity would have been brought into being. This is why *The Prince* ends with the exhortation to the Medici to seize the moment to accomplish this. The true purpose of *The Prince* is not, as is so often remarked, simply to recommend Machiavelli to a potential employer, but to use that figure to realize Machiavelli's vision for Italy.

Machiavelli himself realized how difficult his project would be. In perhaps the most crucial passage in *The Prince*, he writes: 'One always ought to remember that there is nothing more difficult to undertake, nor more dangerous to administer, nor more unlikely to succeed, than to introduce a new political order.'[14]

Chapter 2

Can a Statesman Get into Heaven?

IN 1962 THE editors of *Esquire* magazine published *What Every Young Man Should Know*. Illustrated with sophisticated cartoons and featuring essays on subjects such as Ivy League clothing, the correct form for an invitation, tactics of seduction, and advice on how to choose a college and evade the draft, this book provides a window into East Coast American manners, circa the late 1950s. Books for privileged youths stand within a long line of manuals with titles such as *De regimine principum* ('On princely rule') or often, *Specula principum* ('Mirrors for princes'), of which *The Prince*, as we have seen, is considered to be an example. Often such books were addressed to a king or prince who had recently succeeded to power, but this genre also embraced texts that generally instructed rulers what to imitate or avoid. Their authors included Aristotle and, most definitively, Cicero, whose book *De officiis* ('On duties') became the model for Renaissance humanists. Xenophon, who wrote *Cyropaedia*, Thomas Aquinas, who wrote *On Princely Rule*, and Erasmus, who wrote *Education of a Christian Prince*, all contributed to this literature.[1] What a princely reader could expect from these books was advice on how to behave properly. In the medieval era that meant chiefly how to develop the virtues of a Christian ruler, but there was much in common with the classical examples of this genre, especially the cultivation of the noblest nature of rulers and the expression of universally admired virtues.

There is not much of that in the twenty-six chapters of *The Prince*.

Chapters 1 to 11 concern the various kinds of principalities: hereditary, newly established, mixed (where established principalities annex territory in order to enlarge a pre-existing principality), civil (where the leader is chosen by the people or by the nobility) and ecclesiastical. Were these chapters published alone as a treatise, no one would doubt that the essay was constitutional in nature. Chapters 12 and 13 deal with the armed forces of a principality.

Only chapters 14 to 23 address a prince of this new order. These are the chapters that discuss the training, behaviour and reputation of the prince in a way that might be thought analogous to the advice of classical mirror books, though even these chapters are strictly limited to the prince's deportment as a political head of state who must establish his legitimacy and maintain it. It is these chapters whose recommendations are a studied antithesis of the 'mirror of princes' literature that preceded *The Prince*; they are the ones that both inflamed Machiavelli's critics and entranced his more demonically inclined readers, who chose to ignore completely the significance of the earlier chapters.

Finally, chapters 24 to 26 take up the future of Italy in light of the emergence of this new constitutional order and address the possibility of creating a unified state in the heart of the peninsula. These culminating chapters make clear that the book we know as *The Prince* has a radical *constitutional* purpose, scarcely comprehended by the genre of mannerist essays on propriety for Renaissance dukes and their courts.

In *De officiis*,[2] Cicero writes that a ruler must avoid wrongdoing 'either through force or through deceit; and deceit seems to belong to a little fox, force to a lion. Both of them seem most alien to a human being; but deceit deserves a greater hatred.'[3] By contrast, in one of the most celebrated passages in *The Prince*,[4] Machiavelli writes:

> Everyone knows how praiseworthy it is for a prince to keep his word,
> to live with integrity and not by craft. And yet, one must observe

from recent experience that those princes who have actually accomplished great things are those who cared little for keeping faith and knew how to manipulate men with cunning; indeed they have surpassed those who relied on sincerity. Therefore, note that there are two ways of fighting: one in accordance with the laws, the other with violence. The first is appropriate to mankind, the second to beasts. But because the first way is in many cases insufficient, it is necessary to have recourse to the second . . . Because therefore a prince must sometimes practise the ways of beasts, he should choose from among them the fox and the lion, for while the lion cannot defend himself from traps, the fox cannot protect himself from wolves. It is therefore necessary to be a fox in order to recognize traps, and a lion in order to frighten wolves: those who rely only on the ways of the lion do not appreciate this. A wise ruler, therefore, cannot and should not keep his word when such a strict observance would be to his disadvantage and when the reasons that moved him to make that promise no longer pertain.[5]

This famous remark, with its precise contradiction of an equally notable passage in *De officiis*, might suggest that *The Prince* is a work self-consciously designed to be a mirror book, with the distinction of proposing behaviour that is the opposite of what had usually been advised. In chapter 15 Machiavelli tells us, however, that with respect to the genre of books on the proper conduct of princes, 'I shall depart from the practices of other writers who depict an imaginary world and shall instead describe the ways princes actually behave and how the world reacts.' This remark is easy to misconstrue: instead of confirming that he is writing a book that is simply the inverted advice of mirror books, as is so often assumed, Machiavelli is announcing that he is rejecting the philosophical paradigm of describing a model utopia, towards which we should move and against which the current situation is to be measured. Instead, he plans to report from the front, as it were, those events that he has personally observed in his years as a civil servant and diplomat. From these experiences he will derive rules that avoid the dangerous perils that come with detachment from reality. Thus he goes on to list a number of qualities that elicit praise or blame: generosity/rapacity, compassion/cruelty, affability/haughtiness, sincerity/cunning, and so on, only to say that each of these qualities can be either praiseworthy or the subject of blame depending upon the real-world effects such behaviour brings about. Therefore, he concludes, the prince should not pursue those qualities thought to be the most praiseworthy all the time, when, in some contexts, such behaviour will have the effect of jeopardizing the safety of the state. The prince's first duty is to avoid reproach not for his manners, but for losing his state; he must adopt those qualities that strengthen the state even if they are thought to be vices and avoid those virtues that endanger the state.

This is a crucial distinction: the prince is being advised not on how to comport himself for his own sake, but rather on how to subordinate all other indicia of right behaviour to the one parameter of serving the state. It is not that by following Machiavelli's suggestions a prince will be a better prince; rather, it is that the very notion of what it means to be a prince must change with the advent of the princely state and that, having observed politics first hand, Machiavelli can make suggestions that will prove helpful in this new context.

We can see this in another of his references to Cicero's *De officiis*. Cicero urges that rulers cultivate the virtue of generosity and that 'any suspicion of avarice must be avoided': 'no vice . . . is more foul than avarice . . . particularly among leading men and those who control public affairs.'[6] Yet when Machiavelli takes up the qualities of 'Liberality and Meanness' in chapter 16, he offers a very different view of the matter. Liberality is thought to be a good aspect of reputation; as a Christian, the prince should make his beneficences anonymously. This, however, will only win him a reputation for meanness. If, instead, the prince is overtly generous, this leads to higher taxes on his subjects and poverty for the community, which will offend the many who are taxed, while rewarding only the few who receive gifts. The result is that when danger ensues, the prince will be forced to adopt measures of austerity and thus be thought mean after all.[7] So the prince – acting as a sovereign and not as a Christian – must be frugal and even miserly in order to enable him to be liberal, because by not taxing he gives to all and is really only ungenerous to the few who otherwise would have been the recipients of his bounty. Just such a constraint crippled Piero de' Medici's efforts to imitate his father's *magnificenza*, and the son was ultimately compelled to raise taxes. Thus liberality is a wasting asset that either leads to poverty – which is the loss of the power to be liberal – or, if to avoid poverty, becomes rapacity, which leads to hatred. Machiavelli does not denigrate rapacity in itself but sees it as a quality to be avoided owing to its effect on the standing of the prince, which will affect his capacity for governing. Machiavelli therefore concludes that it is permissible to have a reputation for being miserly, which may lead to reproach, because it does not lead to hatred and therefore does not endanger the state.

This is a subtle distinction and it has misled even some of the most reflective of Machiavelli's critics. Because he believed Machiavelli had detached ethics from politics, Leo Strauss concluded that he was 'a teacher of evil', counselling leaders to avoid the common values of justice, mercy and love in preference for cruelty, violence, fear and deception.[8] Even a more sympathetic reader like Benedetto Croce treats Machiavelli as a 'realist' who suspends ethics in matters of politics. Similarly, some defenders of Machiavelli simply take the view that moral values have little place in the particular kinds of decisions that political leaders must make and therefore that it is a sort of category mistake to assume otherwise.[9] But as we shall see in subsequent chapters, Machiavelli is in fact an intense moralist. It is just that the morality he urges on a prince, when he is acting on behalf of the people and not simply on his own behalf, subordinates the good of the prince to the good of the state. As we shall also see, this view is closely related to Machiavelli's decisive preference for republics over principalities and is one more reason why reading *The Prince* in the absence of its companion volume, the *Discourses*, gives an incomplete and often misleading impression of his views. Whether we *ought* to accept the subordination of our personal morality depends on the nature and purposes of the state.[10]

Machiavelli was among the first to appreciate this distinction,[11] and his argument that the moral imperatives for the official are different from those of the rest of us was a key insight at the birth of the modern state. Indeed, one can account for the timing of this insight by correlating it with the emergence of the state. Whereas feudal princes fused the personal with the political, Machiavelli saw that the state was by no means synonymous with the person of the prince and concluded that the head of a princely state is obligated to govern in light of this distinction.

In his essay 'Political Action: The Problem of Dirty Hands', the American political philosopher Michael Walzer also calls attention to this distinction.* Walzer is seeking an answer to a dilemma posed by a symposium on the rules of war: can a man ever face a situation where he must choose between two courses of action, both of which it would be wrong for him to undertake? The philosopher Thomas Nagel suggested that this could occur when someone was compelled to choose between upholding an important moral absolute and avoiding an imminent human catastrophe.[12] Walzer places

---

* Michael Walzer, 'Political Action: The Problem of Dirty Hands', in Sanford Levinson (ed.), *Torture* (Oxford UP, 2004), pp. 61–76. Jean-Paul Sartre's play *Dirty Hands* has a memorable expression of this point of view. Here, Hoederer, an experienced politician, explains to the naïve young idealist, Hugo, the nature of *realpolitik*: *Moi j'ai les mains sales. Jusqu'aux coudes. Je les ai plongées dans la merde et dans le sang. Et puis après? Est-ce que tu t'imagines qu'on peut gouverner innocemment?* ('Me, I have dirty hands. I've plunged them into shit and blood up to the elbows. And then after? Do you fantasize to yourself that it's possible to govern innocently?')

this dilemma in the context of a government official and draws a conclusion that would have been most unwelcome to Machiavelli:

> I don't think I could govern innocently; nor do most of us believe that those who govern us are innocent . . . even the best of them. But this does not mean that it isn't possible to do the right thing while governing. It means that a particular act of government . . . may be exactly the right thing to do in utilitarian terms and yet leave the man who does it guilty of a moral wrong . . . If on the other hand he remains innocent, chooses, that is, the 'absolutist' [position] . . . he may also fail to measure up to the duties of his office.[13]

In Walzer's view, it is the official's duty that requires him to do things the rest of us would regard as immoral – lying, deceiving, killing, even torturing. This in turn leads to the moral contempt in which the members of the public hold public officials.

> [A political leader] . . . is asked to authorize the torture of a captured rebel leader who knows or probably knows the location of a number of bombs hidden in apartment buildings around the city, set to go off within the next twenty-four hours. He orders the man tortured, con-vinced that he must do so for the sake of the people who might otherwise die in the explosions – even though he believes that torture is wrong, indeed abominable, not just sometimes, but always . . . [H]e is not too good for politics and [indeed] he is good enough. Here is the moral politician: it is by his dirty hands that we know him. If he were a moral man and nothing else, his hands would not be dirty; if he were a politician and nothing else, he would pretend that they were clean.[14]

This conclusion has rather negative implications for the govern-ance of a democratic republic, for what sort of leaders would one choose, knowing they were being obligated to debase themselves, and what sort of men and women would aspire to such roles? Machiavelli's distinction between a personal and a governing ethos, however, redirects the official and leaves his personal morality uncompromised, whereas Walzer's citizen who authorizes the distinctive role of a governing official but disclaims any responsibility for the action of government is a hypocrite, or worse. Far from having dirtier hands, the officials of the Machiavellian state have hands at least as clean as those of the rest of us and possibly a good deal cleaner.

In other words, Machiavelli is not *advising* a prince to disregard the conventional, Christian and classical virtues when this is necessary to protect the state; he *requires* this of a prince who has been given responsibility for the protection of the state, because it is sometimes a necessity.

> If you object to the political methods recommended [by Machiavelli] because they seem to you morally detestable, if you refuse to embark upon them because they are . . . too frightening, Machiavelli has no answer, no argument. In that case you are perfectly entitled to lead a morally good life, be a private citizen (or a monk), seek some corner of your own. But, in that event, you must not make yourself responsible for the life of others . . . In other words you can opt out of the public world, but in that case he has nothing to say to you, for it is to the public world and to the men in it that he addresses himself.[15]

This has important consequences for our understanding of Machiavelli's Christianity. What really drove critics like Gentillet mad was Machiavelli's claim in chapter 18 that, while practising the conventional virtues at all times was bound to be harmful, 'seeming to observe them is useful: for example, to appear to be merciful, faithful, humane, forthright, and religious . . . And there is nothing more indispensable than to appear to have the latter quality.'[16] The notion that religion could be used to manipulate the moral sentiments of the people cannot have truly shocked Machiavelli's worldly readers; but that a prince should be *advised* to detach his behaviour from his religious convictions was shocking indeed. Surely only the devil's voice would counsel the conscience of a prince to act contrary to the commands of religion, yet this is apparently the inference one draws from *The Prince* when princes are advised to 'seem' religious always, rather than be so.

This too was a profound misunderstanding. It has led many readers astray and misled some into conclusions about Machiavelli's Christianity that are at odds with his statements and behaviour; indeed, Isaiah Berlin thought Machiavelli was a pagan.[17] Let us review Machiavelli's argument for a princely morality of state. When we do, we will see that it is grounded in a Christian view of reality.

Machiavelli argues:

(1) It is the nature of man that he will behave badly in order to get what he wants.

As he notes in chapter 17 of *The Prince*, 'One can say, as a general matter, about men that they are ungrateful, fickle, deceitful, cowardly and greedy . . . Men are a wretched lot whose obligations are voided whenever it suits their self-interest.' This obsession with self-interest is an elemental function of man's nature and does not evolve with time.

(2) As a consequence, sometimes this will create a situation in which necessity – the necessity of preserving the state – requires that a prince depart from the customary virtues in order to cope with adversaries who are deceitful, greedy, etc.

For example, trickery is 'detestable yet in the conduct of warfare it is nevertheless praiseworthy and glorious', and all the more so 'with an enemy who has deceived you'.[18] The same thing may be said of other nominal vices – cruelty, dissimulation and deceit. Whether these are in fact virtues or vices depends entirely on whether they are necessary to preserve the state.[19]

(3) Therefore it is a prudent rule that the prince who governs a state must do unto others as they would do unto him.

Accepting man's nature as it is,[20] and accepting that men, not angels, govern states, a prince must avoid the wishful thinking that his competitors will treat him as he wishes to be treated. Instead, the prince must learn to treat others as they would treat him – the language of modern deterrence. Machiavelli derives this fundamental precept of statecraft from the most basic element of human nature.[21]

Three parts of this argument have a theological resonance. First, the account in Genesis of man's expulsion from Eden and fall from grace depicts the nature of man as fundamentally sinful. We will see in chapter 5 of the present work how Machiavelli relies on this description of man's nature as the basis for his jurisprudence.

Second, if it is correct, as Machiavelli argues, that acting honourably will lead to the downfall of the state, then the argument above is one from necessity. Machiavelli writes that a man who wishes 'to behave honourably at all times' will inevitably fail because he is surrounded by so many unscrupulous men; therefore, 'it is necessary for a prince to learn how to behave dishonourably, if he wishes to maintain his authority, and to use this knowledge – or not – according to the dictates of necessity.'[22]

The key phrase here is 'according to the dictates of necessity' (*secondo la necessità*). As Mansfield observes, Machiavelli moves necessity from being a limitation on human action to being a driver – choosing good or evil according to necessity. Thus, Machiavelli writes, 'a ruler should stick to the conventional virtues whenever it is possible to do so, but he must know how to enter into evil when forced by necessity.'[23] In several of his writings, including *The Prince*, Machiavelli reminds us of Moses' various deceptions and uses of horrific violence, including the massacre of the Israelites who worshipped the golden calf. Indeed, Machiavelli goes so far as to claim that those who successfully found a state are, as a consequence, among the most beloved of God.[24] So the question always is: is the proposed use of violence or deception – the lion's way or the fox's – truly necessary for the well-being of the people for whom the ruler is responsible? In Moses' case, God's word and his will frame necessity; in Savonarola's case, his claims to speak with God and to act on his instruction to found a new order are highly dubious and therefore cannot rely on necessity.

Machiavelli never claims divine ordinance for his new constitutional order, but he does stress its necessity. This means that the careful sifting of what is truly necessary must precede any violent or deceitful action.[25]

There is a third and final element: redemption. Sometime between 1525 and 1527 – that is, in the last two years of his life when he was once again active in political and military affairs – Machiavelli delivered a sermon to a religious fraternity of which he was a member. The sermon was entitled 'Exhortation to Penitence',[26] and in it Machiavelli presents God as 'mindful of human weakness' and most merciful, and as opposed to 'the rigours of the vendetta'. It is this last phrase that catches one's eye, for while we see in Machiavelli's work repeated examples of violence, it is always turned to the public good. A vendetta is a private affair.

The worst sin, Machiavelli writes in the 'Exhortation', is ingratitude to God. It leads to the second greatest sin, enmity towards one's neighbour. For 'those who are ungrateful to God cannot avoid being hostile to their neighbours'.[27] Or to put it even more succinctly, as Machiavelli writes in *The Art of War*: 'How can those who scorn God respect men?'[28]

So we may infer that an essential element of a ruler's duty as head of a princely state is reverence for God, because this is the basis for respect for mankind.* *The Prince* is not a tract that disparages

---

* Those who are surprised by Machiavelli's invocations of God might consider Sebastian de Grazia's summation. He writes: 'scattered about his writings . . . like poppies in a field of chickpeas, are many references to God. Together they form an unmistakable likeness. Niccolò's God is the creator, master deity, providential, real, universal, one of many names, personal,

mankind simply because it sees us clearly with our faults; if it were only that, it would be the book that Gentillet thought, but if it were only that, there would be no basis for exalting the common good in the *Discourses* and elsewhere, and no reason for the morality of subordinating the prince's behaviour to the furtherance of the welfare of the state. Nor would there be any purpose in Machiavelli's denunciation of men's envy, counting among the virtues of the prince his ability to conquer this public vice.

Imagine you wish to train yourself to be a professional poker player. Part of that training must be learning all the tricks of the card sharp, dealing from the bottom of the deck, palming a card, marking a deck, etc. You must learn these things so you can spot them when someone is trying to cheat you. But must you practise these tricks yourself? I suppose it depends on how good your game is, and whether the persons with whom you are playing will enforce the rules once you have exposed the cheat. To the question, 'Must it be this way? Can't we do better?' the answer does not lie entirely within your power.

It is instructive that Machiavelli was thoroughly honest in his public dealings. When accused of corruption by jealous courtiers, an investigation cleared him of all charges – in an age not notably scrupulous about converting public funds to private use. And this despite the fact that he was chronically underpaid – he once threatened to sell his horse if his salary was not forthcoming – and often handled large sums for disbursement.

There is something appealing, however, to the present world about the misleading portrait of Machiavelli to which we are accustomed. It is consistent with our current contempt for bureaucrats, for politicians, for lawyers – the superstitious reaction of people

---

invocable, thankable, to be revered, a judge, just and forgiving, rewarding and punishing, awesome, a force transcendent, separate from the operative in the world.' De Grazia, *Machiavelli in Hell* (Vintage, 1994), p. 58.

who are frightened by forces that they identify with those who are trying to master those forces, rather like blaming a volcanologist for a volcanic eruption. Perhaps it was always so, at least since the birth of the state that gave us the bureaucrats, lawyers and politicians that are its creation.

Conclusion to Book I

The Prince is a Constitutional Treatise

IN ROMAN MYTHOLOGY Janus is the god of openings and endings. Niccolò Machiavelli lived at that moment when one constitutional era was ending and another beginning. *The Prince* and the *Discourses* look back to the past for lessons, and forwards to a future that has not yet come into being. Like Janus, *The Prince* has two faces, a topological fact that does not permit reduction to a single consciousness, no matter how conscientious. No coin has only one side.

Book II

Lo Stato – The Relation of *The Prince* to the *Discourses on Livy*

IT IS OFTEN asserted that Machiavelli's use of the term 'state' should be taken to refer to the status or condition of the prince, and it is true that this was the most common use of the term *lo stato* in Machiavelli's time. But his use of this Italian word in the context of a *republic* suggests that he was here, as elsewhere, using a common term in a novel way: to describe an identity linked to, but separate from, the person of a prince.

> *Tutti li stati, tutti e' dominii che hanno avuto et hanno imperio sopra li uomini, sono stati e sono o republiche o principati.*

'All states, all dominions that have had and continue to exercise lawful authority over men were, and remain, either republics or principalities.'[1]

Chapter 3

A Republic's Duty of Consequentialism

I N 1930 THE Cambridge philosopher C. D. Broad claimed that we could define ethical theories on the basis of the priority given either to values or to obligations. He then made the following distinction, which is now in general use:[1]

> [If we say that] concepts of obligation are fundamental and the concepts of value are definable in terms of them . . . [we would conclude] that 'X is intrinsically good' means that it is fitting for every rational being to desire X. Such theories might be called *deontological*.*

On the other hand, if concepts of value are fundamental, and the concepts of obligation are definable in terms of them, such theories may be called *consequentialist*, for it would be held that 'X is a right action' means that X is likely to produce consequences which are at least as good as those of any other action open to the agent at the time.

When we contrast deontological rules ('Thou shalt not kill') with consequentialist rules ('It is permissible to kill an aggressor in self-defence – that is, in order to preserve one's own life'), we are contrasting absolute duties (imperatives) with relative judgements (for example, that a particular means is justified to the degree that it serves a desirable goal).†

---

* *deon* is the Greek word for 'duty' or 'obligation'.
† A third category, aretaic theories, holds that people should act in accordance neither with absolute duties nor with assessments of the consequences of an

During the Second World War and the Cold War, it was frequently said by the leaders of the democracies that they were bound by certain ethical rules of behaviour – truthfulness, compassion and non-aggression – which no peril would justify them violating, while the dictators against whom they struggled felt no such constraints. For the latter, it was said, the rule was: the end justifies the means.

In my view this is at least incomplete. Seeing why this is so will illuminate Machiavelli's commitment to a republican form of government, his hostility to autocracy, and the basis for some of the more shocking statements in *The Prince*, for no phrase is more associated with Machiavelli than the consequentialist motto 'the end justifies the means'.

The origin of the 'duty of consequentialism' lies in the deepest constitutional mandate of republican government.[2] That is because the officials of such a state are bound to behave, *in their official capacity*, in a way that maximizes the ends or goals of the people in whose name they govern. It is this delegation that imposes the duty of evaluating policies in terms of the ends they serve and that displaces the deontological or *a priori* moral imperatives that are so much a part of personal life. By contrast, the dictator or autocrat can say: 'my religion imposes upon me a duty that I, in my governing role, will superimpose on the public regardless of the consequences for them and regardless of their wishes for themselves.' Machiavelli knew such men, perhaps beginning most traumatically with the charismatic priest Girolamo Savonarola.

Savonarola was reputed to have spoken with God. For a half-dozen years, before the death of Lorenzo the Magnificent until two years after the French invasion of Italy, he transfixed Florence. A Dominican friar from Ferrara, he became the prior of San Marco in Florence. He was a spell-binding preacher and

---

act, but rather in accordance with the characteristics a virtuous person should have. I will discuss this alternative in chapter 6.

an innovative legislator, and during the years of his influence he dominated Florentine morals and manners: he persuaded the public to burn its 'vanities' (mirrors, books such as those by Boccaccio, paintings by Fra Bartolomeo and Botticelli among many other painters, carnival masks and even toupees that were thought to be incidents of sin); denounced the papacy and the Medici for corruption; initiated the alliance with France that proved so fateful for Florentine diplomacy; and warned of a terrible revenge by God if the Florentines continued in their worldly ways.[3] One might say he was the apotheosis of the deontological.[4]

After he was excommunicated and tortured, he denied that he had actually spoken with God, but when he was taken from the rack and about to be burned at the stake, he recanted his denial. It was only after Savonarola's fall that Machiavelli was able to enter the civil service as secretary to the Ten of War and to the Second Chancery, posts that fell open when Savonarola's allies were dismissed.

Machiavelli's attitudes towards state power were by no means absolutist. To see this, we must begin with Cicero. In his *De officiis*, Cicero had written that 'some things are so disgraceful, or so outrageous, that a wise man would not do them even to protect his country'.[5] This is an example of a deontological absolute. By contrast, Machiavelli held that 'When the safety of one's country is at stake, there must be no scruple of justice or mercy or blame; on the contrary, one should wholly pursue that policy that saves the life of the state and preserves its liberty, regardless of any other consideration.'[6] Whereas Cicero took the example of Romulus, who murdered his brother Remus in order to achieve sole power for the founding of the Roman state, as having committed a crime that cannot be excused,[7] Machiavelli takes the same example* and observes: 'It is

---

* Bondanella and Musa, *The Portable Machiavelli*, p. 22. Similarly, Machiavelli gives the example of the Spartan king Cleomenes who 'had all the ephors [five elected magistrates who determined public policy] murdered and anyone else who could

surely right that though the act may accuse him, he is excused by the result; for when the result is good, as with Romulus, it will always excuse him because while one should reproach someone who is violent in order to destroy, one should not blame one who uses violence to set things aright.'[8]

The crucial difference is not quite captured in the phrase 'the end justifies the means': for not just any end can justify and not just any means is justifiable. On the contrary, Machiavelli is at pains to argue that only those ends that serve the common good – that are clearly in the public interest and do not simply serve the personal interests of the ruler – can justify violence. Moreover, the means must be narrowly and proportionately tailored to serve that end.[9] As we saw in the previous chapter, this inquiry into necessity is critical to Machiavelli's reasoning. As we shall see in the next section, Machiavelli explicitly condemns many uses of violence, notably expulsions of the population and various sadistic acts, which he claims cannot be justified by necessity because they cannot contribute to the common good.

A good example of Machiavelli's rejection of deontological absolutes for persons governing the state is provided by his discussion of the Roman army's actions after their entrapment at the Caudine Forks in 321 BC. Given the choice of annihilation in battle or a shameful evacuation – passing under a symbolic yoke and returning to Rome disarmed – the Roman legate chose the latter. 'The life of Rome,' he argued, consisted 'in the life of that army . . . [and] one's country is well defended in whatever way one defends it, whether with ignominy or with glory.' Without the army, 'Rome, even if it died gloriously, was lost and its liberty [lost too].'[10]

The Caudine Forks parable is also instructive of another point often made by Machiavelli, which emphasizes the proportionate

---

oppose him' on the grounds that otherwise he would have been unable to restore the just and praiseworthy law of Lycurgus (*Discourses*, book I, chapter 9).

nature of a means/ends analysis. Machiavelli exhorts states to use violence only as a last resort: 'I think that while one must employ arms and force, these must be reserved as a last resort, when all other methods are insufficient.'[11]

These observations suggest that the ends that states pursue matter: predation is ruinous to both the predator and the prey; only necessity imposed by a threat to the common good can justify acts of violence, and even then there are some means that are so degrading that they cannot be employed. Means, therefore, also matter: even when they are justified by necessity, they must be calibrated and judged by their effectiveness in addressing that necessity. At the Caudine Forks, the Samnites sought the advice of their leader, Herennius, who urged them either to let the Romans go free, unharmed, or to kill everyone. His reasoning was that if the army were released, Rome would bear no grudges; and if it were destroyed, Rome would be unable for a generation to reconstitute it and exact revenge. The decision to be avoided was 'a middle way', which Herennius' son had sought but which would leave the Romans eager to retaliate yet not significantly weakened.

Machiavelli criticizes his patron, Piero Soderini, for refusing to employ decisive force, which might have been perceived as dictatorial, in order that good ends might be served:[12]

Piero Soderini believed he could overcome his enemies' lust for a return to power by being patient and good. Although his prudence told him of the necessity of action, and even though fate and the ambition of his enemies offered him the chance to destroy them, nonetheless he could never make up his mind to do so. He ought to have known that his deeds and intentions would be judged by their success and that had he been successful it would have been apparent that he had acted for the preservation of his native city, not out of his own ambition. Instead, he lost both his city and its liberties as well as his reputation.[13]

This theme of the common good runs throughout Machiavelli's work and is indispensable to an appreciation of his ideas.[14] It allows him to distinguish between what I have elsewhere called 'states of terror' and 'states of consent' – states whose legitimacy is claimed on the basis of the coercion of its citizens or on the basis of their volition.[15] For Machiavelli too, the former kind of political arrangement is one in which the citizens 'can be arbitrarily mistreated at any moment, and it is this constant possibility that inevitably creates a fear that generates those servile habits that are utterly incompatible with the status and responsibilities of a free society'.[16]

By contrast, the 'common interest that results from republican self-government' is '*not to be afraid for oneself*'.[17] For this reason, Machiavelli disdains autocracies where a state of terror is always present. He decisively prefers republics to monarchical states,[18] for 'without any doubt, this common good is pursued only in a republic'.[19]

> It is marvellous to think of the greatness Athens achieved in the space of a century once she had freed herself from the tyranny of Pisistratus and even more marvellous to consider the greatness Rome reached having freed herself from her kings. The reason is easy to comprehend: it is not the private, personal good but the common good that makes cities great (*perché non il bene particulare, ma il bene comune è quello che fa grandi le città*).[20]

Machiavelli's insight – that officials must disregard their personal moral codes in carrying out the duties of the state – is seldom assessed within the context of law, even though for the states in which we live today, it is law, and not the judgement of the prince, that guides those who govern. Both princes and republics 'need to be regulated by laws, because a prince who can do simply as he wishes is crazed, and a people who can do whatever it wishes is imprudent'.[21]

Sometimes this point about the necessity of law and the role of necessity itself appear to be in conflict, and this has led some commentators to propose that emergencies – when the life of the state is in peril – justify a departure from the strict observance of law. In the United States the case often cited is that of President Abraham

Lincoln, who suspended *habeas corpus* during the American Civil War – in direct contradiction of a specific provision of the US Constitution – in order to arrest some 13,000 persons under martial law. If we look carefully at this example, however, we see that Lincoln's action was undertaken to preserve a state under law and not out of any personal, moral imperative (such as the destruction of slavery). Defending his decision in a message to Congress on 4 July 1861, he wrote:

> To state the question more directly, are all the laws, *but one*, to go unexecuted and the government itself go to pieces, lest that one be violated? Even in such a case, would not the official oath be broken, if the government should be overthrown, when it was believed that disregarding the single law, would tend to preserve it?[22]

This is plainly a consequentialist argument, but look carefully at how it sorts out ends and means. The objective sought (the end) that justifies the violation of law (the means) is in fact the *preservation* of the rule of law, and the means chosen is indispensable and proportionate to the end of the common good. When a leader consciously violates the law – Jefferson purchasing Louisiana without Congressional authorization, Roosevelt aiding Britain despite the Neutrality Act – he is not in quite the same position as the citizen who commits an act of civil disobedience. Like that person, the representative of a state of consent must be bound to accept whatever punishment is appropriate for his act in violation of law; but unlike the ordinary citizen, he may not act as an official in conflict with the common good – that is, he may not put his interests including his moral code above the public interest, because his official authority derives solely from the public's empowering him to act in its interests.*

---

* Robert M. Cover makes a similar observation with respect to judges: 'The judicial conscience is an artful dodger and rightfully so. Before it will concede

STATECRAFT AS STAGECRAFT

The idea that the perception of a prince's acts and qualities are an important element in his ability to govern is a persistent and subtle theme of Machiavelli's. It is one way in which Machiavelli is able to reconcile his claim that people really do value honesty, generosity, courage and piety with his observation that the exercise of these traits, in some contexts, may undermine the state. By distinguishing between the quality of seeming to be one thing and actually being something else – by cultivating the faculty for convincing hypocrisy, let us call it – the successful prince avoids the contempt of his people while also taking those measures that are necessary to preserve the common good, even when these do not comport with the virtues we admire in individuals.

Once again, we begin with Cicero, who, in *De officiis*, writes that 'men who think that they can secure for themselves unshakeable glory by pretence and empty show ... are wildly mistaken. True glory takes root and spreads its branches [while] everything false drops swiftly down like blossom'[23] – a Roman version of the Americanism, 'You can fool some of the people all of the time, and all of the people some of the time, but you can't fool all of the people all of the time.'[24] Machiavelli gleefully rejects this advice by insisting that hypocrisy is essential to good governance (for the reasons argued above – namely that, as de Grazia summarizes it, 'a prince cannot govern in the way the public idealizes, yet he must appear as if he were doing precisely that in order to secure the support necessary to be successful for the public's own good'[25]), and furthermore that it is not very difficult to do successfully, because 'Men in general

---

that a case is one that presents a moral dilemma, it will hide in the nooks and crannies of the professional ethics, run to the caves of role limits, seek the shelter of the separation of powers. And, indeed, it is right and fitting that such insulation exists.' Cover, *Justice Accused* (Yale UP, 1975), p. 201.

judge by what seems rather than by what is in fact the case – that is, more by their eyes than their hands'.[26] Isolated from the populace at large, the prince appears to everyone as 'the person you seem to be while few know how you really are, and they do not dare to oppose the common opinion'.

> Therefore, it is not necessary for the prince to possess all of the admirable virtues, but it is quite necessary for him to appear to have them. Furthermore, I daresay that having these virtues and practising them in every context is harmful while appearing to rely on these admirable qualities is useful . . . It is essential to understand this: that a prince, and especially a 'new' prince, cannot always observe those rules by which the generality of men are considered good, for he is often obliged to act in order to maintain the state in ways that may be against his own faith, against charity, against humane behaviour, and against religious dogma . . . A prince therefore must be very cautious not to let anything come from his lips that is not imbued with those five qualities; rather, to those seeing and hearing him, he should appear to be all mercy, all faithfulness, all integrity, all kindness, all religion.[27]

There is more to the 'rhetoric of imposture' than hypocrisy, however; illusion is essential to art, including the art of governing. One forgets that Machiavelli, after he was removed from office, became Italy's leading playwright and that *La Mandragola* is still widely performed. Indeed, it was the exercise of his literary talents that became the key eventually to winning over the arts-loving Medici, who were suspicious of him owing to his association with Piero Soderini and the Florentine Republic.

Not just the distinction between being and seeming, which is crucial to Machiavelli's thought, but also two further arts of the playwright manifest themselves in his advice: the creation of quasi-mythical *dramatis personae*, such as Romulus, Moses and Lycurgus; and the cathartic climax by which a prince wins the allegiance of his people and consolidates his power against his adversaries.

In describing the efforts of Cesare Borgia to carve out a princely state from the papal vicarages of the Romagna, Machiavelli gives the unforgettable case of Ramiro de Lorca, whom Borgia had made his governor of the cities he had conquered. Ramiro had overseen the daily governance of these cities with a singular cruelty and was hated by the populace. When his work of intimidation was done, Cesare Borgia staged the following theatrical performance, which Machiavelli witnessed as a young diplomat:

> Because Borgia appreciated that such severe governance had alien-
> ated the people, he wished to dispel their hatred and win their
> allegiance by showing that whatever cruelty had occurred was attrib-
> utable to his deputy, Ramiro. Seizing upon an opportunity to
> demonstrate this, one morning Borgia had Ramiro hacked into
> pieces and displayed the body in the square at Cesena with a block of
> wood and a bloodstained sword beside it. The sheer horror of such a
> spectacle left the people at once satisfied and mesmerized.[28]

Machiavelli, when discussing Romulus and the founding of Rome, had set this criterion for justifying violence: the consequences must redound to the common good. The same standard is applied to Cesare Borgia, whose violence had brought peace to the Romagna and won its approval.

UNACCEPTABLE CRUELTIES[29]

If Machiavelli has a strict criterion for the exercise of those traits that are not considered humane in the individual, it follows that there must be some uses of violence that are unacceptable, and these he portrays in chapter 8 of *The Prince*, a chapter devoted to Agathocles, the Sicilian tyrant.[30] Agathocles was a success as a ruler, if by that is meant that he lived a long time secure in his estate and defended himself from external rivals; there were no successful conspiracies against him within his country. Yet it is plain that Machiavelli despises him and describes him as a man of 'savage cruelty and inhumanity'. It was Agathocles who transformed Syracuse from a republic with citizens into a dictatorship with subjects, from a state of consent into a state of terror.

Machiavelli's view of Agathocles is a pivotal one, for it shows the limits of the instrumentalities of force which Machiavelli is willing to endorse, but it is also a subtle view because Agathocles is not a cartoon villain, but a creature depicted in the round with extraordinary virtues as well as vices. Thus, he is to be admired for his capacity at 'entering into and escaping from dangers, and [for] the greatness of his spirit in enduring and overcoming adversities such that one does not see why he has to be judged inferior to the most excellent captain'. Yet despite Agathocles' intrepidity, Machiavelli ultimately concludes that, 'Nonetheless, his savage cruelty and inhumanity, together with his infinite crimes, do not permit him to be celebrated among the most excellent men.' Machiavelli is quite capable of distinguishing between praise for the tyrant in one respect – 'those who observe [the imposition of necessary cruelties 'at a stroke', as recommended by Machiavelli] can supply some remedy for their status with God and with men, as had Agathocles' – and condemnation for his behaviour taken as a whole.

Although some of his critics might expect Machiavelli to excuse a successful ruler from the indictment that he killed his citizens, betrayed his friends, was without faith, without compassion, without religion, in fact he does not. Indeed, Machiavelli credits Agathocles with courage and determination, yet does not excuse him because the end that Agathocles sought was 'an absolute power, a form of governance that the authors of politics and history called tyranny'.[31]

Analogously, although Machiavelli shocks us when he does not condemn torture – Machiavelli was himself tortured to exact his confession following the Capponi conspiracy – he insists that it is unacceptable when done for the pleasure of the torturer. As an example he cites the duke of Athens cutting out a citizen's tongue 'with so much cruelty that [the man] died of it'.[32] He also condemns unusual torture, citing the duke's torturing citizens 'with new methods',* which earns him the characterization of one who is not *acting* cruelly but actually *is* cruel. 'This duke, as his governing demonstrated, *was* miserly and cruel . . . he deserved to be hated.'[33] Similarly, Machiavelli indicts the duke of Milan, whom he condemns by noting that he was not 'content with putting them to death unless he could kill them in some cruel way'.[34]

By the standard of serving the common good, such pathological sadism is obviously unacceptable. But the point is made even more strongly by Machiavelli's condemnation of the killing – or the expulsion and relocation – of large numbers of the population.[†] It is axiomatic that the destruction of a large part of the population cannot be for the *common* good, for it irretrievably sunders the commonality of the populace.[35] Similarly, Machiavelli requires that executions should always be limited to particular political leaders or military commanders, who are always few in number, and must not be of the kind that 'injure an entire community'.

Machiavelli states that there can be 'no more miserable or unusual example' of what we might today call 'ethnic cleansing' than Ferdinand of Aragon's 'pious cruelty' in expelling the Marranos (Muslims and Jews who had been forcibly converted to Christianity) from Spain. The same might also be said of Ferdinand's expulsion of

---

* Anticipating by some centuries the eighth amendment's prohibition in the US Constitution of 'cruel and *unusual* punishments'.

† Chapter 5 of *The Prince*, which advises the conqueror of a republic to disperse the population for his own safety, is not assessing such a step on the basis of its contribution to 'the common good'. Nor is this principle contradicted by the Roman practice of mass executions within a rebellious army, or against an insurrection, where the objective is to promote the common good and the victims have chosen to take up arms against the state; see the *Discourses*, book III, chapter 49.

Spanish Jews, or his depredations against the Native Americans the Spanish found in South America.

The essential point is that to discriminate between acceptable and unacceptable uses of violence implies that there is some consequentialist standard against which such means must be measured. For Machiavelli that standard is the public interest – common good – that the state is created to serve.

*****

With this background, we can now construe the most famous passage in *The Prince,* from chapter 17, which addresses the issue whether it is better to be loved than feared. The prelude to this passage is quite subtle and might appear to reverse the distinction between seeming and being: Machiavelli observes that sometimes one must seem to be cruel in order to avoid harsher measures later, whereas earlier he had suggested the prince must sometimes be cruel but should take care to appear to be merciful. But if we appreciate that the usefulness of separating seeming from being depends entirely on the contribution made to the common good by the action undertaken, this apparent contradiction vanishes.

> Let me say that every prince ought to wish that he be thought merciful and not cruel. Nevertheless, he must be careful when he exercises mercy. Cesare Borgia was considered cruel, but his cruelty re-ordered the Romagna, united it and restored it to peace and loyalty. This was far more merciful than the Florentines who allowed the destruction of Pistoia in order to avoid a reputation for mercilessness. Therefore a prince, so long as it is a matter of keeping his subjects united and loyal, ought not to fret about being thought cruel. With only a few demonstrations of harshness, he will ultimately prove more compassionate than those who, through excessive clemency, allow disorders to arise out of which come murders and robberies that injure the entire community while the executions ordered by princes injure only particular individuals. Still, a prince must be cautious that he does not inspire

fear of his politics, and he should behave in a way tempered by prudence and humanity so that his trust in the people does not render him incautious nor his vigilance and suspicion make him insufferable.[36]

We can now understand the paragraph from which it is so often mistakenly severed, the controversial assertion that it is better to be feared than loved:

> From this comes the question whether it is better to be loved than feared, or vice versa. Of course, one would prefer to be both loved and feared, but since this is unlikely it is much safer to be feared. For one can generalize about men that they are ungrateful, fickle, fraudulent and deceitful, cowardly and covetous. As long as you succeed on their behalf, they are yours entirely, but when peril approaches, they will abandon you. The prince who relies solely on the promises of men, neglecting other defences, will find himself ruined. For friendships acquired by mere success and not by greatness or nobility of mind may well have been earned, but they are rented, not owned, and in an emergency cannot be cashed in when needed. Men have fewer reservations about injuring someone who has made himself loved than one who has made himself feared because love is maintained by links of obligation that, men being vain, are broken whenever it serves their purpose while fear is preserved by a dread of punishment that never leaves them.[37]

In other words, the promises that the obligations of love impose on others, on which we rely, can always be unilaterally broken, because we can always break the commitments love exacts from us without the consent of the loved one.

By contrast, the fear and dread imposed by another person, a person with the power to execute his threats, creates habits and responses it is not in our power to dissolve unilaterally. Yet it would be an error to suppose that what we dread from government is only the power to inflict harm; just as important is the power to withdraw protection and thereby diminish our security. These observations take us to the next chapter: the bases for law.

Chapter 4

Good Arms, Good Laws

MACHIAVELLI BECAME THE first philosopher of the modern state because he saw the necessity for the emergence of a new, post-feudal political structure in the events that engulfed Italy at the end of the fifteenth century. Such states did eventually emerge in the sixteenth century, confirmed in their status by the Treaty of Augsburg and its famous phrase *cuius regio, eius religio* [the ruler may determine the religion of those within his jurisdiction]. But this prescience is often denied Machiavelli by those historians who date the appearance of the modern state to the period of the Westphalian settlement of the seventeenth century,* and the accounts of sovereignty given by Hobbes and Bodin,[1] though such a portrait of the modern state misses entirely the importance of an earlier development by which the idea of sovereignty was made possible. That this is acknowledged by the concession that Machiavelli simply 'prefigured' Hobbes and his contemporaries misses the point of Machiavelli's insight.

* The 'Westphalian settlement' refers to the idea that the treaties of Munster and Osnabruck that ended the Thirty Years War in 1648 created the international order of sovereign states within which we live today. I have criticized this claim in *The Shield of Achilles*, arguing that the crucial basis for this assertion – the inclusion of the role of the ruler in determining the religion of his subjects, which is predicated on a territorial basis for the state – in fact dates from the Treaty of Augsburg in 1555. See *The Shield of Achilles*, pp. 502–8.

It has always been a problem that, though the idea of the modern, princely state originates in Italy at the end of the fifteenth century, the constitutional arrangement that ratifies the pre-eminence of this constitutional order – the *cuius regio, eius religio* mentioned above, which is so often misattributed to the treaties of Westphalia in 1648 but originated in fact at Augsburg in 1555 – applied to parties that were not Italian states. This is a problem for historians and constitutional and international relations theorists because the general pattern by which a new form of constitutional order emerges and eventually triumphs occurs when an innovative state – the Napoleonic imperial state-nation of the 1790s, for example, or the German industrial nation state that was created in the 1870s – smashes the prevailing constitutional order and, by means of an 'epochal war' extending over decades, brings the new form to a dominance that is recognized by international society at the constitutional conventions that produce the peace treaties that ultimately end such wars.*

But though an Italian thinker initially described the idea of a princely state, the Italian cities never successfully created such a state. Rather, it was the princely states of the Holy Roman Empire that wrested religious perquisites from the empire and so brought this new constitutional order to pre-eminence. These states decisively defeated the idea of a feudal realm as a viable strategic competitor, despite the immense and superior resources of the congeries of Charles V's holdings of which his realm was composed. The epochal war that brought forth the princely state was indeed the Habsburg–Valois conflict that erupted in Italy in Machiavelli's time. But when France was compelled by internal religious strife to quit the field, other states continued forwards with this innovation, and it was their creation that was ratified at Augsburg.

---

* Sometimes innovations in warfare undermine the dominant constitutional order; sometimes the collapse of the prevailing constitutional order provokes changes in strategy and tactics.

No doubt Machiavelli's acute insight was aided by the fact that he was, in his lifetime, a military and diplomatic figure, an administrative bureaucrat, drafter of statutes and at least two constitutions, as well as a gifted biographer and historian, for the state is defined by the interplay of three elements: strategy, law and history. No doubt, too, he was sensitized to the emergence of this new constitutional form by his lifelong interest in the classical states of antiquity, which he seems to have inherited from his father Bernardo, a humanist who trained as a lawyer. But the work of great writers and philosophers is more than the sum of their experiences. Guicciardini was a more careful historian than Machiavelli, and Giovanni dalle Bande Nere was a far more capable military leader, who mocked Machiavelli's inability to get his troops to march properly. Machiavelli's statutes were repealed and his constitutions never adopted. It was Machiavelli's *genius* that was unique, for he saw in the events around him a new phenomenon, while everyone else was still captivated and ensnared by the old structures even as they were crumbling around them. In *The Prince* Machiavelli tells us how, as a young diplomat, he was instructed by Louis XII's immensely sophisticated adviser, the cardinal of Rouen, that the Italians did not understand war, to which he tellingly replied that 'the French did not really understand the state'.[2]

Whereas the political structures of medieval Europe were over-lapping and various, the distinct feature of the modern neoclassical state is its consolidation of strategy and law into one topologically unique structure: strategy concerns the *outer* face of the state, while law concerns its *inner* life. 'Good institutions without military backing,' Machiavelli wrote in *The Art of War*, 'undergo the same sort of disorder as the rooms of a splendid and regal palace which, adorned with gems and gold but without a roof, have nothing to protect them from the rain.'[3]

No state is sovereign whose exterior relations are ruled by another state, and no state is sovereign whose interior life is subject to the laws of another state. Thus the modern state separates itself from other states by this relationship of inner and outer, like the topology of a glove, or a membrane, that cannot have an exterior form without an interior cavity and vice versa. By contrast, medieval political entities interpenetrated, all overlaid by the universal authority of the Church. Perhaps if Charles V had defeated France and absorbed Italy into a vast empire; perhaps if Pope Alexander VI and his successors had not turned the papacy into a principality; perhaps if, while Machiavelli was completing the *Discourses*, Martin Luther had not propounded his ninety-five theses or Henry VIII had not challenged Pope Clement VII over the leadership of the Church in England – perhaps if these events had turned out differently, Machiavelli would have been remembered much the same as he is today, as a mordant and diabolical essayist. But these events did turn out the way they did, and the transformation of the constitutional system of Europe did take place as a consequence. To read Machiavelli as if his work were irrelevant to that development is as much a travesty as to read him as though these events were irrelevant to the development of his ideas.

Machiavelli held a very unsentimental view of how law achieves legitimacy and how it can be effectively enforced.[4] As we shall see, he then applied this assessment of the means of managing internal stability to all state action, encompassing external relations with other states. Underlying this move was his appreciation of the deep relationship between strategy and law, which is reflected in one of his most often quoted remarks from *The Prince*:

> The main foundation for all states, the new as well as the old or 'mixed', is good laws and good arms. Just as there cannot be good laws where the state is not well armed, so it is also true that where the state is sufficiently armed there will be good laws.[5]

On the face of it , this statement seems to betray a gross, logical error: surely it is wrong to conclude that, assuming that there are not good laws where the state is not well armed, there must actually be good laws where the state is well armed. Given the single premise, it must be possible that a well-armed state could also be without good laws, or that it is indeterminate whether a well-armed state will in fact have good laws.

But this error is *too* gross for a subtle mind like Machiavelli's, and it prompts us to ponder what Machiavelli meant by 'good laws' and why he drew the conclusion that a well-armed state would have them. The first question is answered by the preceding chapter in the present book: good laws are those that effectively serve the common good. As Machiavelli himself writes in *The Art of War*:

> All the arts that are provided for in a civil community for the sake of the common good of men, all the statutes made in it so that men will live in fear of the laws and of God, would be vain if for them there were not provided defences, which when well ordered, preserve them, even though they themselves are not well ordered.[6]

Apparently 'good law' may not actually be 'well ordered' even in a state that is well armed. This suggests that good laws are merely laws that are obeyed.

The second question then becomes: why would we think that the condition of a state's arms influences the efficacy of its laws? The answer begins with Machiavelli's judgement of the nature of public behaviour under law:

> As all commentators on civil life have shown, and as every history amply exemplifies, it is necessary for the framers of a republic and its laws to assume that all men are bad and that they will always act out this malignity of their natures whenever they are presented with the opportunity. Men never do good except when they are compelled by necessity.[7]

If this sounds particularly shocking, we should be reminded that it has a sympathetic resonance in American jurisprudence. In *The*

Federalist (no. 51), James Madison observed that 'if men were angels, no government would be necessary'. This view is seconded by the American jurist Oliver Wendell Holmes, Jr., who, in 1897, addressed an audience at the Boston University Law School, telling them: '[i]f you want to know the law and nothing else, you must look at it as a bad man, who cares only for the material consequence which such knowledge enables him to predict.'

It was Machiavelli's next move, however, that reflected his genius, for he took this insight about the interior working of the state and generalized it to all state action, counselling that the state's legitimacy depends upon a successful anticipation of the acts of its competitors and thus that the leaders of the state are compelled to act towards other states as those states would act towards the states those leaders govern.*

One dramatic example will suffice. After Cesare Borgia had ordered the murder and dismemberment of Ramiro de Lorca as a cathartic gesture of reassurance to his subjects, he proceeded on to a meeting with four of his *condottieri* whom he suspected – correctly – of plotting against him. The ensuing events are described in a memorandum by Machiavelli to the Florentine Signoria. Having taken steps to appease his restless lieutenants by executing de Lorca, their rival, Borgia then prepared a trap for them at Sinagallia. The four lieutenants unwisely allowed themselves to be separated from their forces in order to accompany Borgia to his quarters, where they were then made prisoners. Two of them – Vitellozzo Vitelli and Oliverotto da Fermo – were strangled. Two weeks later, the two others – Francesco Orsini, duke of Gravina, and his brother Paolo Orsini – were murdered in the same manner. The very

---

* De Grazia refers to this as the 'Un-Golden rule' and correctly notes that it is a matter of 'moral philosophy [and its role in law] . . . [Machiavelli] propels the Un-Golden rule to the heights of constitution making and asks the legislator to strike first with the law.' De Grazia, *Machiavelli in Hell*, p. 302.

evening of the arrests, Borgia had sent for Machiavelli, who then set out for Florence to report on events. Ten years later, in *The Prince*, Machiavelli wrote:

> In reviewing Borgia's actions, I can scarcely reproach him. On the contrary, it seems to me his behaviour is a model for anyone who has risen to create a state. Anyone who thinks it necessary in his new principality to secure himself against his enemies, to win over allies, to conquer either by violence or by deception, to make himself loved and feared by the people, to win the allegiance of his soldiers, to eliminate those who may harm him, to replace old institutions with new ones, to be both severe and kindly, magnanimous and generous, to eliminate disloyal troops and forge a new military, to sustain alliances with kings and princes so that they must either gladly help him or at least be reluctant to injure him – that person can find no more recent examples than Borgia's deeds.[8]

If this seems appalling, it is necessary to put Borgia's action in context. First, these were not petty, sadistic crimes but rather crucial steps necessary to preserve Borgia's scheme to create a new principality in the centre of Italy by using, but not wholly relying on, self-serving and treacherous *condottieri*. Second, the example set by these notorious events allowed Borgia to be less violent when meeting future challenges because, having established the credibility of his use of force, he could then rely on the fear that credibility ensured to enforce his will.

Machiavelli's constitutional topology – the inner lining of the glove sheathed with an outer coat of fine mail – means that both domestic and foreign security are inextricably linked.[9] 'Everyone knows,' he writes, 'that whoever says empire, kingdom, principality, republic, whoever says men who command, beginning with the first rank and descending even to the master of a brigantine, says justice and arms.'[10]

So we see that Machiavelli by no means assumes that strong arms will inevitably lead to good laws, but only that without such arms effective laws are impossible, while within a well-armed and secure state, the laws are likely to be obeyed.

All this leads to the question whether, as Carl Schmitt has argued, Machiavelli derives his domestic rules for law from the state's strategic imperatives, or whether it is the other way round, as Woodrow Wilson argued. Any answer ought to reflect the relationship between strategy and law, between the internal stability and the external independence, of the state.* For Machiavelli, although different purposes are served by the interior lining and the exterior covering, one cannot exist without the other, and one is not derived from the other, but both exist in a mutually affecting relation. On the one hand, a *condottiere* like Francesco Sforza manoeuvres his way into power and creates a dukedom for himself and his heirs: an example, it would seem (Mansfield cites this case from *The Prince*), of a strategic move – conquest – as the predicate for the constitutional position of the new prince. Similarly, the Malatesta seized power in Rimini. On the other hand, the heir to a throne like the duke of Ferrara (cited by Machiavelli in *The Prince*) withstood the assaults of the Venetians in 1484 and those of Pope Julius II in 1510 'simply owing to the [authority derived] from his long-established rule in that realm';[11] this is an example of dynastic inheritance, a constitutional element, as a predicate for strategic success.

Machiavelli's notion of a mutually affecting relation between strategy and law can be seen most clearly in his obsession with replacing Florence's reliance on mercenaries with a recruited militia.

---

* For example, fascist regimes import strategic conflict into the domestic realm; this is one objective of the 'friend/enemy' distinction that Schmitt claims underlies all politics. Communist parties export the internal class struggle to a universal conflict. One might say that civil wars, like the French Revolution or the Spanish Civil War, which are the occasion for foreign intervention, are gloves turned inside out, as warfare engulfs the domestic arena and the legal legitimacy of the state vis-à-vis other states is put into play.

In *The Prince* he asserts that armies can be described as either hired mercenaries or citizen militias. In Italy the system of *condottieri* – mercenaries bound by a contract, or *condotta* – was the characteristic way that wealthy but relatively small cities sought to protect themselves.[12]

'For many years Italy has been in the grip of mercenaries', with the consequence, Machiavelli writes, that the entire peninsula 'has been overrun by Charles VIII of France, looted by Louis XII of France, ravished by Ferdinand of Aragon, and insulted by the Swiss ... Mercenaries and forces lent by other countries are useless and dangerous ... disunited, ambitious, undisciplined and treacherous ... Their defeat (*sconfitto*) is only postponed until they actually have to fight.'[13] Certainly these claims were amply confirmed by the Florentine experience with mercenaries in the attempt to recover Pisa.

Following Piero de' Medici's abject appeasement, when he granted Pisa its freedom from Florentine domination, and the ensuing expulsion of the Medici in 1494 which this fiasco provoked, Florence began a series of campaigns to retake its former subject city. In 1500, however, the Florentine campaign waged by *condottieri* completely collapsed. In the summer of 1503 Machiavelli collaborated with Leonardo da Vinci to divert the Arno in an attempt to strangle Pisa; throughout much of 1504 this fantastic effort went forwards, to no avail. Again, in 1505, a second offensive was launched, but at the very moment when the Pisan fortress walls were breached, the captains of ten mercenary companies mutinied, being unwilling to risk their capital – their men – in a final assault. By the end of the following week of bickering and escalating demands for new payments, the entire campaign was abandoned.

At this point Machiavelli finally received authorization from Soderini and the Signoria to proceed with recruiting a citizen militia. By the middle of February 1506 he had succeeded in assembling 500 farmers from the Mugello, and in April he recruited Cesare Borgia's notorious lieutenant, Don Michelotto – who had strangled Borgia's *condottieri* at Sinagallia, not to mention Borgia's sister's second husband – to be the militia's captain.[14] By the summer the Florentine militia was fighting in Pisan territory, and by June 1509 a successful siege and blockade had forced the Pisans to surrender. It was the high-water mark of Machiavelli's political life, and he was lionized in Florence by the same aristocratic forces that had feared the militia and attempted to discredit him.

Despite the fact that the Florentine militia collapsed when faced with the highly professional *tercios* of the Spanish that besieged Prato in 1512, ultimately resulting in the collapse of the Florentine Republic, Machiavelli never wavered in his faith in a citizen army. *The Prince*, written a year later, ends with his urging the Medici 'above all else' to recruit a standing militia. Much of *The Art of War* is devoted to arguing on behalf of 'the method of a citizen army'. To see why he persisted after the debacle at Prato is also to see the link he drew between 'justice and arms', as he put it.

The militia that fled so humiliatingly at Prato was never assembled in adequate numbers and thus never drilled in square formation; its company commanders were frequently changed, preventing the men from developing loyalty to their leaders. The failure of the militia to attract a sufficient and stable body of men was the result of Florentine refusal to trust the provincial forces they had recruited, denying them full citizenship and continuing to extract from them heavy taxes. Florence, as Machiavelli wrote in an essay on the ordinance he drafted that created the militia, was behaving unjustly towards its members. If it was true that a republic required an army of free men fighting for their own country, an army created by 'public deliberation', it was correspondingly true that these men had to be treated with justice. The power of the aristocratic party, which feared arming peasants and farmers, to thwart a just relationship with them had led to the collapse of the entire enterprise.[15]

This is an influential example, in Machiavelli's thought, of the mutually affecting relation between the inner, constitutional life of the state and its external, strategic affairs.[16] At the end of the eighteenth century, a militia of citizens with a passionate commitment to their republic would prove the most potent military force ever to sweep Europe.* This strategic result came about as a consequence of a political and constitutional rearrangement, the French Revolution. As we have also seen, however, it was the strategic crisis brought about by French artillery at the end of the fifteenth century that first prompted Machiavelli to promote a militia as an alternative to a mercenary force. So the answer to the question of which dimension controls the other – constitutional or strategic – is that both do.

---

* Napoleon's strategic innovations, especially the 'nation in arms', were a consequence of the political and constitutional events of the French Revolution, while Machiavelli's citizen militia, a profound political and constitutional innovation, was a consequence of changes in the strategic context in Italy. In other words, fundamental strategic change does not simply provoke constitutional change, nor the other way around; they affect one another, so that nothing fundamental happens in the strategic context without equally fundamental constitutional change, and vice versa. See *The Shield of Achilles*, pp. 538–42. See also note 16 above.

Conclusion to Book II
Machiavelli's Philosophy of State

THE HABITS AND ethos of a society will determine its fate because these create the possible ways in which a culture copes with change. For a state, this is a matter of its constitutional forms and practices. The interplay between strategic and legal innovation – the outer and inner membranes of the state – as these confront the vagaries of Fortune shapes the state and brings it success or failure.*

* Moreover, it is my view that when one state develops a more strategically and constitutionally dynamic order, its forms and practices – if not its values – will eventually be adopted by those states it surpasses. See *The Shield of Achilles*.

70

Book III

Virtù e Fortuna – God Does Not Want to Do Everything

MACHIAVELLI BELIEVED THAT there is a vital space for free will in the interstices created by the intersection of events and human character. The random collisions of developments and personality create constantly new contexts, and these new contexts create the opportunities for undetermined human action. Man cannot control Fortune nor can he change his nature, but he can mitigate their effects to the extent that he is foresightful and resolute in exploiting the new opportunities with which he is presented.

Lucretius, following Epicurus, envisioned a universe composed of tiny, indivisible and indestructible particles that fell through infinite space at great speed; at random moments they deviated from their straight paths and collided unpredictably, their collisions thus not being the result of a determined necessity but always leaving some role for chance. By this assumption, Lucretius provided a physical foundation for free will. He describes in the second book of *De rerum natura* how the *clinamen* (the swerve in direction) is 'free will wrested from the fates' (*libera . . . fatis avulsa voluntas*). In his own copy of this work, Machiavelli scribbled next to this text that 'from motion there is variety and from it we have a free will'.*

* Compare the physicist John Wheeler's account of a game of 'Twenty Questions', quoted in Philip Bobbitt, *Constitutional Fate*, p. 238, and its conclusion that we can have only probabilistic predictions.

Chapter 5

Virtù is from Mars, *Fortuna* is from Venus

I N THE FOLLOWING passage, Felix Gilbert describes the heraldry of the Rucellai, an important Florentine family whose gardens were the scene for Machiavelli's *Discourses* (and, after 1512, for his intellectual circle, the Orti Oricellari). On its ornate crest, he writes,

> is a ship, the mast of which is formed by a nude woman who holds in her raised left-hand the mainyard and in her right the lower part of the swelling sail . . . We know that Giovanni Rucellai was deeply puzzled by the fundamental problem which runs as its *leitmotif* through the thinking of Italian humanism from Petrarch to Bruno, namely, the relation of *virtù* to *fortuna*: Is man, even if he applies all his powers of reason and foresight, able successfully to counteract the accidents of Fate? . . . The female figure in the middle of the boat is Fortune, who symbolizes the power of the storm. No one can successfully resist this powerful and inclement goddess, but the man who, like the sailor in the boat, recognizes her strength and adjusts himself to her whim will be able to use her to bring the ship safely into port.[1]

As with the ethical issues discussed in chapter 2, the problem of *fortuna* presents itself in two aspects: that of the individual who struggles to master the unpredictable events that life presents; and that of the society that also must cope with events. And, as with Machiavelli's approach to the ethics of leadership, these two aspects are given very different treatments.

FORTUNE AND THE INDIVIDUAL

Machiavelli draws on a long tradition of depicting Fortune as a woman who influences the world in an arbitrary and unpredictable way: 'without compassion, without law, without right . . . [she] keeps the good beneath her feet [and] raises the wicked up . . . [and often] seats the undeserving on a throne the deserving never attains.'[2] Certainly Machiavelli's own life was testament to the caprice of Fortune.

By his mid-twenties, Machiavelli had observed first-hand the exile of the Medici who had ruled Florence for sixty years, the astonishing rise of Savonarola, his excommunication and fall, and even his burning at the stake. At the age of only twenty-nine, Machiavelli had profited from this astounding turn of events to achieve public office. Within a month of Savonarola's death, Machiavelli had been elected by the Florentine Republic's Grand Council to serve as chancellor (or secretary) of the Second Chancery, and, in only another month, he also became secretary to the Ten of Liberty and Peace, the executive committee of the Signoria that handled defence and foreign affairs. Despite his being unable to be admitted to the bar, he had obtained a government post that had usually been reserved for lawyers. As secretary to the Chancery he had become an accomplished bureaucrat, drafting important statutes on domestic matters and running an office of assistants; as secretary to the Ten he had been an envoy to the most important courts of Europe and had personally represented Florence to the kings of France and Spain, the Holy Roman Emperor, countless *condottieri* and warlords, the pope, and various foreign dignitaries. Denied the title of ambassador because he did not come from an aristocratic family, he was widely recognized as far more brilliant and influential than his nominal superiors. The *gonfaloniere* for life (head of the government of the Republic), Piero Soderini, had made him his protégé.

Machiavelli coolly weathered the false accusations of envious contemporaries,* and by reforming the defence policy of Florence to create a militia he became an heroic figure for his countrymen with the successful seizure of Pisa. A letter from a colleague at the Chancery describes the mood in Florence on 8 June 1509, when news came of the capitulation of the city:

> Here it is not possible to express what happiness, what jubilation and joy, all this people has received at the news of the recovery of that city of Pisa. Every man in some way is wild with exultation; there are fireworks over the city, even at 21 hours . . . I swear by God, so great is the exultation that we have, that I would make you [a eulogy worthy of Cicero] . . .[3]

Yet it is this same militia that flees in ignominy before the Spanish troops at Prato, bringing about the flight of Soderini, the collapse of the Republic, the return of the Medici, and Machiavelli's abrupt fall and exile. In his poem 'On Fortune', written about the same time that he composed *The Prince*, Machiavelli wrote:

> While you are flung around the rim of the wheel [of Fortune], she content and encouraging for the time being / is apt to change her whirling in the middle of the spin / and you are not able to change [your] being / nor depart the trajectory that heaven gives you / in midway you are abandoned by her.

Led by Giovanni and Giuliano, the Medici returned to power. Machiavelli was dismissed, and though apparently innocent, he was implicated in the Capponi conspiracy to murder Giuliano, arrested and tortured. His wrists were tied behind his back with a rope strung through a pulley attached to the ceiling, and he was repeatedly hoisted by his arms and then plunged to the floor, stopping just short so as to wrench his arms from their sockets. Despite this

---

* It is notable that there is no evidence that Machiavelli ever employed violence or deceit to advance his personal fortunes or to get revenge on those who had traduced him.

agony, Machiavelli refused to confess and was languishing in prison when Giovanni de' Medici's election as the new pope provided the occasion for a general amnesty. Machiavelli was exiled from the city to a small farm he had inherited. His career appeared to be at an end. In the rude surroundings to which Fortune had so precipitously flung him, he began to write on a problem that had long preoccupied him.

For both individual and society that problem is the same – heaven has endowed us with immutable individual characters while Fortune is fickle and constantly shifting:

> [I]f one could change one's character with the times and with events, [one's good] fortune would continue, [but] one cannot deviate from that path towards which nature inclines each of us ... [Soderini] always acted with patience and humility. When the times were in accord with his approach, he and Florence prospered, but when things changed and he had to put aside his patience and humility, he did not know how to do this so that, along with his native city, he lost his position.[4]

This passage is from a chapter in the *Discourses* entitled 'How one must change with the times in order to have good fortune'. It is the logical next step from Machiavelli's observation in chapter 25 of *The Prince* that 'as fortune varies while men continue on the same paths, they will prosper only as long as their ways of acting suit the times and they will fail when they are no longer in harmony'. The difficulty is that men are not able to command their natures.

So how is the individual to cope with fortune as the times change? This challenge will help us construe Machiavelli's use of the term *virtù*, which is so central to his thought and has proved so elusive for so many commentators.[5] *Virtù* is not 'virtue' – no matter how many caveats are employed,[6] one simply cannot use the word 'virtue' with English-speaking readers and expect to capture Machiavelli's idea of *virtù*. To read *virtù* as a virtue – or as virtue itself – when Machiavelli clearly states that the highest form of *virtù* in a prince is the ability to do whatever is necessary to preserve the state, would literally make virtue out of necessity.

Fortune is a woman, Machiavelli writes, and is most attracted by *virtù*, the Italian derivative of the Latin word *virtus*, which itself derives from the Latin *vir*, 'man' (our own word 'virility' derives from this origin). It is this Latinate, classical sense of *virtus* that best captures Machiavelli's use of the Italian *virtù*.

Virtù is a congeries of manly traits: courage, fortitude, admiration for craft, competence, ingenuity and above all the resolute exercise of one's talents.[7] True *virtù*, therefore, is judged by the goals pursued and the results of achieving them and for this reason cannot be regarded as a synonym for 'virtue'; indeed, with respect to the states-man, Machiavelli frequently observes that the blind adherence to moral virtues will yield ineffective or even disastrous results. Perhaps the best English words for *virtù* are 'manly virtuosity'.

> Fortune is a woman, and if you want to master her, you must beat her and compel her to struggle. She is more susceptible to impetuous men than to circumspect ones. And, like a woman, Fortune is also inclined to favour young men, for they are less cautious, are more aggressive, and command her with more audacity.[8]

This passage from *The Prince*, which some readers will doubtless find offensive, actually helps us understand Machiavelli's advice on how the individual is to cope with change. He must preserve the essential element of youth, which is hope. He must never give up but always persist. Denied success in one avenue, he must turn to another.

> I wish to claim once more that, as can be observed in history, men can act in harmony with Fortune but they cannot oppose her; they can weave her warp but they cannot disentangle it. Yet they must never give up – not knowing the future, as Fortune moves along paths both familiar and as yet unexplored, men must maintain hope

and, with hope, they must never despair no matter what Fortune brings or what difficulties they encounter.[9]

Machiavelli held it to be 'a great and continuous malice of fortune' that compelled him to leave the public stage at the age of forty-three. Initially, he turned his hand to composing that great treatise which comprises both *The Prince* and the *Discourses*. When these works were ignored by men in power, he came five years later to another genre entirely, and wrote *La Mandragola*, a satirical comedy that ranks among the greatest works of European literature.[10] The play's success was followed by another successful comedy, *Clizia*, and his celebrity as a playwright renewed his relationship with the Medici when the Medici pope Leo X arranged for it to be performed at the Vatican. In the ensuing years Machiavelli returned to the political and diplomatic stage as a counsellor to the Medici. The man who had won fame with his militia in 1509, only to be disgraced in 1512 owing to its collapse, would find himself with access to power because he was famous as a writer of ribald comedies.[11] In the prologue to *La Mandragola*, an actor playing the author appears on stage and apologizes to the audience that he has turned to playwriting owing to his ill fortune:

> For elsewhere he has not /a place to turn his face: /for he has been barred /from demonstrating with other works another *virtù* /there being no reward for his labours . . . and if this material is not worthy/ for being light, even /of a man who wishes to appear wise and serious, /excuse him with this, that he contrives /with these vain thoughts /to make his wretched time smoother.[12]

So as a man cannot change his nature, and as events will inevitably transform the likelihood of success for any given set of traits, he must find a new *context* within which to act, wresting freedom of action from the forces he cannot control, restlessly seeking those new fields that may be propitious for his talents, searching always, never despairing, changing that which he can change – the arena of his efforts.

FORTUNA AND SOCIETY

In the *Discourses* Machiavelli asserts that if a city is to achieve great-ness, it too must exhibit *virtù* – that is, this set of qualities must be possessed by the body of citizens as a whole.[13] The same willingness to do whatever is necessary to serve the common good and to place the interest of the community above private interest is held to be no less essential in the case of the society at large and the citizens of which it is composed.[14] The *virtù* of a society will enable it,

> to honour and reward excellence, not despise poverty, to esteem the
> methods and regulations of military discipline, to oblige the citizens
> to love one another, to live without factions, to esteem private less
> than public good.[15]

Machiavelli writes that, when faced with 'the ultimate decision concerning the safety of one's country', every citizen must recognize that 'no consideration of what is just or unjust, merciful or cruel, praiseworthy or shameful, should be permitted; on the contrary, put-ting aside every other reservation, one should follow in its entirety the policy that saves [the state's] life and preserves its liberty'.[16]

But if the society, like its rulers, must also cultivate the same quali-ties of *virtù*, does it not face the same problem, namely that Fortune will ask of it different actions at different times? Machiavelli's solu-tion is not only ingenious, but also offers a key to understanding the significance of his contribution to thought.

In 1506 Machiavelli wrote a letter to Piero Soderini's nephew, Giovan Battista, in which he observes that different behaviours nevertheless often lead to the same results and that the same behav-iour, in a different context, brings about different results. How is it that Hannibal won widespread admiration throughout Italy for his perfidy, cruelty and scorn for religion, while Scipio achieved the same renown in Spain through piety, faithfulness and reverence for religion? Why was Lorenzo de' Medici able to enhance his power in Florence by disarming the populace, while Giovanni Bentivoglio achieved the same result in Bologna by arming the public? How was Francesco Sforza in Milan able to preserve his state by building new fortresses, while the duke of Urbino achieved the same goal by destroying existing ones? These examples are repeated in chapter 25 of *The Prince*, written more than half a dozen years after the letter to the young Soderini. Machiavelli further illustrates the point with the example of Pope Julius II, whose impetuousness and love of violence won for him a series of unexpected victories despite his maladroit diplomacy. Had he lived longer, he would have outlived his success, Machiavelli believed. That is because 'He would never have deviated from those habits of acting to which his nature inclined him,'[17] while the world in which he operated would have changed – in part by the effect of his own efforts – and thus would demand different 'habits of acting'.

Machiavelli concludes that success depends on whether the actions of men are suited to the times in which they must act; in different contexts, different behaviour can achieve the same result. The problem then is that whether or not the nature of one's times is in harmony with the nature of one's acts seems itself to be a matter of fortune. Indeed, success only tends to confirm men in their preferred modes of action, regardless of whether these cease to be in harmony with the times. Only if men could properly discern the demands of the times and adjust their behaviour accordingly could they govern Fortune – if one wants to seduce Fortune, one must sense her mood. Hence Machiavelli's suggestion that the individual be alert to shifts in events so that he can change the contexts within which he acts. But how was a *society* to do this?

Machiavelli's answer was the creation of the modern state. Remember that Fortune need be no more than 'arbiter of one half of our actions'; to suppose otherwise would be to 'eliminate our free will',[18] but 'God does not wish to do everything for that would deprive us of our free will'.[19] A state, because it is separate from the person of the prince, need not be doomed by the inevitable frustration that comes when the nature and inclinations of a leader become unsuitable for the times. This is the great *virtù* of republics: they allow for the ruthlessness of the *public*, which can replace its leaders according to the demands of circumstances.

While Hannibal gained victories in Italy, the 'hesitant and cautious' Fabius was able to defend Rome's armies. When the Romans, however, debated whether to seize the initiative and invade Africa, Fabius predictably declared himself against this policy. The Romans determined to side with Scipio, whose nature was more aggressive. Because Rome could deploy either Fabius or Scipio, Rome was able to triumph.[20]

> If Fabius had been king of Rome, he might easily have lost that war because he did not know how to vary his actions to suit the change in the times. But instead he was born into a republic, where there were diverse citizens with diverse talents and approaches, and thus while Rome once had Fabius who was the best leader in times that required sustaining a prolonged war, so it later could turn to Scipio who was more suited to those times apt for seizing victory.
>
> For this reason, a republic has greater longevity and more sustained good fortune than a principality because its diversity of citizens allows it to adapt more easily to changing circumstances than can a single prince. A man who is accustomed to conducting himself in a certain manner never changes and therefore when the times change in ways unfavourable to his methods, he is ruined.[21]

In the twentieth century, perhaps the most celebrated example of this was the electoral defeat of Winston Churchill at the very hour of his triumph over Nazi Germany – he was in fact at the Potsdam Conference when news of the British elections arrived. The British public was not ungrateful, but they were perfectly prepared to replace the heroic war leader with the careful and conciliatory Clement Attlee, who could better deliver the welfare state they desired for the post-war period.

Because collective *virtù* can only be manifested in a stable political environment that structures conflict, and thus allows for peaceful transitions of power, it needs a state. The key to ensuring that the citizens of a society are 'well ordered', therefore, lies in the constitution of the state. This solution is posed in the opening chapter of the first *Discourse*. We can discover how it was that 'so much *virtù* was maintained [in Rome] for so many centuries' by determining 'how she was organized'. The succeeding chapter in the *Discourses* emphasizes this point: we must study the republic's *ordini*. *Virtù* will be the consequence of the interplay between the *umori* – the humours or natures of men – and their modalities of action – their *modo di procedure* – within a constitutional framework.

Victoria Kahn has remarked that '*virtù* cannot be called any one thing', that it is not 'concept-oriented' but 'problem-oriented',[22] and this seems right to me, because it portrays *virtù* as completely context-dependent. The flexibility Machiavelli claims is indispensable to success can rarely be achieved by a human being and by no human being perpetually, because the individual has a small number of modalities of action by nature, to which he adheres because of the success they have brought. But the constitution of a state can provide its citizens with many varying modalities of action and the ability to change its leadership as the changing context demands.[23] By moving from the *virtù* of the prince to the *virtù* of the citizens of a state, Machiavelli both introduces the idea of the necessity of the modern state and provides, in his call for a flexible constitution, the means to keep Fortune by its side.

Chapter 6

Machiavelli's View of History

'Jonathan Wild . . . was a master criminal, and he lived last century – 1750 or thereabouts.'

'Then he's no use to me. I'm a practical man.'

'Mr. Mac[Donald], the most practical thing that ever you did in your life would be to shut yourself up for three months and read twelve hours a day at the annals of crime. Everything comes in circles, even Professor Moriarty . . . The old wheel turns and the same spoke comes up. It's all been done before and will be again.'
Sir Arthur Conan Doyle, The Valley of Fear

ONE CAN WINCE when one hears the phrase 'the lessons of history clearly show that . . .' as a prelude to the speaker's advice on some contemporary policy problem. History may rhyme, as Mark Twain said, but it seldom repeats itself, and it is terribly hard to know precisely what inference to draw from one historical context to another. In 2011 a revolution took place in Egypt. But was it a replay of the events in Tehran in 1979, which led to an authoritarian theocracy? Or was the appropriate precedent the removal of Ferdinand Marcos from Manila in 1986, which was succeeded by a functioning if occasionally turbulent democracy? In both cases, an autocrat allied to the US was removed, as has happened in Egypt, but the results for the publics of Iran and the Philippines and for Western interests were strikingly different.

It is deceptively easy to read Machiavelli's insistence on the

usefulness of history as if he, too, were the sort of policy commenta-
tor addicted to prefacing his advice on the diplomatic problems contemporary to him with just such a phrase. There are many passages
in his writings that, taken in isolation and construed in the most
naïve way, might tempt one to do this.* Machiavelli's uses of history,
however, are of a different sort altogether.[1] Once we appreciate his
way of dealing with the formal problems of anachronism – how we
can know how actors in an earlier era really understood themselves
and their own actions when these occurred in a context we dimly
perceive and never fully comprehend – we will then be equipped to
appreciate his methods of historical rhetoric.[2]

The problem of anachronism is a variation on the question of
whether there are eternal truths. On the one hand, we know that historical methods are inevitably uncertain, but that to say the past is so
inaccessible to us that we can never appreciate its import for its writers and their contemporaries is to render history an impossibility and
to make of our ancestors almost another species. On the other hand,
if there are eternal truths – and to say there are no eternal truths is to
propose one – then what makes them true must be accessible to us,
at least in principle, if we know them to be true. But this conclusion
leads us to epistemological arguments, rather than historical ones. It
will become clear in the course of this book that neither do I wholly
endorse the view of one school that Machiavelli's work is an irre-
trievable event that sets other events in motion but is forever confined to his time (the way a meteor might strike the earth and set off
a chain of geophysical events); nor do I wholly endorse the view of
another school that Machiavelli is a materialist, or perhaps a Marxist
avant la lettre, expressing timeless and inexorable truths.

* For example, *Discourses*, book I, chapter 39: 'Thus, it is an easy matter for
anyone who examines past events carefully to foresee future events . . . and to
apply the remedies that the ancients employed, or if old remedies cannot be
found, to think of new ones based upon the similarity of circumstances.'

For Machiavelli, the essential eternal truth is the unchanging nature of man which manifests itself according to context. As Machiavelli writes in the *Discourses*:

> Prudent men usually say that if one wants to see what has to be, one need only look at what has been; that everything in every era has its counterpart in ancient times. This is the case because the actions of men motivated by the same passions, necessarily, lead to the same results.[3]

But knowing that the passions of man do not change – that men will always desire the same things – does not tell us how to cope with what does change, the ever surprising contexts that Fortune creates within which the nature of man must be perpetually revealed.*

That coping is accomplished, not by mechanically transposing the events and actions of the past to those of the present so that current events appear to be mere recapitulations, but rather by inspiring the actors of the present through examples of the wise management of affairs throughout history.[4] Ancient histories, Machiavelli writes, allow us to experience good emperors living in safety among safe citizens,

> a world full of peace and justice . . . its prince glorious and universally respected, its people devoted to him and secure in his rule . . . If a prince will then carefully study the histories of inadequate emperors, he will find them crowded with the atrocities of war, riddled with the dissension that arises from sedition, cruel in times of both peace and war, marked by assassinations, civil and foreign warfare.[5]

Machiavelli's use of historical examples – especially his recounting of the acts of great figures of the past – is not, strictly speaking, a recitation and study of past events so much as the creation of archetypal, mythopoeic figures whose authorship of the precise events

---

* Freud thought that all men desire honour, fame, riches, power and the love of women; what women want, he professed to be baffled by.

related cannot be assumed.[6] These figures are more in the nature of dramatic exemplars, because what they exemplify is the best – or the worst – of human nature, not the actual acts of any citizen or leader. That Machiavelli was a gifted playwright perhaps reinforces the conclusion that he was trying to give his readers an experience that will enhance their judgement in the way that the experience of his diplomatic missions enhanced his. Cultivating such judgement is essential to the *virtù* necessary to protect the state.

In this way, the study of history can arouse *virtù* through the narration of dramatic acts drawn from antiquity, and for this reason Machiavelli argues it is of greater value than the philosophical precepts of moral discourse:

> Who will teach courage, justice, loyalty, self-control, simplicity and the acceptance of grief and pain better than men like Fabricius, Curius, Regulus, Decius, Mucius and countless others? For if the Greeks bear away the palm for moral precepts, Rome can produce more striking examples of moral performance, which is a far greater thing.[7]

It is not by studying the facts of historic events but rather through reading a stirring account of the past that fires our imagination that we achieve 'that *sense* ... that flavour that narratives of the past inherently possess. Failing to get this feeling, the numberless people who have read histories merely take away pleasure in hearing about the various incidents of the past without ever thinking of imitating them.'[8]

Machiavelli believed that history was cyclical but also irreversible – that is, that states went through a cycle of growth and decay, returning to a condition similar to that with which they began, but not going quite back to the original point of beginning, because the action of the cycle created new contexts.[9]

> *Virtù* makes countries tranquil, and from Tranquillity, Leisure next emerges, and Leisure burns the town and villages. Then, after a

country has for a time been subject to lawlessness, *Virtù* often returns to live there once again. Such a course the power which governs human things permits and requires, so that nothing beneath the sun ever will or can be firm. And it is and always has been and always will be, that evil follows after good, good after evil.[10]

The cycle of affairs moves through history, never returning to the context from which it began, yet endlessly repeating its pattern. Rome had been powerful and independent for centuries; by Machiavelli's time, it was desperately trying to survive under a series of corrupt papacies that were incapable of coping with the challenge of foreign invasion. In the time of Rome's dominance France was merely a rustic, fragmented arena for conflict; by the time of *The Prince* it was the strongest and most influential kingdom in Europe. Having described the cycle of growth and decline – monarchies decay into tyrannies, aristocracies into oligarchies, republics into democracies, each degraded order deriving from its superior form – Machiavelli observes: 'Rarely do they return to precisely the same government because almost no republic can live so long as to be able to experience these mutations many times and still endure.'[11] What ensues is that another state, with a more strategically and constitutionally dynamic order, surpasses the state that is in a period of stasis. 'Rather, it happens that a republic, lacking ingenuity and strength, will become subject to a neighbouring state that is better ordered.'[12]

In fact this is precisely what happened to the princely state of which Machiavelli was the architect: it proved a more successful model, strategically and constitutionally, than the feudal system it replaced, and it was itself superseded by the more dynamic order of the consolidated kingly states of the seventeenth century.*

---

* *The Shield of Achilles*, chapters 6–7. Note that it was not the Italian innovation – the first princely states which appeared in Italy – that ultimately dominated the international system, but rather the adoption of this form by other states in northern Europe. Similarly, it was not the American innovation of the imperial

Machiavelli's ideology of mutability – of constant and unpredictable change – which was discussed in the preceding chapter, has led some scholars to conclude that he was an apostle of modernity because it is the essence of the modern that it is constantly changing, always becoming more modern.[13] But this elegant insight about modernity neglects the cyclical aspect of Machiavelli's ideas of historical development. Similarly, many scholars seize upon Machiavelli's cyclical ideas to deny that fundamental, irreversible change occurs, neglecting his keen appreciation of the constitutional developments that are the result of the interplay between popular morale and warfare.[14]

Some readers may be familiar with Parmenides' Fallacy.[15] This fallacy occurs when one attempts to assess a current state of affairs by comparing it with the past, instead of with alternative possible states of affairs that have not been realized; or the fallacy may occur when one tries to assess the future state of affairs by measuring it against the present, as opposed to comparing it to other possible futures. 'Will we be better off in five years if we adopt policy X than we are now?' should be rephrased as 'Will we be better off in five years if we adopt policy X than we will be in five years if we do not?'* Faced with a proposed healthcare reform, for example, we should not ask whether or not it means a rise in premiums for the coverage we have

---

state at the end of the eighteenth century that vanquished the territorial state system, but rather a somewhat later version, Napoleonic France.

* A famous example of Parmenides' Fallacy occurred in the 1980 United States presidential race. During the debate between Governor Reagan and President Carter, the governor criticized the president's record by asking the audience: 'Are you better off today than you were four years ago?' But because the state of the nation will never stay the same for years, regardless of which party is in power, the better question would have been: 'Are you better off now than you would have been if Gerald Ford had continued as president and if he had had to cope with rising oil prices, the revolution in Iran, the Soviet invasion of Afghanistan, and soaring interest rates?'

now, but rather whether our premiums will be more or our coverage less if the reforms are adopted than they would be in the future if they are not.

To complement Parmenides' Fallacy, consider Heraclitus' Fallacy. This is the notion that because everything is in flux – that there are no constants – the future is not only unpredictable and uncertain, it is random and as such appears to be infinitely malleable. The past imposes no constraints. Such a view is behind many contemporary claims that we can create the conditions of the future by simply declaring them.* To take a subtle example of this fallacy, consider calls to remove the Senate from the US Congress or to reproportion it along more egalitarian lines.[16] Such a proposed reform is certainly possible under an entirely new constitution; but it cannot be an ordinary amendment to the one we have now because a Senate pro-portioned by state was the crucial basis – memorialized in the text – for the adoption of the original constitution by a deeply divided convention.† To amend *that* constitution in this way would attempt to appropriate its legitimacy while doing away with its essential basis.

Avoiding both these fallacies, Machiavelli maintains that each political form derives from elements present in its predecessor – there is nothing unique or without origin – because the nature of man is constant, and the successive forms of government are

---

* For example, it was commonly said in the early years of the twenty-first century that it would be unwise to call the conflict arising from terrorism a 'war', as this polarized domestic debate, gave excessive authority to military persons and the executive, elevated the terrorist to the status of warrior, and so on. This ignores the fact that even the most rigid nomenclature cannot dictate reality; if the nature of warfare is changing, an insistence on denying it its name will not alter that fact and, as in the aftermath of the fall of Baghdad, can lead to quite disastrous tactics.

† Article V, which provides for the amendment of the US Constitution, also requires 'that no State, without its Consent, shall be deprived of its equal Suffrage in the Senate'.

reactions to each preceding form as it evolves in its attempts to cope with unceasing change.[17] From this notion of the interplay between the eternal, cyclical narrative of mankind and the fortuitous, contingent choices mankind is compelled to make, Machiavelli derives his conclusion that success leads to failure.[18]

Perhaps it is easiest to see this in an individual's life. Each of us has a strategy for success: some simply outwork their competitors, some rely on inspiration, some on good fortune, some on the goodwill of friends. But sooner or later, if we are successful, we will rise and find ourselves in a competition where our customary strategies no longer succeed. Then we will find it very hard to change, partly because our strategies arise from our individual temperaments and partly because they have brought us success in the past.[19]

Machiavelli is an historical rhetorician, not a scholarly antiquarian. In his hands, history is mined not so much for its 'lessons' as for its effect when expressed in an artful historical narrative. Machiavelli's historiography is both cyclical and directional, with elements that are both circumstantial and eternal. Above all, it is purposeful because its objectives are to take what Machiavelli has observed in his diplomatic and political career and what he has read of the classical world, and forge a new consciousness that will enable the successful creation of a new political order, the modern, neoclassical state. Perhaps for this reason, Machiavelli is sometimes thought not to be an historian at all, but a political scientist.

Thus Ernst Cassirer wrote that '[w]hat Galileo gave in his *Dialogues*, and what Machiavelli gave in his *Prince*, were really "new sciences". Just as Galileo's Dynamics became the foundation of our modern science of nature, so Machiavelli paved a new way to political science.'[20] If this were the case, then Machiavelli would have been a very poor founder of political science indeed, because his 'scientific' methods are so fanciful. Consider, for example, *The Life of Castruccio Castracani*, written by Machiavelli in 1520. Many of the details of Castracani's biography are obviously invented: for example, he is depicted as a foundling, a fact for which there is no evidence, while this offers Machiavelli the opportunity to demonstrate how great men have been born in modest circumstances and are creatures of *fortuna*. In order to allow Machiavelli the opportunity to discuss the subject of letters versus arms, the young Castruccio is portrayed, fancifully, as training with weapons (he was in fact educated by priests). In a deathbed oration, a frequent device of ancient biographies, the dying tyrant concludes that *fortuna*, and not *virtù*, is supreme in human affairs. Finally, a collection of Castracani's epigrams is presented, most of which have been lifted from Diogenes Laertius' *Lives of the Philosophers*.

Nor did Machiavelli display any deference to Aristotle – the first political scientist – or to philosophical writing generally. When Francesco Vettori attempts to persuade Machiavelli that he should not be alarmed by growing Swiss power in Italy, Vettori cites Aristotle's *Politics*. Machiavelli is not impressed; he replies that he does not know what Aristotle might have said about confederations like the Swiss, but that he, Machiavelli, is only persuaded by 'what might reasonably exist, what exists, and what has existed'.[21] History provides many examples of federal republics, he wrote to Vettori, that are quite capable of aggressive expansion, as is evidenced by the history of the Etruscans, who conquered all of Italy.

Doubtless this is what Cassirer has in mind: Machiavelli's resolute reliance on the actuality of politics as he knew it. A 'Galileo' in the study of politics would distinguish between facts and dogma, in contrast to a normative vision of a political science. But as I have tried to show in earlier chapters, Machiavelli does not in fact separate fact from morality, even if he denies that observing the conventional moral virtues will always yield the most efficacious result for the state.[22] Rather, he asserts a vigorous morality that comes with taking responsibility for the state. He is not trying simply to describe facts dispassionately, disinterestedly, but instead wants to move his readers to action.[23]

Machiavelli's approach – the approach of the historical rhetorician rather than the political scientist – has significant implications for intelligence and strategic planning today. As Henry Kissinger once remarked, 'History is not . . . a cookbook offering pre-tested recipes. It teaches by analogy, not by maxims.' It can illuminate the consequences of actions in comparable situations, yet each generation must discover for itself what situations are in fact comparable.[24]

*****

In 1502 Alexander VI had dispatched his son, Cesare Borgia, to the Romagna on the final stage of the campaign intended to create a new, Borgia principality. Borgia was accompanied by Leonardo da Vinci, whom he had hired to be his chief military engineer. Also present was Niccolò Machiavelli, who had been sent by the Florentine Signoria to determine the nature of the threat posed by Borgia to Florence. Some writers have speculated that Leonardo was a principal intelligence source for Machiavelli,[25] and the two Florentines were known to be friends who would later collaborate on the siege of Pisa.

Leonardo's role in the Borgia campaign was to study and improve the fortresses that Borgia conquered as well as to investigate new military technologies.[26] The drawings for many of these machines may be seen in Leonardo's notebooks, and they include sketches for the forerunners of modern tanks and helicopters. But Leonardo's notebooks don't disclose a design for the bicycle, that machine that repeats its orbit endlessly while moving forwards.

So, unlike the pump that inspired Harvey, or the clockworks that pervaded Newton's imagination, Machiavelli had to do without the bicycle. But he had another image, in the popular card games that entranced Florentines of the time. Neither endlessly recurrent like Vico's, nor irreversibly progressive like Hegel's, Machiavelli's universe repeats, reshuffles, and deals us a new hand with the same rather frayed cards.

Conclusion to Book III
Machiavelli's Philosophy of Fate

Human nature is constant through time but manifests itself according to the historical context; because these contexts change unpredictably, no person can be sure of success, which depends on the synchrony of temperament and character with the ever-shifting demands of the time. History is thus both cyclical, because every context returns in time, and irreversible, because human interaction with its contexts brings about change.

Book IV

Occasione – The Interesting Timing
of *The Prince*

THREE TIMES MACHIAVELLI glimpsed what seemed to be the opportunity to create a neoclassical state that could defend Italy from France and Spain. The second time a confluence of events appeared to present a propitious chance for this development, he was no longer in office. Yet it seemed that he might nevertheless influence events through his writing by getting his manuscripts into the right hands. To seize this moment, he broke off his treatise on republics – which ultimately became the *Discourses* – and undertook a book on principalities,[1] a book that we know as *The Prince*.

Chapter 7

The Borgias and the Medici

CHAPTER 26 OF *The Prince* – the final chapter – has always posed a problem for readers of that book.[1] In the first place, its tone and diction are radically at odds with the rest of the work.[2] Its title – 'An exhortation to liberate Italy from the barbarians' – is at obvious variance with the restrained chapter headings that precede it ('On hereditary principalities'; 'How cities or principalities should be governed that lived by their own laws before they were occupied'; 'On whether fortresses are useful or harmful'). Chapter 26's florid plea has seemed to many readers somehow tacked on, as if the author had written it for some other purpose irrelevant to the cautious and gimlet-eyed analytics that compose the first twenty-five chapters.

Moreover, unlike the advice in a classical mirror book, which is intended to govern the generality of princes, chapter 26 is entirely devoted to one particular problem, the expulsion of the French and Spanish forces that had vexed Italian statecraft since 1494. Mirror books, like etiquette books, are of a different genre from, say, pamphlets proposing a return to the gold standard. The scope and approach of a mirror book is determined by its purpose to prepare the reader to cope with the many issues that might arise regardless of the locality, or even the era, of the prince such books purport to advise.

Likewise, many readers who have noted the absurdity of Machiavelli's hortatory dedication to the feckless Lorenzo de'

Medici ('Accept, therefore, Your Magnificence, this little gift . . . that you may attain the greatness which Fortune and all your own capacities promise you') practically choke on the suggestion that this twenty-four-year-old syphilitic should take the field with 'new armies and changing battle formations . . . so that Italy, after so long a time, may behold its redeemer'.[3] The most charitable of commentators has observed that 'Machiavelli dedicated *The Prince* to Lorenzo to inform him of the tactics to use in unifying Italy, though the entire intent behind this . . . is shrouded in mystery.' Most critics simply conclude that chapter 26 confirms the suspicion that these sections of *The Prince* are meant to comprise a grovelling, if implied, suggestion that Machiavelli be hired to help accomplish these grand objectives.[4]

Thus the problem of chapter 26: what is it doing here as it seems to have nothing to do with the rest of the arguments of the book?

Let us try to solve this problem and in doing so also resolve another that has tormented readers of *The Prince* over the centuries: why does Machiavelli present Cesare Borgia as a model for new princes in chapter 7 ('for I would not know of any better precepts to give to a new prince than the example of [Cesare Borgia's] deeds'), even to the point of excusing his catastrophic and ultimate failure ('It was not his fault, but arose instead from an unusual and extreme instance of adverse Fortune') when, as Machiavelli makes clear, it was Borgia's credulous and passive stance towards the papal election that brought his nemesis Julius II to power – with the votes of Spanish cardinals whom Borgia controlled – and led to Borgia's ruin and imprisonment?[5]

Chapter 26 is not a mere add-on, an absurdly flattering *l'envoi* that book-ends an equally otiose dedication (or worse, a toe-curling supplication for appointment). Rather, this chapter asserts the entire point of the book. As I have implied in earlier pages, *The Prince* is not chiefly a mirror book at all, but a detailed essay that sits inside a larger constitutional treatise begun prior to the composition of *The Prince*. The reason Machiavelli broke off writing this larger work on republics and hurriedly began a memorandum on principalities is precisely because he believed he saw an opportunity to create a new principality in the centre of Italy, uniting Rome and the papal vicarages with Florence and its possessions, and thus providing a bulwark against Spain and France. To understand this we must see what Machiavelli saw in the constitutional and strategic turmoil that engulfed Italy from 1492 until 1537 – that is, from the death of the Florentine ruler Lorenzo the Magnificent and the entry into Italy of France and Spain, to the accession of his great-grandson Cosimo as duke of Tuscany with the support of the emperor Charles V.* This will require some patience of those readers who, like the author, are not accustomed to the mingling of family names and international politics, of head-spinningly abrupt changes in alliance, and expressions of soon-to-be-reversed eternal fidelity that would sicken a Hollywood agent; but though such a politics often more resembles the quickly changing moods and alliances of a dysfunctional and quarrelsome set of cousins, it was the socio-political environment that cultured the modern state.

We must revisit this history because it is necessary to have a sensitive grasp of the turbulent conditions that followed the French invasion in 1494, the tempting opportunities presented to the Borgias and the Medici, the dizzying shifts of alliance, within which Machiavelli thrice glimpsed the possible future that he laboured to bring into being. Machiavelli sought the creation of a modern state as a constitutional vehicle to secure the common good and as a strategically dynamic structure that could stand up to the great powers of Europe, France, Spain and the Holy Roman Empire, two objectives he believed to be mutually reinforcing. He exalted

---

* Cosimo was also the great-great-grandson of Lorenzo the Magnificent's uncle, Lorenzo the Elder, because Lorenzo the Magnificent's eldest daughter Lucrezia's second daughter, Maria, married her cousin Giovanni dalle Bande Nere, whose child was Cosimo.

first the Borgias, and then the Medici, because he saw they suffered from a lack of legitimacy, and because they possessed the will, the resources, and above all had the opportunity, to create a new principality uniting Rome and Florence. This is why he praised Cesare Borgia, even though Borgia failed to oust the foreign powers, and did not praise Julius II, who defeated them. As we shall see in the next chapter, Machiavelli believed that once such a state was created, its rulers could be persuaded to cede power to a republican form of government.

We must begin therefore not with the Medici but with Cardinal Rodrigo Borgia, who became Pope Alexander VI in 1492. In this election he defeated Giuliano della Rovere (who later became Pope Julius II), forever embittering him. Although there is scholarly support for the judgement that Alexander's uncle, Calixtus III, the first Borgia pope, was an enthusiastic practitioner of papal nepotism, and though it is well known that his predecessor, Sixtus VI, made his nephew lord of Imola and Forli, two papal vicarages in the Romagna, neither pope was unique in this favouritism for nephews,* nor did either have quite the same ambitions for a secular dynasty that gripped Alexander. After Rodrigo Borgia's election as pope, Giovanni de' Medici, who would later become Pope Leo X, warned: 'Now we are in the power of the wolf, the most rapacious perhaps that this world has ever seen.'[6] To see just how rapacious Alexander was, one has to consider the situation in Italy when he came to power.

Alexander found a papacy that had wealth but little political or military control over the Papal States. The Papal States were an accumulation of territories given to the popes from the fourth century

---

* Pope Gregory XII's nephew became Pope Eugene IV, whose own nephew became Pope Paul II; Pope Sixtus VI's nephew became Alexander's archenemy, Julius II, and there are other examples; indeed, the word 'nepotism' derives from the papal practice of appointing nephews as cardinals.

onwards that lay in the Romagna (including the great city of Bologna, as well as Forlì, Imola, Rimini, Cesena and Faenza); Umbria (encompassing the cities of Perugia, Città di Castello, Orvieto and Spoleto); the Marche (within which lay the city of Urbino, as well as Senigallia, Camerino and Ancona); Lazio (the districts of Rome itself, as well as Bracciano, Palestrina, Viterbo and Civitavecchia); and, across the Alps, the Comtat Venaissin in Provence. In these territories, great families – the Baglioni in Perugia, the Bentivogli in Bologna, the Malatesta in Rimini and Cesena, the Montefeltro in Urbino and Ancona, the Varano in Camerino – held power that, though essentially feudatory in relation to the papacy, often meant little more than an insignificant annual toll on local revenues. These fortified towns and lands were known as 'vicarages' owing to their ostensible fealty to Rome. They and their ruling families now became the targets of the Borgias.

At the point of Alexander's election, the papacy had yet to achieve a secular role equivalent to that of the monarchs of France and Spain. To accomplish this, Alexander commenced a blindingly complex series of diplomatic manoeuvres with those monarchs, culminating in a military campaign against the vicarages to bring them under the control of the pope and to carve out a dynastic realm for his family.[7]

In Milan Ludovico Sforza had been forced to confront a challenge to his legitimacy, arising from his usurpation of the duchy from his nephew, the rightful heir, when the king of Naples – whose daughter had been married to the young duke Ludovico had deposed – mounted a claim to the duchy. To parry this challenge, Sforza encouraged the French king Charles VIII to press his claims for the crown of Naples and invited him to enter Italy via Milan.*

---

* It was this invasion that destroyed Medici rule in Florence when the unfortunate Piero, son of Lorenzo the Magnificent, tried in 1494 to repeat his father's historic embassy to his enemies by a peaceful parley with the French in which he made so many concessions that the Florentines drove him from the

The pope granted French forces passage through the Papal States and Charles VIII entered Naples where he was crowned king. But the next year Alexander organized the Holy League to oppose the French, who retreated back across the Alps, and the Neapolitan king was restored to power by Spanish forces. Savonarola, who had allied Florence with France, was excommunicated by the pope, who then employed the traditional papal tactic of placing Florence itself under an interdict that hugely restricted its trade. The Florentines rebelled against Savonarola, who was burnt at the stake on 23 May 1498, and Piero Soderini, Machiavelli's patron, was made *gonfaloniere* (head of government) of Florence.

In 1499 Alexander switched sides again. In a rapid sequence of ruthless ploys, which included the annulment of the new French king's marriage and a dispensation enabling him to make a territorially advantageous match with his brother's widow, bringing a noble French bride and a French title to his son Cesare, Alexander allied himself with the king of France, Louis XII. Louis entered Italy and deposed Ludovico Sforza.

The pope's son, Cesare Borgia, with Louis' backing, then began a series of campaigns to reduce the power of the vicarages in the Romagna. He first ousted Caterina Sforza, ruler of Imola and Forli. The following year – 1500 – saw a dramatic rise in papal revenues as pilgrims flocked to Rome for the papal jubilee, enabling Cesare Borgia to return to the field, independent of French assistance. He soon took Pesaro from Giovanni Sforza (his former brother-in-law); Pandolfo Malatesta surrendered Rimini; and Astorre Manfredi lost Faenza and was drowned on Borgia's orders. In 1501 Cesare Borgia began the siege of Piombino, which capitulated the next year.

He arranged the murder of his sister Lucrezia's Spanish husband, in order that she could marry the heir to the duke of Ferrara. In

---

city, and the Dominican monk Savonarola was brought to power and the republic restored.

1502 Cesare seized Camarino and Urbino but was unable to draw Florence into an alliance. That year, he also captured Ceri and invested Bracciano, which was surrendered by Giulio Orsini. In early August, however, he and his father, the pope, fell ill – it seems to have been an attack of malaria – and on 18 August 1502 Alexander died.

After a brief interregnum of twenty-six days during which Pope Pius held the papacy, Cardinal Giuliano della Rovere was named Pope Julius II in 1503. Cesare Borgia, deprived of his father's support, attempted to ingratiate himself with della Rovere by effectuating this election, but Borgia was soon arrested, deprived of his lands and titles, and imprisoned. He played no further significant military or political role.

Julius II, by contrast, continued the campaign to subdue the vicarages and reconquered several that had been seized by Venice and by the petty tyrants that Cesare Borgia had ousted, including Faenza, Rimini, Perugia and Bologna. By 1512 the French had been driven across the Alps, the Medici restored in Florence, and papal authority securely established in the Romagna, a record that exceeded even Cesare Borgia's triumphs.

And yet Machiavelli does not exalt Julius II, the 'warrior pope', as he does Cesare Borgia. That is because Julius merely sought to consolidate the Papal States, while Alexander and Cesare attempted to create a new principality, carved out of those states. What Machiavelli saw in the campaigns of the Borgias went well beyond their war aims; he saw the possibility of uniting the influence, money and ecclesiastical authority of the papacy with the wealth and genius of Florence to create a new kind of state in the centre of Italy.

Naples and the south were hopelessly backward; Lombardy and the northern states were divided and vulnerable; Venice was prey to the increasing power of the Holy Roman Empire. But in the very heart of Italy there lay the inchoate realm of the first, truly modern, non-feudal state. This historic insight forms the centre of gravity of

Machiavelli's remarkable genius as a student of the constitutional order of states.

The Borgias' ambitions and power presented the first time that Machiavelli glimpsed this extraordinary possibility (though it was not what they had in mind). Then, when Giovanni de' Medici was elected Pope Leo X and his brother Giuliano controlled Florence, Machiavelli saw this potential future a second time.[8] This explains the urgency with which Machiavelli interrupted his work on the *Discourses* to write *The Prince*, which was originally dedicated to Giuliano.[9] When Giuliano suddenly died, Machiavelli debated for some period whether to change the dedication to Lorenzo, whose character he knew. It was his only chance. This opportunity did not lapse with Lorenzo's death in 1517, however; indeed, he was replaced as ruler of Florence by the more capable Giulio de' Medici. Rather, it was the death in 1521 of Leo X that seemed to foreclose the possibility of the modern state that Machiavelli sought. With the election of Adrian VI to the papacy, the Medici no longer controlled the Papal States and could not consolidate them with Florence and its territories in Tuscany.

This, perhaps even more than the terrible events of 1512 that saw Machiavelli arrested, tortured, penalized and exiled, marked a low point in his hopes. For shortly after the death of Leo, Cardinal Francesco Soderini, the champion of the Florentine Republic and brother of Piero Soderini, Machiavelli's patron, attempted to retake Florence for the Republican forces. The *condottieri* he hired, with French assistance, were defeated. That summer, a plot to assassinate Giulio was exposed, and Cardinal Soderini was arrested in Rome by Adrian VI; the same month Piero Soderini died. Both of Machiavelli's great dreams – the creation of a modern state uniting Florence, Rome and the Papal States and his vision of a republican Florence wrested from the Medici – seemed dashed.

Then, in September 1523, Pope Adrian suddenly died, barely twenty months after his election. Giulio de' Medici was chosen as his successor and took the name Clement VII. Once again, Machiavelli saw the chance that the power of a Medici papacy – in the hands of a man whom he knew well, with whom he had met in March 1520 when Giulio had commissioned a study of Florentine governance from him, and who with Leo X had given him patronage to write a history of Florence – might unite the Papal States with Tuscany to create a modern state in Italy.

Although Giulio had been elected pope with the support of the emperor Charles V, he now detached himself from his ally and began negotiations for an alliance with France. For the next four years, Machiavelli would be engaged with ever-increasing authority in an effort to defeat the imperial forces and drive them from Italy. He seems to have seen in the young Giovanni de' Medici – known as Giovanni dalle Bande Nere for the black stripes he wore in mourning for the death of Leo X – the kind of charismatic military leader who might bring about the consolidation of which Machiavelli dreamed, but this final opportunity too was crushed when Bande Nere died from wounds in November 1526.

Machiavelli's other dream – a republican Florence – did come into being; but without the strategic bulwark Machiavelli envisioned, it could not last. In April 1527 Charles V assembled a force combining German *Landsknechts* and Spanish troops, which advanced on Rome. The papal armies, now without Bande Nere, were under the command of Francesco Guicciardini, who was unable to resist the imperial forces. In May these soldiers sacked Rome, and this shattering event precipitated a revolt in Florence, the Medici were expelled and the Republic was restored. Machiavelli hoped that the Signoria might return him to the Chancery, but he had by now long been identified with the Medici and thus he died in June without returning to office.

The sack of Rome in 1527 ended the possibility that the Papal States might serve as a barrier against foreign power in Italy. Clement, who had taken refuge in Castel Sant' Angelo, was forced to pay a heavy ransom for his life, and ceded Parma, Piacenza, Civitavecchia and Modena to the Holy Roman Empire; Venice exploited Clement's impotence by seizing Cervia and Ravenna, while the Malatesta returned to Rimini. After six months as a prisoner, the pope escaped in disguise; he only returned to a devastated and largely depopulated Rome in October 1528. 'Not just a city,' Erasmus wrote, 'but a whole world has been destroyed.'[10] The grander political ambitions of Renaissance Rome were definitively ended, and thereafter Clement followed a policy of deference towards the empire.

Despite the collapse of the League of Cognac – with whom Florence had been allied in opposing the empire – and the signing of treaties between all of its other participants with the emperor, Florence continued to fight on alone. A siege took place that lasted from October 1529 until August 1530, when the city surrendered, betrayed by Malatesta Baglioni, the sort of *condottiere* of whom Machiavelli had once warned. Alessandro de' Medici was installed as *gonfaloniere*,* Clement having purchased an imperial dukedom for him from Charles V, whose illegitimate daughter Alessandro now married. At his side, as senior advisers, were Machiavelli's two close friends, Francesco Vettori[11] and Francesco Guicciardini.[12] There ensued a reign of tyranny in which all the most violent and treacherous methods described in *The Prince* were signally employed. When Ippolito de' Medici – Giuliano's illegitimate son – went to the imperial court to denounce his cousin's abuses, fell ill and died, there was universal suspicion that Alessandro had had him poisoned. Ultimately, Alessandro was murdered by another cousin, Lorenzino de' Medici, who lured him to his death with the promise of a salacious assignation. Fleeing to Bologna when the uprising for which

---

* Alessandro is thought to have been Clement's illegitimate son by an African domestic, but was acknowledged, however, as the natural son of Lorenzo de' Medici.

he hoped did not materialize, Lorenzino wrote an *Apologia* defending his acts and comparing them to Brutus' assassination of Caesar.

Following Alessandro's death, Guicciardini immediately went to the imperial court, where he promoted the cause of Cosimo de' Medici, the son of Bande Nere. Cosimo was barely twenty when Charles V recognized him as head of Florence in 1537. He ruled for thirty-seven years, having ordered in 1548 the assassination of Lorenzino de' Medici, the last remaining Medici with a claim to rule. In this, as in the predations of Alessandro, Cosimo was ruthlessly following the tactics described in *The Prince,* executing the scions of the great Florentine families, promoting men of humble origin who were dependent on him, and allying himself with a great power.

What Alessandro, Cosimo and their Machiavellian advisers, Vettori and Guicciardini, had never appreciated, however, was the real point of *The Prince,* and indeed of Machiavelli's life's work.[13] Machiavelli had described the tactics by which a new realm – the first modern princely state – could be established and maintained in the centre of Italy. This is the purpose of *The Prince*'s important chapter on ecclesiastical principalities and its concluding reference to Leo X. This state had one paramount objective: to promote the common interest of the public. Guicciardini and Vettori – who both wrote histories of Italy and commentaries on Machiavelli – energetically deployed Machiavelli's most brutal tactics but, ironically, never accepted his crucial objective. Indeed, Guicciardini mocked Machiavelli as idealistic and unrealistic: 'you have always been considered exceedingly grand in your opinions by most people, and the inventor of new and outlandish things.'[14] While Machiavelli had seen 1494 and the French invasion as creating the necessity for the modern state, Guicciardini saw only the end of a golden era.

More than Florentine independence was lost in 1530. The very idea of a state devoted to the common interest was brushed aside and abandoned, and with that, the *raison d'être* for *The Prince*. It would be more than three centuries before the Italian state arose.

Perhaps Guicciardini was right; perhaps Machiavelli was too idealistic. But if this is true, it is not because he was unrealistic, only that his realism was in service of a visionary ideal. If anything, he was the most realistic of his contemporaries, who ultimately stumbled into the foreign domination about which he warned them. Rather, like most visionaries, his insights seemed unrealistic because they challenged the assumptions of the era. Then, as now, the emergence of a new constitutional order loomed over men whose eyes were firmly fixed on the ground, even as it was shifting beneath them.

Chapter 8

Machiavelli's Constitution

M ACHIAVELLI WAS OBSESSED with this question: how can a decision-maker master fate? *Fortuna* – the unribboning, unceasing flow of unpredictable events – was favourable to a leader of *virtù*, a person of resolution, imagination, determination and courage. Such a man was Cesare Borgia in 1502, when Machiavelli first encountered him, when Borgia was indeed much favoured by Fortune. But by 1504 this same figure had been stripped of his command of the papal armies, his lands had been confiscated, and he lay imprisoned, exiled to Spain. It seems it was not enough to have been fortunate and, indeed, that depending too greatly on good fortune was a snare.

Had Cesare Borgia been able to win the favour of the new pope after Alexander VI's death, he might have fulfilled Machiavelli's hopes for a consolidated princely state in the centre of Italy. What he lacked was the diplomatic finesse of his father and the shrewd use of papal funds to suborn the conclave, which he ought to have dominated by virtue of his troops and his control of the crucial Spanish cardinals.

Was his failure then a failure of character? At first, Machiavelli seems to have thought that Cesare Borgia, perhaps owing to illness, had succumbed to weakness and panic. But later he concluded that Borgia had simply relied too much on Fortune – which is a way of saying he had come to depend upon his particular *virtù* being favoured by Fortune.

[O]ne sees a prince successful today and ruined the next day without having seen him change his character or his traits. I believe this happens because . . . the prince who relies wholly on Fortune will come to ruin as soon as Fortune changes.[1]

Machiavelli developed this view, as we have seen, by observing the successes of men whose *virtù* was expressed in diametrically opposed ways. Each of the principal actors on the European stage enjoyed a time of historic success, yet each differed profoundly in character from the others – just as profoundly, in fact, as Alexander VI had differed from his adversary, della Rovere, who became Julius II and destroyed Alexander's son Cesare. Each leader follows his nature – one proceeds cautiously, like the Holy Roman Emperor Maximilian; another impetuously, like Julius II; another cunningly, like Ferdinand of Aragon – and for a time succeeds, while the commands of his temperament are in accord with the demands of the situation.*

What was needed was the ability to anticipate and adapt to the changing demands of Fortune:

I also believe that the man who shapes his plans and methods to comport with the temper of the times will triumph and, likewise, that the man who sets his course of action out of harmony with the times will come to grief.[2]

The difficulty is that a man cannot change his 'way of proceeding', which is the way that *virtù* is expressed in a person's acts, because this

---

* 'For one can see that men . . . proceed in different ways: one by caution, another by impulsiveness; one through force, another through guile; one with patience, another with its opposite; and each one can achieve his goals with his means. And we can also observe that, in the case of two cautious men, for example, one achieves his goal while the other does not; and, likewise, two men may equally prosper though using two different means, the one being cautious and the other impetuous: this is explained by the character of the times that either suits or does not suit the chosen way of acting.' *The Prince*, chapter 25.

derives from his individual nature. 'No man,' Machiavelli wrote, 'is so wise that he knows how to adapt his own nature . . . both because he cannot deviate from the path to which his nature inclines him, and also because he cannot be convinced to abandon a well-known path that has always brought him success by his following it.'[3]

This inflexibility is a fatal vulnerability for feudal realms. While they may achieve greatness for a period, because they are tied to the will of a single person, such dominions will inevitably fail. Collective leaderships, like the oligarchies of Venice and the Florentine Signoria, could mitigate this problem, but they introduced other difficulties such as indecision, procrastination, the diffusion of command and responsibility, and perhaps worst of all, the danger of violent faction. As we have seen, however, Machiavelli did have a solution: while his predecessors had thought of *virtù* as a trait of the individual, Machiavelli conceived of a collective *virtù* that would be found in the character of the people. Resolution and self-reliance on their part would permit the society to marshal the ruthlessness of the public to replace leaders whose particular gifts did not serve the times with those people whose natures were better suited to current events.

Machiavelli had already conceived the neoclassical idea of a modern state in the aftermath of the French invasion of 1494. This ancient Greek (and Roman) conception was to be revived and refined in order for the city to develop continuity of policy across successive leaders, manage alliances, raise greater revenues, and create a militia in light of the new threats facing Florence and the other Italian cities. To these reasons he now added another, derived from his insight about the vulnerability of leadership to the changes of fortune. What is required for the success of a political society is not so much 'to have a prince who governs wisely while he lives', but rather to have 'one who organizes the government in such a way' that its fate rests upon 'the *virtù* of the people'.[4] To marshal a collective *virtù*, Florence required a state in order to institute and maintain the rule of law, and to create and nurture a new civil/military relationship by replacing reliance on *condottieri* with a militia recruited from the people. But to enable that state to change its leaders as necessary, the state needed a certain kind of constitution.

As we saw in chapter 4 of the present work, Machiavelli believed that laws 'make [the public] good' by compelling men to serve the common good and refrain from violence,[5] and by channelling behaviour into 'civil modes and customs'.[6] But feudalism had laws. What the constitution of a modern state requires is that the laws be neutral, general and principled. That is, the law must be applied equally to all parties; its rules must treat similar cases similarly so that the public knows what to expect; and there must be articulable rules that can be stated clearly and which govern behaviour. Crimes must be punished regardless of the position of the person charged, for no state 'ever discharges the demerits of its citizens by counting their merits; but rather, having prescribed rewards for a good deed and punishments for a bad one and having rewarded someone for doing good, it punishes the same man later if he acts badly, regardless of his previous good deeds'.[7] Such rules were incompatible with the hierarchical dominions of feudalism.

The rule of law both evokes and reinforces collective *virtù* in several ways. First, when a leader or notable person holds himself accountable to the law, it sets a fine example of putting the common interest above personal interest.* Second, adherence to the rule of law renders the public safe from depredation by the powerful, and thus frees them from fear so that they may be confident and forthright in their political acts. In Machiavelli's *Florentine Histories*, an exiled statesman is quoted as saying: 'I shall always esteem it not

---

* 'I do not believe there can be a worse example in a state than to make a law and then fail to observe it, and this is even worse when the law is not observed by the person whoever promulgated it in the first place.' *Discourses*, book I, chapter 45 (entitled 'It is a bad example not to observe a law that has been passed, especially on the part of its author').

much to live in a city where the laws do less than men, because that fatherland is desirable where [one's] possessions and friends can be securely enjoyed, not where they can be easily taken from you, and friends – for fear of themselves – abandon you in your greatest necessity.' Freedom from terror is essential to collective *virtù*, as we have seen in our own time, for terror is a more merciless master than any individual tyrant. While the tyrant may relent or lapse in his vigilance, terror enlists our own wills to enforce its mandates and silences our consciences.

In the second book of the *Discourses*, Machiavelli lists a number of rights that are enforced by adherence to the rule of law: marriage, private property and inheritance, access to elected office and the enjoyment of the fruits of one's labour. Collective *virtù* – like the *virtù* of the individual – depends upon both self-confidence and sufficient resources. In a state that respects the rule of law and the rights just mentioned,

> Wealth increases more rapidly – including from agriculture and from the arts and commerce – because each person more willingly multiplies those goods that, once acquired, he believes he will be able to enjoy. Thus it happens that men in competition think of both public and private goods, and both increase miraculously. The contrary of this phenomenon occurs in those countries that live in servitude, and the further they move away from the customary good, the harsher is their servitude (*servitù*).*

A modern state was necessary to enforce the rule of law on all parties neutrally; and it was also necessary to create a citizen militia. But why was such a militia crucial to summoning and sustaining collective *virtù*?

---

* *Discourses*, book II, chapter 2. This passage is reminiscent not only of Adam Smith's invisible hand, but also of the work of the contemporary author Hernando de Soto, who argues that the rule of law and respect for the rights of property are essential preconditions for democracy.

As we saw in chapter 4, Machiavelli had long been an advocate of a citizen militia, partly as a reaction to the *condottieri* on whom Florence depended and whose mixture of extortion and aversion to battle had so frustrated their employers. It was Machiavelli's militia that had brought him his highest standing with his fellow Florentines after the siege of Pisa, and also his deepest disgrace, after the rout at Prato. In his *History of Florence*, Machiavelli asserted that Florence had formerly fielded a citizen militia of 1,200 cavalry and 12,000 infantry; indeed, when the manuscript was presented to Clement VII, Machiavelli seized the opportunity to lobby for a papal militia recruited from the Romagna and was promptly dispatched there by the pope to investigate its feasibility. One can see why Machiavelli wished to create such a militia, and why it would call on reserves of martial *virtù*; but how would it arouse such *virtù* in the general public?

Consider Machiavelli's assessment of the French constitutional system. Having praised the French for their adherence to the rule of law (the French kings are 'constrained by countless laws and [are bound] to decide every [domestic] question according to what the laws provide'),[8] he disparages the king of France as one, no matter 'how great his kingdom', who 'lives as tributary to' foreign mercenaries. His reason for this criticism goes beyond simple dependence on mercenaries, but is rather the consequence of a more fundamental civil/military relationship – namely the reluctance of the French crown and nobility to arm the populace for fear that the mass of people would turn their weapons against them. Disarming the people is a blunder resulting from,

> having chosen to enjoy the immediate gratification that comes from plundering their people to flee an imagined rather than a true danger, rather than undertaking policies that would make their own position secure and their realm perpetually happy. This [disarming of the public] though it may bring temporary tranquillity, will ultimately produce damage and irreparable [*irrimediabili*] harm.[9]

Such harm arises because the *virtù* of the public is sedated. Indeed, in *The Art of War*, Machiavelli concludes that the life of the state varies with the military preparedness of its subjects; if they are dependent on others to defend them, they grow passive and enervated.

Beyond requiring a state, however, nurturing collective *virtù* also demanded a certain constitution. That constitution had to be one that compelled the public to oversee crucial decisions by the state. There was one overriding reason for this: making choices is the basis for *virtù*, which it both reflects and evokes.[10] A constitution that did not provide a decisive role for the people in political decision-making could never summon and maintain collective *virtù*. (This is one more reason why Machiavelli was convinced of the need for a modern state. Only a more strategically dynamic constitutional order could preserve moral choice from the imposition of external constraints: 'Among private persons, faith is kept by laws, agreements and constitutions; among rulers, it is kept only by arms.'[11])

Machiavelli was well aware of the general opinion among historians – Livy included – that the populace was an uncertain mass who were unreliable, easily reversed their opinions, and were either arrogant in power or servile without. But he attributed these characteristics to publics acting outside the law and asserted that legal procedures could compel the populace to make specific judgements rather than simply voice generalities, and that 'the people do not deceive themselves in particular matters, even if they delude themselves in generalities'.[12]

But this raised another problem: how to engage the public in governmental affairs in such a way that the common interest would be served. To this question, which also haunted the framers of the US Constitution,[13] Machiavelli gave a surprising answer: it was conflict, structured and managed in a particular constitutional way, a way under laws, that would assure the state of public participation based on the common good. This we could learn by studying the way that

Rome managed political conflict and contrasting it with Florentine methods.[14]

In the *Discourses* Machiavelli had written: 'Men act either out of necessity or by choice',[15] and in *The Prince* he had twice observed that whatever the personal dispositions or natures of men, they still had free choice.[16] It is by the action of free choice that we know what the actor values as the good; without some commitment to the end towards which the choice contributes – without some notion of value – the chooser would be unable to make a decision one way or the other. By the same token, without the opportunity to choose, the chooser is unable to actualize her commitments. Even when conditions of poverty, adversity, fear or necessity have narrowed the scope for choice, free will redeems our status as moral agents.[17]

Recall Machiavelli's marginalia in his copy of Lucretius, that from the random clash of particles, we are freed from determinism. This image of the constant negotiations of *fortuna* and *virtù* suggests a cosmos ordered like a republic, from which ceaseless collision of eternal interests there emerges the opportunity for freedom.[18]

For the state, a constitution creates the basis on which governmental choices are made. As I have observed elsewhere,

> If tort law may be said to be a system of allocating the cost of accidents, and contract law a system of allocating the transaction costs of market decisions, then constitutional law may be thought of as the allocation of roles – who is to have the authority to make what sort of decision.[19]

But if a constitution can require choices by the people – a necessary condition for collective *virtù* – how can such a constitution also ensure that these choices are likely to be made on the basis of the common good when most men 'are more prone to evil than to good' and tend to subordinate the interests of the community to their own interests, preferring to act 'according to the wickedness of their spirits whenever they have free scope'?[20]

Machiavelli's answer was derived from his study of the Roman Republic.[21] He noted the role played by inspiring individuals, harsh and firmly applied laws, a religion whose rituals reinforced the state, and a 'mixed government' that included both patricians and plebeians (this last observation will play a role in the forthcoming discussion of Machiavelli's constitutional design). Most remarkably, he grounded Rome's institutions and practices in the city's fundamental social conflicts and the modalities it had evolved to cope with these conflicts.[22]

> I must say that it seems to me that those who condemn the conflicts between the nobles and the plebeians damn those very things that were the principal cause of Roman liberty . . . they do not consider that in every republic there are two opposing predispositions, those of the people and those of the powerful, and that all of the laws that encourage liberty have arisen out of the conflict between the two, as can easily be observed in the history of Rome. From the Tarquins to the Gracchi, a period of more than 300 years, the disturbances that roiled Rome rarely led to exile and even more rarely to bloodshed . . . The Roman method was such that when the people sought a new law, either they [demonstrated in the streets, or closed the shops, or abandoned the city altogether] or they refused to be recruited for war, so that to placate them it was necessary to offer them some response to their wishes . . . [if the public has been misled] there is the remedy of public assemblies in which some respected speaker demonstrates to the public that they have deceived themselves, for as Cicero observes, the people, though ignorant, can apprehend the truth and will readily yield when the truth is explained to them by a person in whom they trust.[23]

This is Machiavelli's answer, then, to the difficult question of how a collective *virtù* can be brought forth and maintained: *virtù* arises from conflict,[24] and it is maintained by constitutional practices that channel this conflict into reasoned discussion leading to formal decision-making practices under law. Given such institutions, the popular party will police its constitutional guarantees and prevent an aristocratic party from achieving tyranny.

Machiavelli concedes that he is departing from the widespread opinion that reliance on a prince is to be preferred to empowering the people, but he explains that the examples on which such opinion relies are cases in which the people were acting outside the law, and that were these incidents to be compared to those in which princes acted lawlessly, a different conclusion would be reached. The critical move in Machiavelli's argument, however, is not his speculation that, compared to princely decision-making, the public is still to be preferred ('in matters of practicality and stability, I suggest that the populace is more prudent, more stable, and has wiser judgement than a prince.'[25]) Rather, it is that law provides the crucial structure for governance. '[A]ny ruler who is not held in check by laws is likely to make the same mistakes as an unruly multitude.'[26] Linking *The Prince* and the *Discourses* in the constitutional way I have proposed, Machiavelli concludes:

> If princes are better than the public at establishing laws, creating new constitutional orders, and organizing law and new institutions, the populace has been far superior in maintaining institutions in an orderly way . . . [T]he states of princes have long endured – as have republics – when they have been regulated by laws. [I]f one studies a prince and a populace bound by laws, one will see that the people are more adroit than the prince.[27]

This is made even more emphatic in the *History of Florence* where Machiavelli contrasts Rome's method of dealing with factional strife with that of Florence. In Rome conflicts between groups were addressed by a competition of arguments whose results were manifested in law; in Florence social conflicts were resolved by street combat and assassination, resulting in the exile and death of many citizens. In Rome the plebeians sought to share the honours and political roles given to the nobility; in Florence the popular party sought to strip the nobles of their honours and their military and political roles, and this provoked the Florentine aristocracy to violence.

It is tempting to enlist Machiavelli in the debates of political philosophers today. Do his calls for reasoned elaboration prefigure – or perhaps endorse – the programmes proffered by the advocates of deliberative democracy in our time; or does his admiration for Rome's tumults lend authority to those who admire extra-legal measures as a radical way of forcing change? Rather than discourage this speculation, let me suggest a different way of resolving this division, a way that is less programmatic but may be more sympathetic to Machiavelli's larger perspective. What is at stake is his view of the realities of politics and the cultural nature of legal constraints. It is hard to imagine Machiavelli describing politics as quite so predictable as a discursive democracy. But at the same time, I think it is a mistake to portray Rome's tumults – the closing of shops, the refusal of the plebs to be conscripted, for example – as de facto 're-foundings' on the order of the extra-legal acts of Romulus. Indeed Machiavelli is explicitly impressed that the Roman Republic lasted six hundred years without the need for a re-founding. The difference between Florence's 'tumults', which he deplored, and Rome's is the former's addiction to public violence. This isn't so much a matter of the rule of law as it is a recognition of the implicit limits without which law cannot function.

In *The Prince* Machiavelli had observed that in every city one found that 'the people want to be free of domination by the nobility, while the nobles wish to command the people; out of these two opposing desires, there arises in cities one of three consequences: a principality, liberty or anarchy'.[28] (This remark supports the view that *The Prince* and the *Discourses* should be read as one constitutional treatise, for we may assume that Machiavelli preferred liberty to either oppression or anarchy.)

Machiavelli sought a constitutional order that would preserve a certain kind of equality – an equality in which no group would be powerful enough to oppress any other group and thus in which conflict would never result in such violence as would endanger the state. He proposed to frame a constitution that would sustain an equilibrium between the opposing groups,* each of which would 'keep watch over the other' and so prevent both 'the rich men's arrogance' and desire to oppress and 'the people's licence' and tendency to anarchy.[29]

Collective *virtù*, therefore, is a consequence of constitutional arrangements, emphasizing yet again the principally constitutional nature of Machiavelli's work.[30] The repeated resolution of fundamental social conflicts and dissension will bring the result that only those 'laws and institutions' that are 'conducive to public liberty' will be adopted. Although acting to serve the interests of their respective groups, the competing factions will be guided to act in the public interest – 'as if by an invisible hand'[31] – so that 'all of the laws which are passed in favour of liberty are born from the rift between [them]'.[32]

In this book and elsewhere,[33] I have asserted that Machiavelli formulated the idea of the first modern state; and in support of this view, I have noted that the words *lo stato* often appear in *The Prince* in a way that is quite distinct from the ways those words were used previously (to indicate a status or condition). Machiavelli's controversial use of the term *ragione di stato* ('reasons of state'), for example, reflects this new meaning, for that term itself only makes sense if the state has become objectified, separated from the person of the prince or ruler. But when Quentin Skinner made a similar claim regarding the term *lo stato*,[34] Harvey Mansfield responded that Machiavelli's *lo stato*

---

* I am indebted to my student, Rob Goodman, the co-author of *Rome's Last Citizen: The Life and Legacy of Cato* (St Martin's, 2012), for the observation of the late Senator Patrick Moynihan that 'The central conservative truth is that it is culture, not politics, that determines the success of a society. The central liberal truth is that politics can change a culture and save it from itself.' Or, one might add, destroy it.

refers to a personal possession, a patrimony more like a feudal realm than a state in the Weberian sense of an impersonal form of rule within a consolidated territory.[35] How should we reconcile the views of these two erudite and penetrating commentators?

At least part of their difference lies in an elision of the constitutional order of the early modern state with that of later periods, an elision that tends to confuse state and status. As I observed in *The Shield of Achilles*, '[t]he princely state allied the dynastic conventions of medieval feudalism with the constitutional innovation of a distinct and objectified state.'[36] The principal purpose of this constitutional innovation was to legitimate new dynasties by means of the imprimatur of a state. The state's enduring characteristics – permanent legations, the persistence of treaty obligations after the death of a signatory, new fortress architecture, the territorial, sectarian commitments of states (*cuius regio, eius religio*) – were in sharp contrast with their feudal predecessors. The constitutional order of the princely state promised to protect the person, property and perquisites of the prince, most importantly his sectarian preferences, and though it was quite unlike the Weberian state, it was thus a distinct constitutional innovation and a 'state' nonetheless. This analysis perhaps may capture the innovative constitutional spirit that animated Machiavelli when he wrote that he had set out on an 'unknown' path to find 'new modes and orders' of governance. As Machiavelli's most compelling biographer, Sebastian de Grazia,[37] puts it:

> Once, at the beginning of his *Discourses* on the histories of Titus Livy, Niccolò alludes to the great explorations. His own explorations, evidently, are to be no less rewarding and fearful. He is entering on a path not yet tread by anyone, seeking new ordering principles, 'to find new modes and orders', a political phrase pointing to reform measures and new constitutional dispositions.[38]

We actually can discover what Machiavelli conceived as a constitution for a princely state not only because this can be found in his essays, but also because he was twice asked by the Medici to submit such a constitution for governing Florence.

The dispute as to whether Machiavelli's *lo stato* really means a modern state is not settled by the common assumption that the post-Westphalian state is the first modern state, or the equally common and thoroughly anachronistic assumption that the nation state is the only post-feudal constitutional order we have known. Indeed, when we free ourselves of these assumptions, we can usefully categorize different modern constitutional orders of the last five centuries according to the way in which they claim legitimate power and their methods of maintaining that power.*

All the paradigmatic, pre-modern constitutional orders were unstable – monarchy degrading into tyranny, aristocracy into self-serving oligarchy, democracy into anarchy – each generating political corruption as each form empowers a class that inevitably neglects the public interest and eventually degenerates into a violent faction. 'All the forms of government just listed are defective, owing to the too-brief duration of the three positive ones, and the inherent evil of the three negative ones.'[39] For this reason Machiavelli disdained a constitution that put any one class in sole authority; but also for the even more important reasons noted above concerning the need to instill collective *virtù*, Machiavelli favoured a 'mixed constitution', in which each class has an assured role.

---

* As I have summarized elsewhere: 'To vastly oversimplify, the 16th century princely state sought to aggrandize the personal possessions of the prince; the 17th century kingly state attempted to [consolidate] the holdings of a ruling dynasty; the 18th century territorial state tried to enrich its country as a whole (and its aristocracy in particular) by acquiring trading monopolies and colonies; the 19th century [imperial] state nation struggled to consolidate a dominant national people and sought empire; the 20th century [industrial] nation state fought from 1914 to 1990 to establish a single, ideological paradigm for improving the material well-being of its people.' *Terror and Consent: The Wars for the Twenty-First Century* (Knopf, 2008).

A mixed government is one like Sparta's, where the founder Lycurgus 'so structured the Spartan constitutional order that, by allocating different roles to the kings, aristocrats and the people, he was able to create a state that stood for more than 800 years, achieving the highest accolades for himself and peace for his city';[40] or like Rome's, which became a 'perfected republic' when it achieved a mixed constitution by establishing tribunes for the plebeians to serve alongside the aristocratic elements in the Roman Senate, a kingly element in the Roman consuls, and popular representation in the Roman assembly.[41]

To this structural element of plural authority, Machiavelli added two specific requirements, also derived from his views about the inculcation and exercise of collective *virtù*. Machiavelli noted that in the Roman Republic, 'either a tribune or any other citizen could propose a law and . . . any citizen was entitled to advocate or denounce it before it was voted on, so that when the people had heard what each had to say, they could then decide which was the best course'.[42] It follows that the constitution must protect the marketplace of ideas where political decisions can be debated. 'When the people hear two advocates of equal ability speaking on behalf of opposing proposals, it is very rare that they do not choose the better course and that they fail to understand and be persuaded by the truth they are presented.'* Not only is this forum necessary for robust discussion and accurate decision-making, it will be recognized as one of the dramaturgical elements by which collective *virtù* is cultivated.

A second constitutional requirement is that office and honours must be open to all and allocated on the basis of merit. In such a state, the citizens are confident that their children 'can become the leaders of the city' if they are men of *virtù*; in a principality,

---

* *Discourses*, book I, chapter 58. This is a conclusion frequently reported by advocates before juries, the members of which – with some exclusions – are randomly chosen from the public.

by contrast, such opportunities are precluded, because the prince 'cannot dare to bestow honours on any citizens . . . no matter how valiant or good, for fear that he will then have cause to be suspicious of them'.[43] A republic under law rewards its citizens 'only for forthright and particular reasons, and apart from this practice confers no rewards or prizes to anyone'.[44] A prince, however, will often find it useful to bestow public honours on corrupt men.[45] In the Roman Republic, 'poverty was not a bar to anyone for any office or for any honour whatsoever, and exceptional talent was sought wherever it happened to be found'.[46] Therefore, the public should appoint magistrates, rather than the magistracies being inherited, because this will make it likelier that these offices will be filled by more competent persons.

In July 1520 Niccolò Machiavelli was commissioned by the Signoria – the ruling executive body of the Florentine government – and by the leading personage of the city, Cardinal Giulio de' Medici, to go to Lucca to settle a complicated bankruptcy to which Florence was a significant party. That summer, he used his leisure time to write two short works: *The Life of Castruccio Castracani*, the ruthless *condottiere* of the early fourteenth century who became master of Lucca; and the *Summary of Lucchese Affairs*, a study of the city's constitution. It has been suggested that the latter essay was written for Cardinal Giulio, who was known to be interested in a model constitution for Florence and had been urged by his cousin, Pope Leo X, to employ Machiavelli.* The Lucchese constitutional arrangements were flawed, Machiavelli concluded, because the terms of office were so brief, and the exclusions from office owing to class hostility so all-embracing, that the officials thus selected were inadequate to the tasks of governing. As a result, resort was continually had to the counsel of private persons, 'which is not usual in well-organized

---

* A passage in the essay ('anyone organizing a republic should not imitate [the Lucchese constitution]') may support this claim.

republics where the greatest number elect to office, the medium number gives advice, the minority executes . . . Thus did the people, Senate and consuls of Rome; thus do now in Venice the Grand Council, the Senate and the Signoria.'[47] This idea of a mixed and accountable governance structure follows, as we have seen, from Machiavelli's thought about the purposes of constitutional institutions. Moreover, these sentiments foreshadowed the two examples Machiavelli provided of a model constitution for Florence.

After he returned from Lucca and had received the commission from the Medici pope Leo to write the history of Florence, Machiavelli was asked by Cardinal Giulio de' Medici to draft a memorandum setting forth his ideas on the best governance for the city. This paper was to be prepared for Leo. There is some dispute over Giulio's real motives: after the disastrous public reception of Lorenzo's rule, there was a need to take soundings about the standing of the Medici, and it has been suggested that Giulio hoped to pacify the intellectuals and aristocrats of groups like the Orti Oricellari by consulting them on such matters (and indeed Buondelmonti and Alamanni were both approached as well as Machiavelli). But the overriding fact was that both Leo and Giulio held ecclesiastical offices and could have no legitimate offspring. Giuliano and Lorenzo had both died without legitimate heirs, and thus the problem of legitimacy that had haunted the Medici would, in the not-distant future, come to a crisis.

Machiavelli's draft constitution adheres closely to the principles outlined in this chapter: he advocates a mixed constitutional structure, with the three principal organs of government in the hands of the three distinct classes, and various overlapping *ex officio* representatives to ensure confidence and allay suspicion. He confronted one enormous problem, however, in drafting this advice: he had to reassure Cardinal Giulio that, for the lifetimes of the cardinal and the pope, the Medici influence would be paramount. Thus, consistent with his objections to a government that is part monarchy and part republic, he proposed a monarchy that, when the two cousins had died, would develop according to an agreed plan into a complete republic. It was a machine that would run of itself, evolving in accord with the constitutional blueprint and not dependent on the leadership of one figure or family.

Machiavelli's proposal, the *Discourse on Florentine Affairs after the Death of Lorenzo*, thus has two parts: a preamble that assesses the current status of the Medici in Florence after Lorenzo's disastrous interlude; and a detailed structural diagram for instituting a state that maintains an equilibrium among all classes, first under the Medici and then under a free-standing, republican structure.

The preamble addresses the question whether Florence could not simply return to the informal oligarchy of Cosimo and Lorenzo the Magnificent. Machiavelli decisively concludes that it cannot:

> The Medici in power then had been brought up and educated with the citizens and behaved with so much familiarity that they had their goodwill; now they have grown so grand that they have lost all sense of their common citizenship and the same intimacy can no longer exist. Then there were no armies or powers in Italy that the Florentines could not resist with their own arms . . . now that Spain and France are here, [Florence] must be allied to one or the other. If their ally loses, [the Florentines] are immediately at the mercy of the victor . . . The citizens [then] were used to paying heavy taxes . . . to try to accustom them to it again would . . . arouse their hatred.

Thus he concluded that rule by the Medici was not sustainable in the long term.

He then turns to his proposed constitutional structure: 'Anyone setting up a republic must allow for the three different classes of men who exist in every city: the upper, the middle and the lower . . . [S]ince there are three classes of men . . . there should also be three bodies in a republican government and no more.' Accordingly, Machiavelli proposed an assembly (the council) to elect officers, a Senate to deliberate and adopt legislation, and a Signoria to execute:

[T]here are in Florence some superior people who feel that they should have precedence over the others. They must be satisfied within the republican structure. The regime [under Soderini] fell for no other reason than that it did not meet these aspirations. These people can only be satisfied if the chief offices in the republic are clothed in majesty, and this majesty is vested in their own persons. [Therefore,] [t]o give majesty to the government, choose ... sixty-five citizens of over forty-five years of age, fifty-three from the Greater and twelve from the Lesser Guilds,* who will be life members of the government and [divided into four groups who] should reside ... in the palace for three months [with a *gonfaloniere*, chosen from among them, revolving every year] ... [A]ll together they should be called the Signoria.

Now we come to the second body, a Senate. 'I would set up a council of 200, 40 from the Lesser and 160 from the Greater Guilds, all over forty years old. [T]hey would be appointed for life. [This Senate] would be called the Council of the Elect.'

* Florentine guilds were corporations that controlled the arts and trades from the twelfth to the middle of the sixteenth century. The guilds were organized into three classes: major, middle and minor. The seven major guilds included those of cloth merchants, lawyers and judges, bankers and physicians; the middle group of five included guilds for tailors, masons and shoemakers. Together these two guilds, the *arti maggiori* and the *arti mediane*, constituted the twelve Greater Guilds. The *arti minori* included guilds for vintners, innkeepers and locksmiths, and were nine in number. The *minuto popolo*, composed of unskilled labourers, boatmen and others comprising the majority of the population, was forbidden from forming guilds. Membership of each guild was both hereditary and professional – that is, the candidate had to show proof that he was the legitimate son of a member and competent in the relevant craft. Each guild had its own constitution, which had the force of law within Florence. Six of the nine members of the Florentine Signoria were selected from the Greater Guilds, and two were chosen from the *arti minori*. Thus, in addition to protecting their members from competition and establishing standards for production, the guilds were a source of political power for their memberships.

It now remains to satisfy the third and last class of men, which is made up of the main body of citizens. They will never be satisfied . . . if they are not given, or promised, power. But if you [Leo] gave it back all at once, you would forfeit the safety of your friends and your Holiness's own power . . . For this reason, I think that the Hall of the Council of the Thousand, or at least that of the 600 citizens, must be reopened, and they should appoint all the officials and magistrates, as they once did, except the sixty-five [of the Signoria] and the 200 [of the Senate] . . . which during your Holiness's and the Cardinal's lifetimes should be appointed by you.

Like the American Constitution, this structure is not one of separated powers, so much as linked and sequenced so that no one body can rule, as a general matter, without the cooperation of the others. A representative of the popular local administration was to sit with the Signoria, and a special court of accusations was provided for – with 'subject matter' jurisdictional limits that remind one also of US provisions ('there may be no appeal in cases of fraud where less than fifty ducats were involved, or in cases of violence where no bones had been broken or blood shed, or where the damage done did not amount to fifty ducats').

Machiavelli concluded that he sought a 'constitution [that] can stand up on its own. It will always stand firm when everyone has a hand in it, when everyone knows what he must do and whom he can trust, and when fear or ambition is not prompting any class of citizen to look for changes'.* Machiavelli's first requirement is: will a republic's constitution build a strong state by giving a stake in that state to the important interest groups in a society?

Machiavelli's proposals had not been acted upon when Leo died on 1 December 1520; this event actually gave new momentum, however, to constitutional reform in Florence. With the rejection

---

* One might say that the idea of 'statesmanship' arises with Machiavelli. I am indebted to the philosopher Mark Sagoff for this observation.

of Cardinal Giulio de' Medici by the papal conclave and the election of Adrian VI, the Medici became more anxious about propitiating Florentine public opinion. In May Giulio offered to restore the *Consiglio Maggiore*, as Machiavelli had urged in his memorandum ('the main body of Florentine citizens will never be satisfied if the Hall of the Great Council is not reopened . . . Your Holiness must realize that if anyone plans to oust you from power, the first thing he will do is to reopen it'). Again Machiavelli's views on a new constitution were sought, and in 1522 he prepared another memorandum, *A Discourse on Remodelling the Government of Florence*. It was drafted in the form of a decree, putting into effect the principal proposed provisions of the first memorandum.[48]

Giulio's temporizing about constitutional reform, however, provoked a plot against the Medici, organized by the very members of the Orti Oricellari with whom Machiavelli had been communing since the summer of 1517. Machiavelli himself opposed such conspiracies where there were channels for political change, as he had written in the *Discourses*. Nevertheless, two friends to whom Machiavelli had dedicated his books – Zanobi Buondelmonti[49] and Luigi Alamanni[50] – were the leaders of the conspiracy, which included a plan to assassinate Cardinal Giulio de' Medici. Despite Machiavelli's opposition to changing the Florentine regime by force, others in the Orti Oricellari circle – Iacopo Nardi, for example – were convinced that his championing of a republican constitution had been the inspiration for the conspiracy. An intercepted communication foiled the plot, and while Buondelmonti and Alamanni were able to escape, the other conspirators were tortured and executed.

It may well be that Cardinal Giulio never intended to carry through the reforms he promised and to which Machiavelli had given careful elaboration; the possibility that Giulio might become pope – as indeed happened on the death of Adrian in 1523 – would have encouraged a new generation of Medici (though illegitimate) to hope that they might continue to rule Florence with the money and

power of the papacy behind them. Machiavelli seems to have anticipated this; in the second draft constitution he explicitly includes
Alessandro and Ippolito as having interests that need to be protected. What he did not foresee was the extent to which the Medici
were prepared to sacrifice Florence's independence to perpetuate
their power.

The year that Machiavelli died, the people of Florence revolted
against the Medici and restored the Republic until, after an eleven-
month siege, the Medici were reinstated. In 1532 the Republic
ceased altogether, and Pope Clement VII, as Cardinal Giulio had
become, made his illegitimate son Alessandro de' Medici duke of
Florence. Machiavelli had warned that a Medici dukedom – a 'monarchy' in his constitutional terms – was not sustainable in Florence.
There was no armed aristocracy to protect the monarch, and even if
there had been, the city would be at the mercy of foreign powers. By
essentially becoming clients of the Holy Roman Empire, the Medici
addressed both these problems and traded Florentine sovereignty
for the legitimizing of a ducal house by the emperor. The problem,
it turned out, was not collective *virtù* after all – the question that
dominated the *Discourses* – but the drive for legitimacy by a powerful
figure: the issue addressed in *The Prince*.

Perhaps it all had to end this way. It was, after all, Lorenzo the
Magnificent, a man of considerable *virtù*, who had set events in
motion that would eventually change the hegemony of the Medici
into a monarchy. Following the Pazzi Conspiracy in 1478, in which
Lorenzo and his brother were attacked, and the brother, Giuliano,
killed, Pope Sixtus VI – who had supported the conspiracy – had
allied with Ferdinand of Naples to mount an armed attack on
Florence. This war went on for months, during which the city was
put under a papal interdict, and was only ended when Lorenzo put
himself in real jeopardy by travelling to Naples to negotiate an end
to the conflict. One consequence of this dramatic act of *virtù*, however, was a series of constitutional changes within the Republic's

government that enshrined Medici power. Here is Lorenzo's dramatic appeal – an appeal to the common good – that sowed the seeds of the republic's eventual downfall and its replacement by a principality:

> In the dangerous circumstances in which our city is placed, the time for deliberation is past. Action must be taken . . . I have decided, with your approval, to sail for Naples immediately, believing that as I am the person against whom the activities of our enemies are chiefly directed, I may, perhaps, by delivering myself into their hands, be the means of restoring peace to our fellow citizens. As I have had more honour and responsibility among you than any private citizen has had in our day, I am more bound than any other person to serve our country, even at the risk of my life. With this intention I now go. Perhaps God wills that this war, which began in the blood of my brother and of myself, should be ended by any means. My desire is that by my life or my death, my misfortune or my prosperity, I may contribute to the welfare of our city . . . I go full of hope, praying to God to give me grace to perform what every citizen should at all times be ready to perform for his country.[51]

Yet perhaps Machiavelli's dream should not be confined to Renaissance Italy. Writers as diverse as the American conservative Harvey Mansfield, the European social democrat Maurizio Viroli and the New Left critic Gopal Balakrishnan all appear to agree that Machiavelli is the 'spiritual forefather'[52] of the US Constitution. A free and powerful republic, with a civil religion (the reverence Americans have for their constitution) and both a Roman founder (the Cincinnatus-like figure of George Washington) and a re-founding redeemer (the advocate of total war, Abraham Lincoln) – all are elements of Machiavellian polity that has, thus far, been a remarkable success.

Conclusion to Book IV

Machiavelli's Vision

WE ARE MUCH beholden to Machiavelli and others, that write what men do, and not what they ought to do. For it is not possible to join serpentine wisdom with the columbine innocency, except men know exactly all the conditions of the serpent; his baseness and going upon his belly, his volubility and lubricity, his envy and sting, and the rest; that is, all the forms of and natures of evil. For without this, virtue lieth open and unfenced. Nay, an honest man can do no good upon those that are wicked, to reclaim them, without the help of the knowledge of evil.

Francis Bacon

The Machiavelli Paradox Resolved

T HIS BOOK BEGAN by listing five framework assumptions about *The Prince* that have for centuries generated scholarly and popular debate concerning its meaning. This continuing debate reflects this paradox about the great Florentine: how can his stature be so high, and his influence so pervasive, when there is such dispute as to what he wrote?

Niccolò Machiavelli has continued *influence* owing to his grasp of the etiology and evolution of the state as a consequence of many, separate strategic and legal encounters with human desire. He described this interacting, organic morphology long before Charles Darwin or Adam Smith. This influence is confused with the continuing *interest* in his work, which arises from his provocative, even dramaturgical, Mephistophelean writing style. The latter doesn't have to be understood or even coherent to be memorable ('people should be either caressed or crushed', for example). But it is the former – so often overlooked – that accounts for his sustained impact. The neoclassical state is his intellectual and moral creation. That is the world he envisioned and that we have made. Thus the impact of Machiavelli's work has nothing to do with the assumptions that have provoked the most enduring controversies, and these assumptions are based on a deep misreading that ignores the constitutionalist nature of his writing. It is this contribution – and the clear-sighted and ingenious craft which is meant to serve it – that has held our attention since the birth of the modern state, even when we were unsure of its source.

Those five background assumptions are: *The Prince* is a mirror book, Machiavelli's contribution to a well-known genre of manuals of admonition and advice for rulers; *The Prince* advocates autocracy, in contrast to the republicanism celebrated in the *Discourses*; *The Prince* separates politics from ethics; *The Prince* lauds the methods of Cesare Borgia as a man who showed that *fortuna* could be conquered by the exercise of manly, if cruel, *virtù*; the final, notorious chapter of *The Prince* bears no real relation to the rest of the work. These are, by and large, rarely contested maxims about the work, the general knowledge that countless students can recall from undergraduate lectures.

Each one is responsible for the sharp divisions and abundant controversy that have arisen about Machiavelli's most famous essay, and each one is deeply misleading.

THE PRINCE IS A MIRROR BOOK

Considered as such, it is a shocking example of the genre, because it turns classical and Christian advice on its head. That tradition held that the good is the true – that to be an effective leader, one had only to follow the moral standards of conventional virtue, because the most rational course of behaviour was always the most moral. The conventional virtues, enshrined by Plato, were wisdom, justice, courage and equanimity. These are faithfully reflected in Cicero's mirror book, *De officiis*, to which were added – especially for princes – the virtue of honesty (by which Cicero meant keeping one's word and dealing honourably with others), princely magnanimity and liberality.[1] Cicero stresses that, while many men believe 'that a thing may be morally right without being expedient, and expedient without being morally right',[2] they are deceived because expediency and properly moral behaviour are always consistent.[3] This notion was adopted and expanded by the writers of mirror books for Renaissance princes, such as Patrizi's *The Education of the King*, which added the Christian idea that even if, in this life, a ruler were to gain by taking a more expedient route at the expense of traditional virtues, he would suffer sufficiently in the next life so that, all in all, it was still irrational to be immoral.

As we have seen, this view is entirely contradicted in *The Prince*. Machiavelli holds that no successful prince can maintain his success by relying on the virtues 'generally supposed to be good [for] that which appears to be a virtue, if acted upon, may bring about [the prince's] destruction; while another course, which reflects that which seems to be a vice, will result in his safety and his well-being';[4] and indeed that, far from exacting retribution in the next life, God exalts those leaders who, acting contrary to the conventional virtues, have founded lasting regimes. The ruler, Machiavelli maintained, must be guided by the imperatives of necessity and judge each action by its consequences for the state. 'It is essential to understand this: that a prince – and especially a "new" prince – cannot always follow those practices by which men are regarded as good, for in order to maintain the state he is often obliged to act against his promises, against charity, against humanity, and against religion.'[5] Far from counselling liberality, he writes that 'Above all else, a prince must protect himself against being despised and hated. Generosity leads you to both one and then the other.'[6] Instead of requiring a prince to keep his commitments, Machiavelli advises that there are contexts in which a prudent ruler should renounce rather than observe his treaty commitments.*

These passages are well known because they are so shocking, though like those well-thumbed pages in a Henry Miller novel, the late twentieth century has made them less so. Nevertheless, because

---

* 'A wise ruler cannot and should not fulfil his promises when such an observance of his word would lead to his disadvantage and when the reasons for his original undertaking no longer pertain.' *The Prince*, chapter 18.

they contradicted everything we had been led to expect from a mirror book, a number of vexing questions arose: was *The Prince* a satire on the genre of mirror books, not meant to be taken seriously, as Garrett Mattingly proposed?[7] Or was it meant as a warning, a cautionary tale that tells us what a tyrant could do, in order to enable us to resist him, as Spinoza, Rousseau, Ugo Foscolo and Luigi Ricci believed? Or as a snare to undo the Medici by offering them advice that, if followed, would destroy their hegemony, as Mary Dietz has argued?[8] Is it written in code because Machiavelli did not dare to arouse the further distrust of the Medici and the Church? And if written in code so that it does not mean what it appears to mean, what is the key?[9] Or if it really means what it seems to mean – a book of advice for boys written by Charles Addams – should it be proscribed? After its publication was underwritten by the pope in 1532, it was put on the *Index librorum prohibitorum* by the Catholic Church in 1559.

I have argued that *The Prince* is not really a mirror book, but rather that it is a constitutional treatise. Machiavelli's specific advice to statesmen is entirely to be subordinated to his more general constitutional goals. As Machiavelli explained to Francesco Vettori when he first discussed the matter, 'I have composed a little work, *De principatibus*, where I delve as deeply as I can into thoughts on this subject, discussing what a principality is, what kinds there are, how they are acquired, how they are maintained, why they are lost . . . [I]f it were read, it would be seen that I have been at the study of statecraft for fifteen years . . .'[10] Xenophon is the *only* writer of a mirror book for princes that Machiavelli mentions* and his citations are for exclusively historical purposes. Many readers have been misled by the opening passage of chapter 15 of *The Prince*:

---

* 'Pontano, Patrizia and Castiglione are not mentioned in *The Prince* nor does Skinner offer any external evidence for Machiavelli's concern with them.' Nathan Tarcov, 'Quentin Skinner's Method and Machiavelli's *Prince*', *Ethics*, vol. 92, no. 4 (July 1982): 704.

It now remains for us to consider what ought to be the conduct and bearing of a Prince ... And because I realize that many have written on this subject, I fear I may be thought presumptuous to write of it also, all the more because in my analysis I depart from the views that others have taken.

But when we connect this famous passage with the sentences that immediately follow, we see that Machiavelli is not addressing the authors of mirror books, but rather those political philosophers – like Plato – who created ideal worlds towards which the ruler was to strive.

Because it is my objective to write what shall be useful to those who understand my work, it seems to me better to follow the real truth of things rather than an imaginary view of them. For many republics and principalities have been imagined that were never seen nor known actually to exist.

THE PRINCE ADVOCATES AUTOCRACY, WHILE THE *DISCOURSES* ENDORSE A REPUBLICAN FORM OF GOVERNMENT

So it seems that, taken together, the two books are in opposition to one another. This, too, leads to a number of difficult questions. Did Machiavelli become disillusioned and come to view the possibility of a Medici monarchy with disfavour as the years lengthened and no employment came his way? Or was *The Prince* an insincere and cynical tract to begin with,[11] designed to rehabilitate an ardent republican in the eyes of a powerful family that had ousted the author's patron? Or, as Renzo Sereno has suggested, is *The Prince* itself the fantasy of an embittered man that should not be taken to present considered thoughts on statecraft, whereas the *Discourses* are the outcome of some years of discussion within a cultivated circle of intellectuals?[12]

Some critics have argued that Machiavelli sought to deceive princes with his advice, trapping them into actions that would destroy principalities so that they could be more easily replaced by republics.[13] Or is Machiavelli simply an incoherent writer, heedless of the profound contradictions between the two works?[14]

I have suggested that there is no contradiction whatsoever between the two works. I believe that Machiavelli first began the *Discourses* when he was exiled from Florence in the spring of 1513 and that he took up *The Prince* that summer, pausing his work on republics.[15] As he remarks in chapter 2 of *The Prince*, he 'shall set aside any discussion of republics, because I have treated them at length elsewhere [and] shall consider solely the principality [and] how these principalities can be governed and maintained'. For this reason, I think Machiavelli is best understood as having written one great constitutional treatise – *Lo Stato* – with chapters on republics and chapters on principalities.

This is why reading *The Prince* in isolation gives such a distorted picture of Machiavelli's views. It is not that he changed his mind about the comparative efficacy of principalities and republics when he came to finish the *Discourses*. It's rather that he saw these constitutional orders as better at different roles – princes at establishing the state, popular republics at maintaining it – and that the initial step he sought, the establishment of a state in central Italy, had to be undertaken by a prince; hence, the *princely state* that he so accurately foretold.

Giovanni Sartori once called attention to 'the term that symbolized more than any other [a] vertical focus [of power] . . . that term is "Prince". It was no accident that *Il Principe* (1513) was the title chosen by Machiavelli.'[16] Except that it wasn't. It is worth emphasizing that *The Prince* was published posthumously in 1532, five years after Machiavelli's death. In 1513, and throughout his lifetime, Machiavelli entitled the work *De principatibus* ('On principalities'), and not *The Prince*.[17] Moreover, Machiavelli repeatedly refers to the work as 'my treatise on principalities' both during its composition and thereafter.* Nowhere in *The Prince* does he advocate monarchical rule over republicanism as the preferred constitutional method for sustaining the state. It is an ironic travesty that Machiavelli's posthumous publisher translated the Latin *principatibus* into the Italian *principe*, because he also did not appreciate Machiavelli's path-breaking distinction between the prince and the princely state, which has such profound consequences for his ethics and his republicanism, and which reflects his fundamental insight into the new, emerging constitutional order.

It is true that *The Prince* focuses a good deal of attention on the acts of a single person and not on the collective will that is so important an issue in the *Discourses*. But this is misleading, for in the *Discourses*, too, we find extensive discussion of a single leader acting from individual *virtù* to found the state, even though rule by a single person is inadequate to the task of preserving the state over the long run. The founder's role is, on Machiavelli's view, essential to the birth of republics, just as the proper *ordini* is essential for the *virtù* of the founder to be generalized to the citizenry.

THE PRINCE SEPARATES ETHICS FROM POLITICS

'The view of the separation of ethics from politics is more explicitly associated with Machiavelli . . . He not only insists on this dichotomy but also recommends, in his concise and famous thesis named *The Prince*, to the ruler or prince to trample upon every ethical consideration so as to fortify his power.'[18] This proposition, like the ones that preceded it, is widely and tenaciously held, though it gives rise to a great many controversies.

* See, for example, *Discourses*, book II, chapter 1 (*nostro trattato de' Principati*).

Is Machiavelli, then, a humanist, as Croce claimed, who divorced the province of politics from ethics so that rulers might legitimately choose the lesser evil when deciding? Or is Machiavelli, as Leo Strauss argued, the figure who inaugurated the modern era with its detachment from governing moral rules and, as Jacques Maritain concluded, brought forth with that detachment a 'mutation' of the intellect? Or was Machiavelli the first political scientist, doing for politics what Galileo had done for physics, drawing conclusions from a disinterested empirical base, as Ernst Cassirer,[19] Augustin Renaudet,[20] and Leonardo Olschki[21] have asserted?

Machiavelli was in fact a rather thoughtful ethicist, with a very demanding code that I have called 'the duty of consequentialism'. Nor is this ethical code antithetical to Christianity. Roughly speaking, Machiavelli's ethics recognize that different forms of life require different ethical rules. When I act on behalf of myself, I should behave in concert with the classical and Christian virtues; when I am acting at the command of God – like Moses, who slew countless numbers – I should behave in obedience to his will, and not my own; and when I am acting as an agent of the state, I ought to behave in accordance with the common interest, subordinating my own will and preferences. Rather than say that Machiavelli no longer holds that it is always rational to be moral – which is easy to misconstrue – one might say that he implicitly asserts that it is always moral to be rational when one is acting on behalf of others.

This position is easy to confuse with 'role morality', the notion that certain roles override our customary moral obligations.[22] For example, the role of religious confessor may require one to keep confidential matters – such as the commission of a crime – that one might otherwise feel an obligation to disclose. Codes of ethics for lawyers often admonish an attorney to give her client's interest such fidelity that she need not act in a way that gives equal moral concern to both her client and her adversary. She need not present a truthful account of events, may attempt to destroy the credibility of an adversary's account that she believes in fact to be truthful, can legitimately further the client's objectives even when she believes these to be socially harmful, and must refuse in some cases to alleviate the suffering of others simply because the client refuses to permit it.[23] This, and other examples drawn from professional fields such as accountancy and medicine,[24] are often portrayed as contrasting 'role' morality with 'ordinary' or 'background' morality. I am inclined to think that this is a mistaken account of what actually constitutes morality,[25] which arises from specific forms of life and does not exist as a brooding omnipresence, but in any case it is not what Machiavelli is advocating.[26]

Indeed, to assimilate Machiavelli's approach into role morality misses the principal point of his endeavour as well as mistaking his insight.[27] For Machiavelli, the duty of consequentialism – the obligation to serve the public good when one is acting as the public's agent in preference to serving one's own objectives, including one's personal moral objectives – arises from the fact that the agent wields power solely because it has been delegated to him by the public. The agent has no legitimate authority to act in contradiction to the common good.

Now for some this will raise what one might call the 'Nuremberg' problem. This is a problem that arises when an official disclaims responsibility for his acts on the grounds that he was simply following orders. From Machiavelli, one can derive a solution to this problem which lies in his insistence that a state official owes a fidelity to the rule of law. Nazi officers, who at the Nuremberg Tribunal's proceedings in 1945 pleaded in defence of their actions that they were only following the lawful commands of their superiors, were nevertheless part of a formidable war machine that launched an unprovoked attack upon the lawfully acting state of Poland when aggression had been recognized as illegal under international law in such circumstances.[28] Similarly, officials who engage today in genocide, slavery, piracy, torture or other violations of internationally recognized peremptory norms cannot excuse themselves because they were following local law. It is hopelessly anachronistic to apply this solution to the state system of Machiavelli's day – there being no state system as such – and to a period when wars of aggression were sanctioned by international norms but it is no less anachronistic to suppose that Machiavelli's duty of consequentialism means that officials are excused condemnation when they violate some fundamental norms intrinsic to the common interest even when they were not recognized in law. That is made clear by Machiavelli's condemnation of Ferdinand's mass expulsions of populations in Spain, and Agathocles' cruelty in Syracuse.

Skinner has argued[29] that Machiavelli does not address the question whether, even if in this life it may prove expedient to act in contradiction of Christian morals, it cannot ultimately be so because in the life to come we will all be held to account, for eternity, on the day of judgement.[30] But this neglects the most important constitutional aspect of Machiavelli's work – that he reifies and objectifies the state, detaching it from the Christian personality – and it assumes that God demands that we not do the same. It contradicts Machiavelli's view – and that of many Christian theologians of his time and ours – that necessity is God's will.[31]

Perhaps we can see the distinction between having no ethical or moral principles, on the one hand, and having a distinct set of such principles that apply with respect to certain duties, on the other, with the following example. Machiavelli writes, in a famous passage:

> A wise ruler cannot and should not fulfil his promises when such an observance of his word would lead to his disadvantage *and* when the reasons for his original undertaking no longer pertain.[32]

Read as an important maxim in the ethics of diplomacy,[33] this passage simply states what is known in public international law as the doctrine of *clausula rebus sic stantibus*.[34] This doctrine provides that, when the circumstances existing at the time of agreement to a treaty have changed and when this change is such that had they occurred before agreement, the parties would not have undertaken their treaty obligations, the effected provisions are not enforceable. This is not unethical; indeed, it is an essential element in the ethical jurisprudence of treaty law because it binds parties only to the extent that they contemplated being bound in the first place. This is the import of Machiavelli's often quoted line, 'a prince never lacks *legitimate* reasons to break his promises' (emphasis supplied), which is followed by the less quoted sentence, 'one could cite an endless number of modern examples to show how many pacts, how many promises, have been *made* null and void because of the infidelity of princes' (emphasis supplied) – that is, examples of a treaty party being released from his obligations owing to the violation or renunciation of his obligations by the treaty partner.

One more example will suffice to demonstrate that Machiavelli's proposed ethics for state actors is not simply an apologetics for power, a rationalization of the claim that 'might makes right'. When he writes that a new prince who wishes to be absolute must transform everything he finds in the state – destroying its cities and forcibly transporting its citizens *en masse* to new territories – he adds:

> These are such utterly vile practices, not only incompatible with a Christian way of life but with any civilized form of living, that every man should abhor such methods and decide to live as a private citizen rather than rule at the cost of such devastation to others.[35]

This suggests that, even when the power of the ruler is at stake, there are ethical rules that must govern his behaviour, in contrast to the case where the survival of the public interest is at stake. In our own day, we have seen the UN Security Council recognize in 2011, for the first time, that the UN Charter permits intervention against a regime that plans to slaughter its own people, even though it intends no harm to other states – a doctrine that recognizes Machiavelli's distinction.[36]

MACHIAVELLI BOTH ASSERTS AND CONTRADICTS THE CLAIM THAT MAN CAN CONTROL HIS FATE

On the face of it, this common view has some important textual support. In chapter 25 of *The Prince*, Machiavelli writes:

> I assess it to be the case that Fortune is the arbiter of but a half of our actions, leaving us in control of the other half, or almost that. She is comparable to those destructive rivers that, when they become enraged, flood the plain, destroying woods and structures, churning up the earth. Everyone flees in front of this rampage, everyone yields to its forces, unable to oppose it in any way. But that does not mean that, when nature is mild and things are calm, we cannot take precautions and build dikes and dams so that, when the waters rise again, they will be channelled off or their force mitigated.

And in chapter 7 he writes of Cesare Borgia:

> I believe I am correct in suggesting that he is to be imitated by all those who have risen to power by relying on Fortune and the armies of others. He possessed great courage and visionary intentions, and he could not have conducted himself in any other way; his schemes were frustrated by Alexander's death and by his own illness.

Taken together, these passages might suggest that a man of sufficient *virtù* could in fact control his fate, were he clever enough and lucky enough.[37] But this focuses on the wrong question, because it looks at *The Prince* as though it were the story of one exciting figure, and not of a new constitutional order. Even in the case of this one man, Machiavelli concludes in his poem 'The First Decennale' that Borgia met the fate he deserved 'as a rebel against Christ'. That is, by using the papacy to further the ambitions of his family alone, he was to be censured, not admired, however much a *virtuoso* he may have been in the techniques of statecraft. Better than the slogan 'the end justifies the means' as a tag for Machiavelli's views would be 'ends matter'.[38]

In fact, we have a rather coherent picture of Machiavelli's views about the relationship of *virtù* to *fortuna* because the wheel of Fortune – unlike the character of a man that gives rise to his *virtù* – keeps spinning. If one may determine one's fate half the time – say, at roulette – one will nevertheless sooner or later lose everything. Of Julius II's remarkable string of successes, for example, Machiavelli writes:

> No other pontiff, exercising the greatest prudence, could possibly have accomplished what Julius did with his recklessness ... All his actions were like that, and they all succeeded remarkably, for the shortness of his life prevented him from experiencing his ruin.[39]

Machiavelli attempts to solve this problem by inventing collective *virtù* – a quality of the people who, acting in their collective capacity, can do their own spinning of the wheel, changing leaders as the circumstances demand. It is the ruthlessness of the *public*, not of the *prince*, that will save the state. For example, General de Gaulle was the leader who could make peace in Algeria, precisely because only he could fulfil the public's pitiless wish to renege on its commitments to the *pieds noirs*.

In our own times, we have seen many examples of this. Gerald Ford was the right person to restore a sense of integrity to the presidency after the trauma of Watergate; that he was trusted by his peers tended to hasten the departure of Richard Nixon. But those very associations with the Washington establishment led the public to reject him in favour of an outsider, a former one-term governor of Georgia, Jimmy Carter, who not only radiated honesty but came to office without any taint of the party-based corruption against which the public revolted. If he was the right person to restore the honour of the office of the presidency, he was not the right man to rally the country against an increasingly aggressive Soviet Union, perhaps because of his hostility to violence. Rather, a practised rhetorician like Ronald Reagan was chosen by the public in part because he did not burden himself, or the public, or the Soviet Union, with the complexities of *détente*.

CHAPTER 26 OF *THE PRINCE*, WITH ITS FLAMBOYANT EXHORTATION TO LIBERATE ITALY, IS A DRAMATIC DEPARTURE FROM THE REST OF THE BOOK

Felix Gilbert once observed that 'Of all the writings of Machiavelli, none has been so much commented upon as *The Prince*, and of the various sections of *The Prince*, none has been discussed so much as the last chapter', which he described as 'suggestive, puzzling and elusive'.[40] In the final chapter of *The Prince*, Machiavelli – as in the dedication – directly addresses Lorenzo de' Medici. He suggests, a little absurdly, that Lorenzo is the person to liberate Italy from the 'barbarian', the French and the Spanish. This chapter – which Harvey Mansfield refers to as a 'sudden burst of Italian patriotism' – has long been thought to be an anomaly when juxtaposed with the rest of the text; there is an arresting contrast between the matter-of-fact tone of the preceding treatise and the highly coloured last chapter, which ends with a quotation from the poem 'Italia Mia' by Petrarch. For Allan Gilbert the chapter explained Machiavelli's defence of cruelty, treachery and deception: any form of government and any mode of action that might unite Italy was acceptable. Similarly, it has been urged that the last chapter of *The Prince* contradicts the view that Machiavelli was a detached, scientific observer of events committed to objective techniques and without political passions (something that enabled him to serve both the Medici and the Florentine Republic).[41] It has been suggested that the chapter was added two years after the completion of the rest of the text in response to Lorenzo's changed status after Giuliano's death and the

invasion by the French in early August 1515.[42] Some have suggested
that the chapter has rather little to do with the book and should be
considered no more than a purely rhetorical, humanist peroration.
And it is most common today to read that, if anything, the chapter was tacked onto the book to flatter its recipient in the hope of
getting an appointment for the author.*

Indeed, Leo Strauss identified this fault line running between the
concluding chapter and the rest:

> While the last chapter of *The Prince* is thus a call to a most glorious
> imitation of the peaks of antiquity within contemporary Italy, the
> general teaching of *The Prince* . . . is the opposite of an imitation, how-
> ever perfect: while the greatest deed possible in contemporary Italy is
> an imitation of the greatest deeds of antiquity, the greatest theoretical
> achievement possible in contemporary Italy is 'wholly new'.[43]

But if we see the four preceding propositions in the light I have
drawn – if, that is, we see *The Prince* as a constitutional treatise that is
to be read, together with the *Discourses*, as part of a larger treatise, *The
State*; which proposes an ethics of service to the state; which measures the success of leaders by their contribution to the *common* good
(as opposed to the personal gain of the prince); and which favours
republicanism and the rule of law because these have the best chance
of furthering that good – then the fifth problematic also dissolves.
The creation of a unified, new state in the centre of Italy is not the
objective of the book, nor is it superfluous: it is the culmination of
the book's argument. It is not that the methods of the preceding
chapters are in service of this nationalistic ideal, but rather that such
a state is the way of bringing about a political governance in service

---

* It is notable that Machiavelli turned down the offer of a lucrative secretaryship
with the *condottiere* Prospero Colonna, as well as the offer to become chancellor
of the Republic of Ragusa, even though he was at the time largely unemployed
save for the modest commission to write the history of Florence.

of the common good. This reading accords with the structure of classical rhetoric in which the argument culminates in a call to action.

As we have seen, *The Prince* was written on the occasion of the second of three chances for the creation of an Italian princely state – a 'new' constitutional order.[44] These came in 1502 with Cesare Borgia, whose father, the pope, sought to carve out a dynastic, feudal dukedom for his family from the papal vicarages in the Romagna; again in 1513, when it seemed possible that Pope Leo X would unite the Papal States with Florence and its possessions, then ruled by Giuliano de' Medici, the pope's brother; and finally in 1520, when another Medici pope, Clement VII, sought to restart the project of an hereditary Medici realm.[45] That is why Machiavelli abruptly stopped his work on the *Discourses* in 1513 and originally addressed *The Prince* to Giuliano. That is also why, in 1520, he advocated that the Medici begin a transition to a republican state in Florence. It was the spur of the *Occasione* that prompted *The Prince*, and the background concept of the modern state, of which Machiavelli was both the prophet and the poet, that stands behind the twenty-sixth chapter of that work.[46]

Here it is useful to attend to the fact that *The Prince* is addressed to 'new' princes – that is, those who cannot rely on a dynastic legal basis for their legitimacy. The Medici would have been a 'new' dynasty; they had no hereditary legitimacy to rule. A Borgia dynasty would also have been 'new' in the sense in which that term is used in *The Prince*. But behind these problems of legitimacy lies a larger one, the problem of the 'new' constitutional order, the princely state which requires a single founder – hence the extended discussions in *The Prince* of Moses, Romulus, Theseus and Cyrus, all constitutional founders. As Leo Strauss notes of chapter 26, the 'liberator of Italy is described as a new prince, for the liberation of Italy presupposes the introduction of new laws and new orders: he must do for Italy what Moses had done for the people of Israel'.[47] Similarly, it is useful to recall that Cesare Borgia is not the only model for the new prince in the preceding chapters. In chapter 21, Machiavelli says of Ferdinand of Aragon that he might

> [a]lmost be seen as a 'new' prince, because he has gone from being a weak dynastic king to, by means of his fame and glory, becoming the pre-eminent monarch in Christendom. His actions we may regard as very ambitious and occasionally extraordinary ... He was able to fund his armies with revenues from the Church and the people and thus, through a long struggle [with the Moors], lay the basis for the military power that has brought him honour.

That is, Ferdinand did for Spain what Machiavelli hoped Cesare Borgia would do in the Romagna, and what he exhorts a 'redeemer' to do for Italy in chapter 26. But Machiavelli is perfectly forthright in saying that, while creating a new state requires a single founder, a man of *virtù*, maintaining such a state will require a republic. Thus his constitutions of 1520 and 1522 for Florence follow directly from his great, unacknowledged treatise, *The State*, whose constituent parts are *The Prince* and the *Discourses*.

*****

What of Machiavelli's own *virtù*? Did it enable him to shape his ideas and their advocacy to suit the times? It did not. The intellectual and moral climate within which he happened to live was far more hospitable to Vettori and Guicciardini, as we saw at the end of chapter 7. Indeed, Machiavelli was so out of step with his contemporaries that he was said to be 'satanic' even in his own lifetime.

The fact that Machiavelli was quite so out of tune with his times – that he was not able to be 'a great man' who mastered Fortune – is related to his genius: he saw the necessity and inevitability of the emergence of a new constitutional order, the modern state, even though his actions were trapped within the expectations and institutions of the dying feudal realm. It is striking that the three great works presaging this death – More's *Utopia*, Luther's *Ninety-Five Theses* and

Machiavelli's *Prince* – were all written in 1513. It is his insight rather than his virtuoso performances – including his provocative aperçus – that have given him continued (and perhaps increasing) influence during the five-century evolution of the state since his death, and which assures him of relevance today.

Epilogue

Satan's Theologian

'I am not a great man, but sometimes I think the impersonal and objective quality of my talent and the sacrifices of it, in pieces, to preserve its essential value, has some sort of epic grandeur.'
Letter from F. Scott Fitzgerald to his daughter 'Scottie', 1940[1]

IGNORING THE CONSTITUTIONAL dimensions of Machiavelli's life and writings deprives us of some of the assistance his great works can provide us today. No element is more important, in this respect, than Machiavelli's appreciation of the emergence of a new constitutional order in his time, for we are now about to experience another example of this historic phenomenon.

We do not live in princely states (though there are vestigial elements of this form, and even a few examples, like Brunei). We live in industrial nation states, the constitutional order that arose in the United States and Germany in the latter half of the nineteenth century and which, following the Second World War, superseded the imperial state-nations that had dominated Europe and the world from the end of the eighteenth century.

The watermark of any particular constitutional order is its claim to legitimacy. Give us power, the nation state said, and we will improve your material well-being. Lloyd George and Franklin Roosevelt said this, but so too did Vladimir Lenin and Adolf Hitler, for they were all leaders of the same fundamental form of the state (though they had different ideas about how to fulfil this promise). The constitutional order of the industrial nation state brought us mass, free education; the mass franchise, giving the vote not only to property-less males but females as well; old-age pensions and unemployment compensation; the public funding of science; state-owned enterprises such as airlines and railways, telecommunications and other national industries; and also total warfare – that is, warfare against the *nation*. We have lived so long in nation states that we are inclined to forget that a nation is not a state; indeed, some nations – the Kurds, the Palestinians, the Cherokee – do not have states. Machiavelli reminds us that we did not always live with the structures of the modern state, and indeed have not lived since 1648 – as so many unthinkingly claim – within the current form of the nation state.

That is important because if we believe that the only constitutional order we have known since feudalism is the nation state, we will be quite disinclined to believe that our present constitutional order is on the wane or that a new one is emerging. On the contrary, we are more likely to think that the only alternatives are that deep, structural change is illusory or that the state itself will vanish (a most unlikely event). But when we see that the turn of the wheel that will bring one constitutional order to an end and replace it with another is simply the latest iteration of a process going back to the Renaissance, we may be more sensitive to the changes currently under way.

Those changes include: a global system of communications that prevents any nation state from controlling its culture, because the interconnected system penetrates every society and enables social networking technology within them; an international system of trade and finance that prevents any state from wholly managing its national economy and which brings an increased vulnerability to every state arising from the decisions made by markets assessing the financial behaviour of states; a system of international human rights that pre-empts any state's national laws and has most recently been the basis for prosecutions of democratically elected leaders as well as dictators before international tribunals and that has served to legitimate an armed attack on a state that posed no threat to any other state but appeared on the verge of attacking its own people; transnational threats like AIDS and SARS or climate change and global, non-national terrorism, which no state can hide from or arrest by its own efforts alone; and finally, the commodification of weapons of mass destruction, where crucial components can either be sold or bartered on a clandestine market (such as the means by which the A. Q. Khan enterprise enabled the creation of the Pakistani nuclear arsenal) or simply downloaded via the internet (such as the information by which mousepox can be transformed into a human pathogen).

At the beginning of the twenty-first century, we still live in nation states, and their legitimating mission – to better our material well-being – still defines the contemporary state. Yet this mission is becoming harder and harder to fulfil, and publics know this. Few contemporary national groups, except those such as the Palestinians, Tamils and Basques who are without states, seek their fulfilment in a relationship between their nation and the nation state. It is increasingly difficult for the nation state to execute the functions that it added to its portfolio when it superseded the state-nation: not simply the maintenance of an industrial war machine of immense cost that is able to assure the physical security of its citizens, but also the preservation of civil order by means of bargaining among constituencies, the administration of juridical norms that embody a single national moral tradition, the control of the economy of the society in order to provide a continuous improvement in the material conditions of life for all classes – a control that has passed to markets – and an ever-widening scope of material benefits through government entitlements that is proving more difficult to fund as national populations age and the costs of maintaining these entitlements soar.

As the British statesman Douglas Hurd put it:

The world is run on a paradox. On the one hand, the essential focus of loyalty remains the nation state and there are nearly two hundred of these. On the other hand, no nation state, not even the single superpower the United States of America, is capable of delivering to its citizens single-handed the security, the prosperity, and the decent environment which the citizens demand.

These difficulties do not augur the end of the state, even if the constitutional order of the nation state will give way to a new form; rather, the state will change the terms of its bargain with the public, redefining its promises so as to maintain its legitimacy. What will the new constitutional order look like?

Robert Cooper, the distinguished diplomat and theorist of international relations, has called this new form 'the postmodern state'. Along very similar lines, some have named this phenomenon the 'market state'. What is a market state?

One definition holds that it is 'the emerging constitutional order that promises to maximize the opportunity of its people, tending to privatize many state activities and making representative government more responsible to consumers. It is contrasted with the current nation state, the dominant constitutional order of the twentieth century that based its legitimacy on a promise to improve the material welfare of its people.' As the 2005 Royal Dutch Shell Scenarios put it:

> The gradual transition from the nation state to the Market state model implies a redefinition of the state's fundamental promises: from maximization of the Nation's welfare toward maximization of opportunities for . . . civil society and citizens. States in the advanced market democracies do not define their own success in terms of being able to resist market forces, as in Europe not long ago, but in terms of fostering market expansion to [provide] a wide range of public . . . goods.

Such a state depends on the international capital markets and, to a lesser degree, on the modern multinational business network to create stability in the world economy, in conjunction with management by national or transnational political bodies. Its political institutions are less representative (though in some ways more democratic) than those of the nation state. The Open Markets Committee of the Federal Reserve and the electronic referendum (to take two extremes) are more characteristic of the market state than the elegant electoral representative institutions envisioned by Hamilton and Madison or the mass election campaigns of Roosevelt and Johnson. Like the nation state, the market state assesses its economic success or failure by its society's ability to secure more and better goods and services, but in contrast to the nation state it does not see the state as more than a minimal provider or redistributor. If Washington and Napoleon were the chief architects of the imperial state-nation, Lincoln and Bismarck were the initial innovators of the industrial nation state. The nation state defines its operations against the market, which it distrusts and seeks to master. Thus Lincoln issued the Emancipation Proclamation in 1863, while less than two decades later Bismarck proposed a programme of old-age social security and disability insurance. By contrast, the market state manages its operations by using the market and market mechanisms. Whereas the nation state justified itself as an instrument to maintain the welfare of the people (the nation), the market state exists to maximize the opportunities enjoyed by all members of society and accepts that some will make better use of these opportunities than others, inevitably leading to widening inequalities. Thus we see the paradox that while equality of opportunity—for women, minorities, and others—is increasing, economic inequality is also increasing. For the nation state, full employment is an important and often paramount goal, whereas for the market state, the actual number of people employed is but one more variable in the production of economic opportunity. If it is more efficient to have large bodies of people unemployed, because it would cost the society more to put them to work at tasks for which the market has little demand, then the society will simply have to accept large unemployment figures with all the cost to social cohesion and community that implies.

The market state is classless and indifferent to race, ethnicity, sex and sexual orientation; its yardstick for evaluation is the quantifiable. Indeed, to a far greater extent than the nation state, the market state is culturally accessible to all societies: the statistics and media images that carry its messages do not require proficiency in any particular natural language. If the nation state was characterized by the rule of law, the market state is largely indifferent to the norms of justice, or for that matter to any particular set of moral values so long as law does not act as an impediment to economic competition. Because market states are also indifferent to the values of loyalty, reverence for sacrifice, political competence, privacy and the family, they pose an important challenge to civil society: either these values must be supported without government backing or we will replace them with the values of the market, which seem largely to exalt entertainment and the accumulation of wealth.

One can already see the elements of the constitutional order of market states entering the practices of states. When states go from reliance on law and regulation so characteristic of the nation state to deregulating not only industries but, far more importantly, women's reproduction; when states move from conscription to an all-volunteer force to raise armies, as all the most powerful states of NATO have done; when states end their policies of tuition-free higher education in favour of a combination of top-up fees and merit-based scholarships; when we go from direct cash transfers like the dole and workmen's compensation to providing job training and skills to enter the labour market; when state-owned enterprises are replaced by sovereign wealth funds; when regimes of direct democracy like referenda, recall votes and voter initiatives begin to spread in preference to representational systems – in all these instances we are seeing the beginnings of a change in the constitutional order. The market state says: give us power and we will maximize your opportunity (what you do with it is pretty much up to you).

Not only will this bring an added ferocity to our politics, as different groups feel abandoned by government or their values betrayed,[2] it will also pose the problem that it will be much harder to get the publics of such states to risk their lives and fortunes on behalf of a state that is no longer the champion of their cultural values. The sense of a single polity, held together by adherence to fundamental values, is not a sense that is cultivated by the market state. This cultural indifference does, however, make the market state an ideal environment for multiculturalism. Operating through the imperial state-nation, the state sought to enhance the nation as a whole. In the era of the nation state, the state took responsibility for the well-being of groups. In the market state, the state is responsible for maximizing the choices available to individuals. This means lowering the transaction costs of choosing by individuals and that sometimes means restraining rather than empowering governments. Thus we see measures like the proposal to limit the percentage of GDP taken by government; and actions by courts that have struck down affirmative-action plans for racial preferences, or limited federal power to regulate commerce for goals no one would object to (for example, keeping guns out of schools) and disallowed certain criminal sanctions (like those against contraception or abortion or homosexuality). At the same time maximizing opportunity for the citizenry can also mean expanding the powers of governments to enable them to maintain an infrastructure – both tangible like the internet and intangible like health and education – that is largely in private hands; and to intervene abroad when potentially irreversible developments – the acquisition of weapons of mass destruction, campaigns of national genocide, the emergence of a deadly epidemic – must be precluded.

At a meeting of the Royal Institute for International Affairs at which the topic of Europe's future was discussed, the principal speaker began: 'Europe doesn't have a future. The past 60 years of post-modern integration have been an experiment to fit certain historical circumstances [that] no longer obtain ... so Europe

will return to the nation state of Westphalia in 1648.' He continued, noting that the principal conditions that had brought about
European integration – the need for Franco-German reconciliation,
the threat from communism, the division of Germany and the US
commitment to European security – were irrelevant now, and so the
Westphalian system, within which Europe had 'lived for 300 years',
would now reassert itself.

Except that Europe didn't live in nation states for 300 years, and
the Peace of Westphalia didn't inaugurate the modern state in which,
the speaker said, 'the external power of the Church was exchanged
for the security of the state'.* That exchange actually occurred much
earlier, as evidenced by the Treaty of Augsburg, which established
the principle that local rulers could determine the religious allegiance
– Protestant or Catholic – of their subjects.

Augsburg enshrined the pre-eminence of the princely state,
whose pre-eminent political philosopher was Niccolò Machiavelli.
His lesson for us is that Europe and the world have known a number
of constitutional orders besides the twentieth-century industrial
nation state. Such a lesson would loosen the grip on our minds of
the one-constitutional-order myth which has had such a paralysing
impact on political imagination. It is because the speaker could not
conceive of any alternative to the nation state that he was forced
to assume that either Europe must become a super-nation-state,
spanning the continent (the 'United States of Europe' so beloved of
many in Brussels), or that it must revert back to the ordinary nation
states it had attempted to integrate.

Machiavelli is most relevant here, for he could have told us to
imagine *new* constitutional orders, such as the market states that the
EU, the US and China are rapidly becoming. Like the princely states
of the sixteenth century – indeed, like all subsequent constitutional
orders – the market state is coming into being as a response to

* Quoting, after a fashion, Robert Cooper.

changes in the strategic context, and like its predecessors, it will in turn revolutionize that context. Far from being 'super-nation-states', market states are decentralized, networked, have global interests and depend upon using markets rather than defying them to maintain the legitimacy of the state.

In market states, the media act in direct competition to the government of the day. The media are well suited to succeed in this competition because they are trained to work in the marketplace, are more nimble than bureaucrats hampered by procedural rules, are quick to spot public trends, can call on huge capitalizations and the consolidated power in a handful of media empires, and are the most capable users – far outpacing politicians – of the contemporary techniques of information exchange (including, unfortunately, the collection of personal information) and public relations. Finally, the media are protected in many countries by statutes and constitutional amendments, and are thus free of many of the legal and political restraints that bind government officials.

In fact one can say that one principal consequence of the transition to a market state is an enormous increase in the power of the information media. This may seem paradoxical when we think of the apparently inexorable collapse of newspapers and magazines across the English-speaking world, but it is hardly so puzzling when we realize that the constitutional order that is emerging is an informational one just as the order it is replacing was an industrial one. While conventional sources of information may be withering, the very forces destroying them are giving birth to countless new sources of information that are both more available and cheaper. As public opinion plays a more insistent role in governance – through polls, referenda, voter initiatives and the like – the power of the media that instruct the public is growing concomitantly. *Vox populi*, *vox rumoris*, and, thanks to the profusion of internet 'publications', vice versa.

The competitive, critical function of the media in the market state is similar to that of the political parties of the Left in the nation state.

The Left is always a critical organ in constitutional government – reproving, harassing, questioning the status quo. But of course the Left sought a governing role even though, when Left parties held office, they often quickly moved to the centre, co-opting or being co-opted by the Right. Now, with the discrediting of the Left in the market state, its competitive critical function has been taken up by the media.

Machiavelli would probably have approved of this development, because he ardently sought a role in the Florentine state for public watchdogs akin to the tribunes of the Roman state. These tribunes represented the interests of the plebeians.[3] They could veto resolutions passed by the Roman Senate, and did, reversing a plan to distribute grain in a way that disfavoured the poor. It remains to be seen whether the media will in fact serve as tribunes for the under-represented.

In confronting this historic change – the kind of turbulent upheaval that has come only every century or so – we cannot be guided by Machiavelli, but we can be alerted by him. It was the failure of his contemporaries to appreciate the coming age of princely states that doomed Italy to foreign domination. In our case, it is not the hegemony of foreign states that threatens us – though we are so accustomed to thinking in these terms that we scan the horizon restlessly for potential competitors – but rather internal dissolution and disgust with our own institutions. It is, one might say, the reverse of the situation that Machiavelli and Florence faced at the end of the fifteenth century. This, too, however, is a resonance (though a discordant one) with our sublime predecessor.

Yet while it is not these important resonances with contemporary life that have kept Machiavelli's name alive – and that of the mistaken image of him as Satan's Theologian – they are not irrelevant to his enduring interest for us. That is because, though changes in the constitutional order come rarely, we have a continuing and intense interest in the state, and we regard it with as much dread and suspicion as we do hope.

Machiavelli's sensibility in the popular mind promotes these mixed emotions. The legendary Machiavelli seems to anticipate the liberating, existential despair that comes when one realizes that 'all is permitted' and that the notion of God is dead to many people, even when they live in the midst of a Christian or sectarian world. The depiction of Machiavelli as the devil – 'Old Nick' – also holds a magnetic attraction for us: after all, it is said of Milton, who deplored Machiavelli, that he gave Satan the best lines (indeed, many of them seem to be drawn from *The Prince*).

Nevertheless, Machiavelli is a profoundly ethical writer. This fact, more than the instrumental value of his advice, accounts for his passionate insistence that we look at the world as it is and do not pretend it is otherwise, lest we harm the public as a consequence of acting on our platitudes. We need his insights because he cautions us against our illusions. And yet, ironically, it is his reputation for cheating fate – the greatest illusion – that we associate with his name.

The lesson of Machiavelli's advice to statesmen is: don't kid yourself. What annoyed and frustrated Machiavelli was the willingness of his contemporaries to pretend that quite simple formulations were adequate to the task of governing in the common interest: 'a prince should always keep his word'; 'a prince should be liberal and generous with his funds'; 'a prince should be mild and clement, and always exercise mercy'. One can see him squirming impatiently when he explains that it was not really merciful of Scipio to pardon rebels, because this led to further rebellion and the need for more drastic repression;[4] or denounces the extravagance of princes who overtax their subjects and are ultimately driven to be more miserly than they would have been had they been less eager to impress the public with their liberality;[5] or suggests that when acting on behalf of the public it may not always be in their interests for the prince to bind them to commitments he has unwisely made.[6] One has only to attend to the daily incidents of wishful thinking and appalling hectoring tantrums – the editorial pages of one of our most prominent newspapers would not be a bad place to start – to see that, in this respect, things have not changed much since Machiavelli's day. It is a common error – perhaps we should call it Soderini's Fallacy – to apprehend a problem in a way that structures it as if it were amenable to the methods that have brought us success in the past. A person who hitherto has achieved his objectives by reasoning with others may be inclined to think all of his adversaries are reasonable; a successful litigator may think that the trial process is the only way to deter terrorists, while a distinguished soldier may think that the tried and true methods of warfare hold the key. The random waltz of Fortune will always be of compelling interest to societies that believe that, if only they could run faster, stretch out their arms further, they could grasp the future and bend it to their goals and away from the freighted trajectory of the past. Machiavelli's counsel to us, by contrast, is that we must wake up and face the music.

The lesson of his *life* is something else: do not be surprised if your ideas are ignored or assimilated into those of your contemporaries, so that what is truly new and illuminating will be mistaken or misrepresented to fit the common perceptions that underlie the political orthodoxies of the day.

This book began with a perhaps pedantic discussion of how Gentillet, a serious scholar and gifted linguist, though perhaps something of a mediocrity, so very largely determined how Machiavelli would be perceived by the generations that followed. He was, as the movie script says,[7] a small man who tried to destroy a larger man. Today, undergraduates, one hopes, will get a more appreciative view of *The Prince* than did those earlier generations, who were the heirs to Gentillet's artful amputations. I suppose we must have faith that future scholars will sort out the true from the distorted. That would be comforting, for the phrase 'Satan's Theologian' was not, in fact, applied to Machiavelli; it was applied, by a critic of *The Shield of Achilles*, to me.

I sometimes fear that the lesson of Machiavelli's study of the state

– which his statecraft is meant to serve – might indeed be lost to the future. If we attend only to his tactical advice, then, as my colleague Sanford Levinson has observed, every successful state is self-validating. The Nazi state is as legitimate as the parliamentary democracies it tried to destroy.* This mistake underscores the importance of appreciating the constitutionalist nature of Machiavelli's work, for that perspective makes clear that the nature of the state – its commitment to the common, public interest which embraces all classes and groups under law – is what makes the state a worthy recipient of the devotion that Machiavelli felt is its due.[8] Ends matter, and not just any ends will justify just any means.

The last word must belong to Machiavelli. Here, in the most famous passage of the most famous letter written during the Renaissance, he is writing to Vettori, describing his life in the country after his exile:

> I am living on my farm, and since my latest disasters, I have not spent a total of twenty days in Florence . . . I get up in the morning with the sun and go into one of my woods that I am having cut down; there I spend a couple of hours inspecting the work of the previous day and kill some time with the woodsmen who always have some dispute on their hands either among themselves or with their neighbours . . . Upon leaving the woods, I go to a spring; from there, to one of the places where I hang my lime-traps for thrushes. I have a book under my arm: Dante, Petrarch, or one of the minor poets like Tibullus, or Ovid. I read about their amorous passions and their loves, I remember my own, and these reflections make me happy for a while. Then I make my way along the road towards the inn, I chat with passers-by, I ask news of their regions, I learn about various matters, I observe

---

* In fact, the example of the fascist dictatorships brought many readers to study Machiavelli, perhaps because it was thought they were reflections of 'the pure doctrine of Machiavellianism'. See the Introduction by A. P. d'Entreves to Chabod's *Machiavelli and the Renaissance* (Bowes & Bowes, 1958), pp. xvi–xvii.

mankind: the variety of its thoughts, the diversity of its tastes and dreams. By then it is time to eat; with my household I eat what food this poor farm and my modest patrimony yield. When I have finished eating, I return to the inn, where there usually are the innkeeper, a butcher, a miller and a couple of kilnworkers. I chat with them for the rest of the day, playing *cricca* and backgammon, and these games lead to a thousand squabbles and endless abuses and vituperations ... When evening comes, I return home and enter my study; on the threshold I take off my workday clothes, covered with mud and dirt, and put on the garments of court and palace. Now clothed appropriately, I step inside the venerable courts of the ancients, where, graciously received by them, I nourish myself on that food that alone is mine and for which I was born; where I am unashamed to converse with them and to question them about the ends they sought by their actions, and they, out of their human kindness, answer me. And for four hours at a time I feel no boredom, I forget all my troubles, I do not dread poverty, and I am not terrified by death. I absorb myself into them completely. And because Dante says that no one understands anything unless he retains what he has understood, I have jotted down what I have profited from in their conversation and composed a short study, *De principatibus*, in which I delve as deeply as I can into the ideas concerning this topic, discussing the definition of a princedom, the categories of princedoms, how they are acquired, how they are retained, and why they are lost.

Dramatis Personae

The Medici

Lorenzo (I) the Magnificent (1449–92), ruler of Florence (1469–92), the ideal Renaissance ruler, patron of the arts; he was the grandson of Cosimo de' Medici, the 'Father of his Country'.

Giuliano (1453–78), brother of Lorenzo the Magnificent, murdered during the Pazzi Conspiracy by assassins who also wounded Lorenzo.

Piero the Unfortunate (1472–1503), eldest son of Lorenzo the Magnificent, ruled Florence from 1492 until he was expelled by the Florentine public in 1494, when Charles VIII of France invaded Tuscany en route to Naples.

Giovanni (1475–1521), second son of Lorenzo the Magnificent, ruler of Florence (1512–13), who was elected pope as Leo X in 1513.

Giuliano (1479–1516), third son of Lorenzo the Magnificent, ruler of Florence (1513–16), who was succeeded by Lorenzo (II).

Lorenzo (II) (1492–1519), son of Piero, ruler of Florence (1513–19), who was succeeded by Giulio.

Giulio (1478–1534), son of Lorenzo the Magnificent's brother Giuliano, archbishop of Florence, who ruled (1519–23) until he was elected pope as Clement VII in 1523. He was succeeded as ruler of Florence by Ippolito.

Giovanni dalle Bande Nere (1498–1526), son of Caterina Sforza and Giovanni de' Medici, a cousin to Lorenzo the Magnificent and his brother Giuliano. Bande Nere was a highly celebrated *condottiere* employed by Pope Leo X and Pope Clement VII.

Ippolito (1511–35), illegitimate only son of Lorenzo the Magnificent's son Giuliano, whose authority was exercised by a regent, Cardinal Passerini, from 1523 until 1527, when the Medici were again expelled by the Florentine public following the invasion of Italy by imperial forces.

Alessandro (1510–37), illegitimate son of Giulio, recognized as the only son of Lorenzo II and made ruler of Florence in 1531, following the return of the Medici and the final end of the Florentine Republic; the last member of this branch of the Medici and the only one to have been made an hereditary duke.

THE PAPACY

Alexander VI (1492–1503), Rodrigo Borgia
Pius III (22 September–18 October 1503), Francesco Piccolomini
Julius II (1503–13), Giuliano della Rovere
Leo X (1513–21), Giovanni de' Medici
Adrian VI (1522–3), Adriaan Boeyens
Clement VII (1523–34), Giulio de' Medici

THE MONARCHS

Charles VIII of France (1483–98)
Louis XII of France (1498–1515)
Francis I of France (1515–47)
Maximilian I, Holy Roman Emperor (1486–1519)
Charles V, Holy Roman Emperor (1519–58)
Ferdinand II of Aragon (1479–1516)

OTHER CHARACTERS

Cesare Borgia (1476–1507), Duke of Valentinois

Francesco Guicciardini (1483–1540), Florentine political figure and historian

Livy [Titus Livius] (59 BC–AD 17), Roman historian

Bernardo Rucellai (1448–1514), Florentine aristocrat

Girolamo Savonarola (1452–98), Dominican priest and political leader

Caterina Sforza (1463–1509), Countess of Forli

Ludovico Sforza (1452–1508), Duke of Milan

Piero Soderini (1450–1522), Republican leader of Florence

Francesco Vettori (1474–1539), Florentine diplomat

Chronology

The following is a brief, parallel history of events in Machiavelli's life (in *italic type*) juxtaposed with contemporaneous political and military events in Italy.

Niccolò Machiavelli is born in Florence on 3 May 1469 and baptized the next day at San Giovanni. His father is Bernardo Machiavelli, a doctor of law – although apparently a default on debts owed to the city (perhaps debts originating in the estates of his father and uncles) precludes him from joining the guild of practising lawyers. The lives of father and son embrace the ascendancy of the Medici, their fall, restoration, and second expulsion from Florence.

Bernardo is only a child in 1434 when Cosimo de' Medici takes over the Florentine government and makes himself the head of an oligarchy of allies and clients. In 1454 Cosimo concludes the Peace of Lodi, which confirmed a balance of power among the city states of Milan, Florence and Venice. These states are soon joined in this relationship by the Papal States, adding Naples and various smaller cities to form the Italic League.

In 1469 Cosimo's successor, his son Piero, dies and the leadership of Florence passes to Piero's son Lorenzo, whom we know as the great Renaissance figure Lorenzo the Magnificent.

The peace arranged by Cosimo's balance of power is his greatest achievement and largely prevails until 1494, when the new king of Naples, Alfonzo, allies himself with the Borgia pope Alexander VI and claims dynastic rights to the duchy of Milan, which had been seized in 1450 by the *condottiere* Francesco Sforza (who had been a signatory to the Peace of Lodi). Sforza's fourth son, Ludovico, now ruler of Milan, attempts to parry this threat by allying himself with the king of France, Charles VIII, and inviting the French into Italy with the alluring promise of the throne of Naples. Thus begins a period in which outside powers – France, Spain, and the Holy Roman Empire – vie for conquests in Italy. One consequence of the ensuing French invasion is the threat posed to Florence by the French army as it moves south from Milan through Tuscany en route to Naples. When Piero de' Medici, eldest son of Lorenzo the Magnificent and now ruler of Florence, attempts to propitiate the French by surrendering the fortress city of Pisa, the Florentine public revolts in disgust and the Medici are compelled to flee. The city, though nominally still ruled by the Signoria, the ruling executive council, now comes under the influence of the Dominican firebrand Girolamo Savonarola.

In 1498, however, Charles VIII dies, following his defeat at Fornovo and the French army's evacuation from Italy. That same year, Florence is the subject of a papal interdict and Savonarola is excommunicated for his attacks on the papacy; he falls from power in Florence, and is executed.

Partly as a result of this change in the leadership of Florence, Niccolò Machiavelli is appointed head of the Second Chancery (roughly the equivalent of a permanent undersecretary in the British foreign office, or an undersecretary of state in the American system) and secretary to the Council of Ten of Liberty and Peace, who oversee foreign and military matters (perhaps the equivalent of the US national security adviser, who is also the secretary to the National Security Council).

The next year, Florence realigns itself with Pope Alexander VI, along with Venice, against Ludovico Sforza of Milan, who now seeks protection from Spain. Supported by his father, the pope, Cesare

Borgia – holding a French title, the Duke of Valentinois – begins a campaign of conquest in the Romagna, a region nominally held by the papacy but in fact controlled by local lords, or vicars, whose lands are known as vicarages.

In 1499 Machiavelli undertakes his first diplomatic mission on behalf of the Signoria when he is sent to negotiate with the condottiere *Jacopo d'Appiano, the ruler of Piombino, who is demanding more money to continue Florence's siege of Pisa. Later that year, Machiavelli undertakes his second mission, to Forlì, to persuade the legendary Caterina Sforza to induce her elder son, Ottaviano, a young* condottiere, *to renew his contract with Florence without an increase in pay.*

At this time, Florence is led by Piero Soderini, a moderate and conciliatory figure who had been voted *gonfaloniere* – head of government – by electors chosen by the *Consiglio Maggiore* (Grand Council). His policy is to align Florence with France, with the aim of preserving the Florentine Republic while keeping the Medici (and the Borgias) at bay.

In 1500 Machiavelli is dispatched to Lyon to negotiate with Louis XII of France over various difficulties arising from the behaviour of mercenaries lent to the Florentines by France, who had promised to restore Pisa to Florence in return for a substantial payment that Florence had not provided.

In 1501 Machiavelli is sent to Pistoia to restore order after civil war had broken out between two factions in that city.

In 1502 the Signoria elects Soderini *gonfaloniere* for life. Previously the eight members of the Signoria, as well as their presiding officer (*gonfaloniere*), were elected to two-month terms, during which they take up residence at the Palazzo della Signoria. These brief tenures were necessary because officials were drawn from the various guilds and such limited public service was all they were willing to contribute away from their personal and commercial affairs.

Machiavelli had drafted the law enabling Soderini, his patron, to extend his term of gonfaloniere *indefinitely.*

In June 1502 Machiavelli is sent on his first mission to meet the illegitimate son of Pope Alexander VI, Cesare Borgia, who had conquered the dukedom of Urbino a few weeks earlier through a masterful deception. Borgia threatens to remove the Florentine government and to reinstate Piero de' Medici unless the Signoria commits to the recognition of his conquests and the payment of money he is owed for his services as condottiere *for Florence.*

In October 1502 Soderini sends Machiavelli back to Imola to report on the activities of Cesare Borgia, who is now threatened by disgruntled condottieri *who covertly sought support from Florence.*

In December Borgia travels to Cesena, where he brutally executes his deputy, Ramiro de Lorca. He then departs for Senigallia, to confront his hostile *condottieri* who have captured the city.

Machiavelli writes On the Measures Adopted by the Duke of Valentinois to Kill Vitellozzo Vitelli, Oliverotto da Fermo and Others *(Borgia's restive commanders).*

In August 1503 Pope Alexander VI dies.

In September 1503 Machiavelli is sent to Rome to observe the papal elections.

Pope Pius III is elected by the conclave, but after a pontificate of only 26 days he dies and Giuliano della Rovere is elected Pope Julius II. Although della Rovere had long been an enemy of the Borgias, he wins the papal election by inducing Cesare Borgia to deliver the votes of the Spanish cardinals he controlled in exchange for a promise to retain Borgia as commander of the papal forces. Once elected, della Rovere revokes this promise and has Borgia stripped of his titles and arrested. Without his father's political and financial support, Cesare Borgia's nascent principality in the Romagna collapses.

In December Spanish forces decisively defeat the French army at the battle of Garigliano, just north of Naples.

In January 1504, as a consequence of the Spanish victory, Machiavelli undertakes a mission to the French court, seeking reassurance for Florence; he wants Louis XII to confirm that he will protect Florence from the Spaniards should the Spanish army turn north from Naples.

This assurance becomes unnecessary when, at the end of the month, the Treaty of Lyon is signed and Naples is ceded to Spain. It is agreed that France will control northern Italy while Spain will control Sicily and southern Italy.

Machiavelli writes the Discourse on the Arming of the State of Florence, *urging the creation of a citizen militia to defend the Republic, the great military project of his life.*

In 1505 the Signoria adopts a law, drafted by Machiavelli, that establishes the militia. The following year a Council of Nine is created to oversee the activities of the militia; Machiavelli is appointed secretary to the Council.

In 1506 Machiavelli writes The Purpose of Military Force *and is dispatched to Rome to meet with Pope Julius II and to assess the pope's objectives.*

In 1506 Julius II – known as the 'warrior pope' – takes command of the papal forces and begins a campaign to reclaim the Papal States from the local warlords who had seized various towns and fortresses in the Romagna and Umbria after the fall of Cesare Borgia; this year he reclaims Bologna and Perugia.

In the spring of 1507, as the Spanish threat to Florence recedes, another great power seems on the verge of imperilling central Italy. Maximilian I begins preparations for a journey to Rome to be crowned Holy Roman Emperor. The French fear that this will prove the occasion for the empire to oust the French from Milan in order to vindicate Maximilian's own claim to that city. Alarmed, the Florentine Republic, which has allied with France, sends Francesco Vettori, a young aristocrat, to assess the situation; over Soderini's objections, Machiavelli is kept in Florence and does not accompany Vettori.

In December Soderini is able to persuade the Signoria to send Machiavelli to the imperial court. Machiavelli's reports are sceptical, arguing that Maximilian is incompetent to manage an invasion.

Machiavelli is vindicated when, in February, imperial troops attack Venetian forces near Vicenza and are decisively defeated. When Maximilian signs a three-year truce, the threat to Florence abates.

In 1508 Julius II organizes an alliance – the League of Cambrai, which includes France, Spain and the Holy Roman Empire – to oust Venice from its possessions in the Romagna, and in 1509 Venice is defeated at Agnadello.

In 1508, Machiavelli is sent to Pisa to oversee the siege of that city by Florentine forces that he had organized.

In 1509 Pisa finally capitulates.

Early in 1510 Julius II smashes his own creation, the League of Cambrai, and makes peace with Venice, whom he then recruits to join Spain, the Holy Roman Empire and forces he hires from the Swiss cantons to oppose France. This puts Florence in a vulnerable position because, following an assassination attempt widely believed to have been sponsored by the Medici and the pope, Soderini has deepened the Florentine Republic's alignment with the French.

At the end of June 1511 Soderini sends Machiavelli back to the French court. His instructions are to encourage Louis to propitiate the pope in order to avoid a conflict in which the Florentine Republic would find itself besieged by papal forces who might reinstate the Medici.

On 2 January 1511 Julius leaves his sickbed in Bologna and leads the papal army in person through deep snow to besiege Mirandola, a city allied with the French. The French king, exploiting his relationship with Florence, attempts to convene a council of bishops in Pisa to overthrow Julius. Although the French triumph at Ravenna in April 1512, Charles I, king of Spain, and Maximilian, Holy Roman Emperor, are able to finance a Swiss force to invade Lombardy, resulting in a French withdrawal from Italy. In June Julius demands Soderini's removal from power.

Spanish forces then march on Florence. Following a bloody sack of Prato, a possession of Florence since the mid-fourteenth century, the Florentine Republic collapses when pro-Medici forces storm the Signoria. Soderini flees to Rome, and the Medici are restored to power on 1 September 1512, when Giuliano de' Medici, third son of Lorenzo the Magnificent, enters Florence; his brother, Cardinal Giovanni de' Medici, follows on 14 September.

Soderini had asked Machiavelli to negotiate his safe conduct from Florence to Rome. Following the Medici restoration, the principal Republican institution, the Consiglio Maggiore *(Grand Council), is dismissed, and the Florentine militia, which had disgraced itself at Prato, is dissolved. On 7 November Machiavelli is removed from office; on 10 November he is required to post a crippling bond and is sentenced to internal exile. He is then banned from entering the Signoria. He is forty-three years old; he has been in office for fourteen years and will never return to the Signoria as one of its officials.*

In February 1513 a plot to murder Giuliano de' Medici and his nephew Lorenzo is uncovered. The conspirators were unmasked when their leader, Agostino Capponi, accidentally dropped a paper listing some twenty persons whom he and his co-conspirator Pietro

Paulo Boscoli had hoped to enlist in the conspiracy. These two are arrested, tortured and beheaded.

Machiavelli's name is seventh on the list. On the night of 18 February 1513 he is arrested and taken to prison. He is tortured but does not confess; it appears that he was approached by at least one of the conspirators but did not offer any support for their efforts.

On 21 February Julius II dies, and on 9 March Giovanni de' Medici, second son of Lorenzo the Magnificent, is elected Pope Leo X. Though a cardinal since childhood, on 15 March he is ordained as a priest; two days later he is consecrated as a bishop; he is crowned pope on 19 March. He is 37 and will remain pope for eight years.

In the enthusiastic celebrations that engulfed Florence, a general amnesty is declared, and on 11 or 12 March Machiavelli is released.

Sometime in the spring and summer of 1513, Machiavelli begins writing a series of essays on republics; when his former colleagues in the Second Chancery are restored to their posts, he apparently breaks off this endeavour in order to write an extended essay on another form of the state, the principality, which he addresses to Giuliano de' Medici.

In June 1513 the French are defeated by a Swiss force and driven from Milan, which is restored to Massimiliano Sforza, son of Ludovico.

In December 1513 Machiavelli writes to Francesco Vettori, asking him to review the as yet uncompleted manuscript De principatibus *(as* The Prince *is at this point entitled), with an eye to presenting it to Giuliano when the book is completed.*

In December 1514 Vettori requests a memo from Machiavelli for Leo X, to help the pope decide whether to ally with France or Spain and the Holy Roman Empire.

Early in 1515 Machiavelli begins meeting with the papal secretary Paolo Vettori, Francesco's brother. If the pope were to succeed in making his brother Giuliano the ruler of the Romagna, it seems likely that Paolo would be appointed to govern one of the cities in the new realm. Machiavelli advises that the Medici should unify the Romagna into a single princely state. But Machiavelli's hopes for employment are thwarted by Giulio de' Medici, first cousin of Leo and Giuliano, who tells Vettori to have nothing to do with him.

In 1515 the new king of France, Francis I, defeats the Swiss at Marignano and reconquers Milan.

When Giuliano dies in March 1516, Machiavelli changes the dedication of De principatibus *and sends it to Lorenzo de' Medici, Giuliano's nephew and successor as ruler of Florence.*

In the Treaty of Noyon of 1516, Spain once again recognizes French claims to Milan, while the French, once again, renounce their claims to Naples, which remains Spanish.

By the summer of 1517, Machiavelli has joined a group of patrician intellectuals and humanists in a symposium that convenes regularly. This group comes to be known as the Orti Oricellari, named after the gardens of the Palazzo Rucellai where they meet.

Leo wishes to create a duchy of Urbino in the Romagna for the Medici, so he organizes a new alliance against France, receiving 150,000 ducats from Henry VIII of England and enlisting the aid of Spain. The ensuing War of Urbino lasts from February to September 1517 and culminates in the confirmation of Lorenzo de' Medici as duke of Urbino.

In 1518 Machiavelli composes La Mandragola, *a satirical comedy, explaining that he has turned to playwriting because he has been 'reduced to indolence / And has no other way to turn / Condemned to an enforced sojourn / All worthwhile occupations barred . . .' The play, first produced for the Orti Oricellari, is a rousing success.*

In May 1519 Lorenzo dies of syphilis at the age of 26. Thereafter, Florence is ruled by Giulio de' Medici, archbishop of Florence.

In June 1519 Leo X endorses the election of Charles I of Spain as Charles V, Holy Roman Emperor, a move that further alienates the French.

In March 1520 Giulio meets with Machiavelli and commissions a study on how to govern Florence. This treatise – the Discourse on Florentine Affairs after the Death of Lorenzo *– lays out a constitution for Florence that would preserve the Republic (the Great Council would be revived along with a* gonfaloniere *for life) but allows a transitional role for Medici pre-eminence during Giulio's and Leo's lifetimes.*

In April a member of the Orti Oricellari reports to Machiavelli that Pope Leo wishes to have La Mandragola *produced at the papal court and plans to commission further projects from him.*

In the summer of 1520 Machiavelli is sent on a mission to Lucca to recover debts from a bankrupt Lucchese merchant. Shortly thereafter, he composes a brief biography – the Life of Castruccio Castracani *– of a fourteenth-century* condottiere *who ruled Lucca. This book is dedicated to two members of the Orti Oricellari, Luigi Alamanni and Zanobi Buondelmonti.*

In November 1520 Machiavelli receives an important commission from Giulio and Leo X to compose the official history of Florence.

In the spring of 1521 Machiavelli is sent by the Otto di Pratica, the Florentine board overseeing foreign affairs, to Carpi in order to assert control over the Franciscan Order there.

In May 1521 Leo X concludes a treaty with Charles V to oust the French from Milan, which had been taken by Francis I after Marignano. Leo had once contemplated an alliance with France, England and Venice against the emperor Maximilian, but Charles had dissuaded him from this course. Now, in November, Milan falls.

In August 1521 Machiavelli publishes The Art of War, *the only one of his works to be published in his lifetime. In the form of a dialogue, it is set in the gardens of the Orti Oricellari.*

On 1 December 1521 Leo X dies. Immediately, Cardinal Francesco Soderini, the brother of Piero, allied with France, hires *condottieri* to remove the Medici from Florence, but his forces are defeated by the *condottiere* Orazio Baglioni, the illegitimate son of the ruler of Perugia.

In June 1522 a plot to kill Giulio de' Medici is exposed. Francesco Soderini is arrested in Rome by Adrian VI, who has been elected pope to succeed Leo. On 13 June Piero Soderini dies.

The two would-be assassins of Cardinal Giulio are members of the Orti Oricellari and ardent republicans, Zanobi Buondelmonti and Luigi Alamanni, to whom Machiavelli had dedicated the Life of Castruccio Castracani.

Pope Adrian VI dies in September 1523, barely twenty months after his election. Giulio de' Medici is elected as the second Medici pope, Clement VII. Although Giulio had supported an alliance with Charles V (who is partly responsible for his election as pope), once in the papal office Clement detaches himself from his former ally, the emperor, and begins negotiations for an alliance with France.

In November 1524 the French recapture Milan, and in December Clement signs a secret treaty with Francis against the Holy Roman Empire.

Early in 1525 Machiavelli completes his History of Florence.

In February 1525 French forces are destroyed by the emperor's mercenaries at Pavia. Francis is taken prisoner, the first reigning French monarch to be captured in battle since Poitiers in 1356. Milan is retaken by the imperial forces. In May a treaty is signed between Charles V and the Church.

Machiavelli travels to Rome to present Clement with his History of Florence. *The dedication to Clement concedes that the book is often critical of the Medici. In his audience with the pope, Machiavelli tries to persuade him that the establishment of citizen militias throughout the Papal States would serve as a bulwark against foreign invaders. Clement sends Machiavelli to the Romagna to assess the feasibility of such a project. There he meets with Francesco Guicciardini, the governor of the region.*

In January 1526, by the Treaty of Madrid, Francis cedes Milan to Spain and reaffirms Spanish authority in Naples. Once he is released and returns to France in May, however, Francis renounces the treaty and allies with Clement, Sforza, Venice and Florence in the League of Cognac to drive Charles V from Italy.

The Art of War has earned Machiavelli a reputation as a military engineer – the book has a lengthy section on fortifications – and in the spring of 1526 he is invited to Rome to report to Clement on the condition of the Florentine fortifications in anticipation of an attack by the imperial forces. He is subsequently named Secretary and Quartermaster of the Curators of the Walls.

In the summer of 1526 Machiavelli is ordered to Lombardy to reorganize the infantry at Marignano under the command of the famed condottiere *Giovanni de' Medici.*

Giovanni de' Medici – known as Giovanni dalle Bande Nere – is the twenty-eight-year-old son of Caterina Sforza by Giovanni de' Medici Popolano, a member of the cadet branch of the Medici. This great-grand-nephew of Cosimo de' Medici is perhaps the most celebrated *condottiere* in Italy, and it is in his hands that the pope places his fate.

Machiavelli negotiates the surrender of Cremona to the papal alliance, the Holy League.

On 25 November 1526 the imperial army – including a large German contingent known as *Landsknechts*, many of whom are followers of Martin Luther – engage troops commanded by Bande Nere, in the aftermath of which he dies. Facing the imperial forces without Bande Nere, Clement decides to bribe them. In January 1527 he signs a treaty with the emperor promising to pay 200,000 ducats to induce the imperial forces to retreat across the Alps. But a minor victory by Holy League forces prompts Clement to repudiate the treaty. Augmented by Spanish infantry, the imperial army begins marching south on 31 March in the direction of Florence.

Confronting Machiavelli's fortifications, the imperial army determines to bypass Florence.

On 4 May the imperial army reaches Rome, where they demand 300,000 ducats from the pope. Clement refuses and an assault on Rome begins on 6 May. The ensuing occupation and sack of Rome is the most widely deplored predation of the century.

Machiavelli, now in Florence, is dispatched to Civitavecchia, to arrange the evacuation of the pope from Castel Sant' Angelo.

In the wake of the imperial seizure of Rome, on 16 May the Medici government of Florence is overthrown. The Republic is restored and the Grand Council, as well as the Ten of Liberty and Peace, is reconvened.

Machiavelli now hopes that he might be reappointed as secretary to the Chancery, but despite the urging of Buondelmonti and Alamanni – who have returned to Florence from exile – he is not appointed. To the republicans, whose cause he had championed in the Discourses, *he is now too closely associated with the Medici, just as in 1512 he had been seen by the Medici as too close to Piero Soderini, the champion of the Republic. He falls ill, and on 21 June 1527 he dies.*

Pope Clement remains a prisoner in Castel Sant' Angelo for six months before escaping in disguise. In June 1529 he signs the Peace of Barcelona with the emperor, Charles V, one provision of which requires the restoration of the Medici to power in Florence. In 1530, after an eleven-month siege, the Florentine Republic falls to imperial forces, and Alessandro, the pope's illegitimate son, is installed as duke. He is assassinated in 1537 at the age of 26 by a distant cousin, who attempts, unsuccessfully, to restore the Republic.

Acknowledgements

I T SEEMS SLIGHTLY absurd to agree to write a short book on Machiavelli's masterpiece, *The Prince.*

In the first place, *The Prince* is itself a short book, and it is written in a pithy, accessible style. It needs no summary which would, paradoxically, detract from the brevity of the masterpiece it supplemented.

In the second place, there is already an excellent short book by Quentin Skinner, describing the arguments, historical context and philosophical perspective of *The Prince*, appropriately entitled *Machiavelli: A Very Short Introduction*, and an even shorter, though necessarily less comprehensive, fine book by Maurizio Viroli, *How to Read Machiavelli*.

Thirdly, the present book was commissioned as part of a series of ten books, the other nine by very distinguished authors who all turned in their work on time. I think with shame that my failure to do the same may have delayed their publication or detracted in any way from this very successful series that I was honoured to join. But the project did present a problem: as scholars of Machiavelli will quickly appreciate, almost all my quotations and references to his work are familiar ones. Whether or not my readers are persuaded by my thesis, they will not claim that it relies on recondite sources. Yet I strained at every juncture of the argument not to put in scores of other references, principally from the *Discourses*, but also drawn from Machiavelli's letters and memoranda, that are evidence for my claims. That would not have been possible in a book of the length I agreed to write. Some readers will doubtless be grateful for this, but it still vexes me.

When asked by Toby Mundy, the publisher of Atlantic Books, to write a short book on *The Prince*, I acknowledged that I had long wanted to write about Machiavelli, but I didn't say why. Perhaps when I began writing, I didn't know precisely why myself. It is true that I wanted to treat more extensively some of the claims about and interpretations of Machiavelli offered in previous books of mine. But perhaps there was more to it than that.

For attentive readers of the notes to the present work, it will soon become obvious that my rendering of Machiavelli is an example of what Jorge Luis Borges called a writer's creating his own precursors. The notion of a constitutional order that supplanted the feudal order and began the era of the modern state a century before Westphalia, which I introduced in *The Shield of Achilles* – as well as the 'field' relationship between strategy and law that is so important to that book, and the 'duty of consequentialism' that is imposed on public leaders and is such an important element of *Terror and Consent* – are instances of just such a process of creation.

In his lifetime, Niccolò Machiavelli was successively a civil servant, a playwright and a jurist. In each of these roles he displayed a rare ability to portray life as it really is, with its contradictions and complexities, its historical determinants and twists of unexpected fortune. Rarer still was his faculty of withstanding those crosscurrents, of staying on his feet as the feudal tectonic plates shifted and opened up the chasm before modern Europe.

As a civil servant, Machiavelli did not have the power to place his views above those in the Signoria whom he served. After Soderini's downfall, which was brought about in part by Soderini's reluctance to accept the advice of his protégé, Machiavelli was thrust from the office where for fourteen years he had laboured as Florentine secretary, and the republic which he had served was effectively overthrown by the Medici. Machiavelli believed that *The Prince* would demonstrate to Florence's restored rulers how they might legitimate the new principality they were creating in everything but name, and he hoped that this demonstration would win him a return to his former role. For those who have not served in government, it may be hard to accept that a person of integrity could seek to play both sides – republican and monarchical. But if we see that Machiavelli believed, with good grounds, that he understood Florence's situation better than many others, and that, out of office, he could do his beloved city little good, we may be more sympathetic.

Machiavelli became a playwright by default. When *The Prince* failed to interest the Medici in bringing him back into government, he turned to a new genre entirely, composing *La Mandragola*, a satirical comedy. He did not pretend that playwriting was his preferred life's work.[1]

Yet there can be little doubt that Machiavelli composed his plays with great skill; *La Mandragola* itself is a comic masterpiece that is ranked among the greatest works of the Italian theatre. What distinguishes Machiavelli as a playwright is the roundedness of his characters. Anticipating Shakespeare by more than half a century, Machiavelli does not create wholly unsympathetic villains and unflawed heroes, but makes all his characters subject to human folly and never without a rueful appreciation of their predicaments.[2] To this situational irony, Machiavelli juxtaposes dramatic irony (for example, *La Mandragola* depends upon a cuckolded husband's ignorance of the plot to seduce his young wife, of which the audience is aware), and the dialogue is salted with comic ironies as each character reveals himself to be subject to vices that contrast with our expectations (for example, it is the priest, masquerading as a doctor, who persuades the husband to sacrifice an unwitting victim in order to secure an heir; it is the virtuous wife who, having been reluctantly persuaded to allow a stranger into her bed, then convinces herself that this turn of events is divinely ordained and should be perpetuated). Victoria Kahn puts this well when she observes that 'Machiavelli's irony does not involve simply saying one thing and meaning its opposite; it more often describes an attitude that embraces two possibilities at the same time.'[3]

Machiavelli's father, Bernardo, had been trained as a lawyer and was a member of the lawyers' guild – a prestigious and powerful Florentine group. Though Niccolò did not follow him into law – the father may have been barred from practice owing to a default on a municipal debt that would also have prevented the son from practising law[4] – there is a lawyerly cast to much of Machiavelli's jurisprudence. His fundamental idea that moral autonomy is distinct from – and not necessarily privileged above – the practice of governing is a lawyer's idea, and no doubt a source of the common hostility to lawyers. For example, Machiavelli's use of the term *ragionare* can be better rendered as 'rationalizing' – in the sense of offering a rationale – rather than reasoning,[5] and this, too, is characteristic of lawyers and judges, who must account for the application of a rule in order to legitimate its use, in contrast to the desire to explain the use of a rule (by reference to politics, or psychological or sociological predispositions).[6] For the advocate, it is the predicament of the client that provokes action, and this is a paradigm for Machiavelli's constitutional solutions to the iron necessities of God and the fickle constraints of Fortune. It is conflict – which is the consequence of desire confronting constraint – that animates Machiavelli's constitutional proposals, not only setting the terms of the problem but also providing the basis for his solutions.

Machiavelli's three lives also intrigued me, for my own professional life – on a far more insignificant scale – has careered from the academy, to government, to the writing chamber. And finally, for me, as for Machiavelli, the greatest source of consolation and encouragement has come from friends.

I should like to pay tribute to them, for they have contributed in so many ways – often unknown to them – to this book. First, I must thank my old Austin circle – Steve and Louise Weinberg, Paul

Woodruff, Lawrence Wright, and especially Betty Sue Flowers – for commenting on the manuscript. No less have my London friends – Philip Ziegler, Sir Simon Jenkins, Anthony Smith, Sir Max Hastings, Sir Lawrence Freedman, and especially Sir Michael Howard – been supportive and generous.

It will not be surprising that I have turned to diplomats for help with this work. I would like to single out ambassadors Sir Peter Westmacott, Lord Hannay, Sir Jeremy Greenstock, Sir Robert Cooper, Rolf Ekeus, Robert Hutchings, Ivo Daalder, and especially the former US Secretary of State, Henry Kissinger. Nor should it be unusual – in light of my thesis – that I should also turn to scholars of constitutional law, including my colleague of thirty years, Sanford Levinson, as well as professors Akhil Amar, Henry Monaghan, Jack Goldsmith, and Robert Post; the distinguished jurists Judge Michael Boudin and Judge Guido Calabresi; international lawyers Kenneth Anderson, Sarah Cleveland, Michael Reisman, and Ruth Wedgwood; former government officials, including my old friend Gregory Treverton, Richard Danzig, Steven Simon, Paul Monk, Edwin Williamson, Matthew Waxman, and the late Sir Michael Quinlan; philosophers John Gray, Gilbert Harman, Dennis Patterson, and especially Mark Sagoff; social critics Richard Sennett and Michael Lind; historians Margaret Macmillan, Niall Ferguson, and Roger Louis; foreign policy analysts Charles Kupchan and Timothy Garton Ash; journalists, including the late Christopher Hitchens, Matthew d'Ancona, and Benjamin Wittes; and especially my dear editor Ashbel Green, so recently lost to us in this life, and the editor and publisher Henry Reath; economists Sir John Vickers and James K. Galbraith; the playwright Richard Brockman; poets Robert Pinsky and David Ferry; and the polymaths Edward Binkowski and especially David Bodanis. As I observed above, in his time Machiavelli was all of these: diplomat, constitutionalist, civil servant, philosopher and social critic, historian, essayist, playwright, and poet.

My gifted secretary, Jennifer Lamar, has once more midwifed a book of mine. Her colleague, Terri Germany, and his family have seen to it that I might work in happy and beautiful surroundings. My young friends, Travis Pantin, Tom Schmidt, and Winthrop Wells – law students when I was working on this manuscript – and my supremely hard-working research assistant Jacob Fiddelman and, more recently, Rob Goodman – all contributed diligently and tirelessly to this book.

The dean of the Columbia Law School, David Schizer, contrived to get me a leave of absence from teaching. Since my coming to New York, he has been a steadfast friend. Roger Hertog, who has single-handedly brought seminars on grand strategy back into the university curriculum through his foundation, supported a class on Machiavelli for undergraduates and law students at Columbia. My courageous friend, Bill Powers, president of the University of Texas, and the dean of the law school there, Lawrence Sager, and my former colleague at the National Security Council, James Steinberg, all collaborated to find support for my writing time.

At Atlantic Books, I have been much blessed by the temperate patience of its chief executive, Toby Mundy, and two hard-working editors, Orlando Whitfield and, following his departure for the glittering art world, the diplomatic but firm Margaret Stead. Ben Dupre, a gifted writer of his own books, has proved to be a superb copy-editor – the best I have ever had – of the present one.

On 30 June 2012 my life changed when Philip Baines Nizami Bobbitt – whose mother, Maya Ondalikoglu Bobbitt, and I call 'Pasha' – was born. One of Machiavelli's tenderest letters is addressed to his son, Guido; now I think I know how he felt. The world into which Pasha has come is in many ways a far better one than the world into which I was born, and a far less dangerous one than Renaissance Florence, but it is not without formidable challenges. I should like for Pasha, some day, to pick up this book and profit by his exposure to the constitutional aspects of Machiavelli's thought, for it is in the dimension of the changing nature of the state that his world will be most fraught, as was Machiavelli's. Perhaps Pasha will play some part in shaping that evolution.

Finally, my grateful thanks to a Providence that has brought me the incomparable Maya. Her tender encouragement and unfailing wit are making my life poetry, though I had been accustomed to and content (I thought) with prose. We first met in a seminar on *The Prince* and the *Discourses* and it now seems that, for all my many debts to Machiavelli, this will prove to be the greatest.

Philip Bobbitt
Istanbul
1 January 2013

A Note on Translation

THE QUOTED PASSAGES from *The Prince* and the *Discourses* are the work-product of my collaboration with the Italian Renaissance scholar – and novelist – Ms Lisa Hilton Moro, but this fine writer must not bear the blame for my authorial decisions. I have tried to produce *semblances* of Machiavelli's sentences – that is, restatements that capture the tone, style and objectives of his writing and are not merely literal translations. To correct for this presumption, and the mistakes I may have introduced through ignorance and folly, I have provided in the bibliography excellent editions by my favourite translators of Machiavelli. Of course the responsibility is entirely mine.

Notes

PROLOGUE: *ARTE DELLO STATO* – THE MACHIAVELLI PARADOX

1. Within the last year, three new biographies and three new major studies have appeared in English alone: John McCormick, *Machiavellian Democracy* (Cambridge UP, 2011); John M. Najemy (ed.), *The Cambridge Companion to Machiavelli* (Cambridge UP, 2010); Miles Unger, *Machiavelli: A Biography* (Simon & Schuster, 2011); Niccolò Capponi, *An Unlikely Prince: The Life and Times of Machiavelli* (Da Capo Press, 2010); Maurizio Viroli and Antony Shugaar, *Machiavelli's God* (Princeton UP, 2010); Paul Oppenheimer, *Machiavelli: A Life Beyond Ideology* (Continuum Books, 2011).

2. Harvey C. Mansfield, Jr., *Machiavelli's New Modes and Orders: A Study of the 'Discourses on Livy'* (Cornell UP, 1979), p. 7.

3. For the thesis that a new constitutional order, the 'market state', is emerging, see Philip Bobbitt, *The Shield of Achilles: War, Peace, and the Course of History* (Knopf, 2002), pp. 213 ff.; see also Robert Cooper, *The Breaking of Nations: Order and Chaos in the 21st Century* (Atlantic, 2003); and see *Shell Global Scenarios to 2025: Trends, Trade-offs, and Choices* (Shell International Ltd., 2005).

4. John T. Bookman, 'Machiavelli Scholarship: An Essay and List of Works in English', *Philosophy Research Archives* 9 (1537) (1983); Eric Haywood, 'Touring The Hall of Fame', *Review of Politics*, vol. 62, issue 4 (Autumn 2000): 833.

5. Machiavelli letter to Francesco Vettori, 10 December 1513, in James B. Atkinson and David Sices (trans. and ed.), *Niccolò Machiavelli, Machiavelli and His Friends: Their Personal Correspondence* (N. Illinois

UP, 1996); see also John Najemy, *Between Friends: Discourses of Power and Desire in the Machiavelli–Vettori Letters of 1513–1515* (Princeton UP, 1993).

THE UNHOLY NECROMANCER AND HIS KORAN FOR COURTIERS

1. Peter Bondanella and Mark Musa (ed. and trans.), *The Portable Machiavelli* (Penguin, 1971), p. 21.
2. Maurizio Viroli, *Machiavelli: Founders of Modern Political and Social Thought* (Oxford UP, 1998), p. 95. See also Patricia Vilches, *Discourses on Livy* (reviewing the *Discourses* translated by Julia Conway and Peter Bondanella), *Sixteenth Century Journal*, vol. 36, issue 1 (Spring 2005): 27; Albert Russell Ascoli, *Speculum* 70, 4 (1995): 952 (essay on Najemi's *Between Friends: Discourses of Power and Desire in the Machiavelli–Vettori Letters of 1513–1515*).
3. Victoria Kahn, 'Reading Machiavelli: Innocent Gentillet's Discourse on Method', *Political Theory*, vol. 22, issue 4 (Nov. 1994): 539; Antonio D'Andrea, 'The Political and Ideological Context of Innocent Gentillet's Anti-Machiavel', *Renaissance Quarterly*, vol. 23, issue 4 (Winter 1970): 397.
4. L. Arnold Weissberger, 'Machiavelli and Tudor England', *Political Science Quarterly* 42 (1927): 589–90.
5. See also the English author John Case, who knew Machiavelli's writing well but was willing to accept Gentillet as having provided an adequate summary of his doctrines. See N. W. Bawcutt, 'The "Myth of Gentillet" Reconsidered: An Aspect of Elizabethan Machiavellianism', *Modern Language Review*, vol. 99, issue 4 (Oct. 2004): 863, 871.
6. 'One that writteth of matter of state, and gouernment, and against Machiavell, the Courtiers and suchlike mens *Summun Phytagoreum*, saieth, hee seeth no reason, but his books may rightly be called *Alcoranum aulicorum*, the Courtiers Alcoran, seeing as they haue them in no lesse estimation, then the Turkes haue the Alcoran & dreames of Mahumet.' Quoted in Bawcutt, 'The "Myth of Gentillet" Reconsidered', p. 873.

7. Bawcutt, 'The "Myth of Gentillet" Reconsidered', p. 866. 'I doubt not, but many Courtiers, which deale in matters of Estate & others of their humor, will find it very strange, that I should speake in this sort of their great Doctor Machiavell; whose bookes rightly may bee called, the French Courtiers Alcoran, they have in them so great estimation; imitating and observing his principles and maximes, no more or less than the Turkes doe the Alcoran of their great prophet Mahomet.'

8. For a discussion of Gentili and his work, see Philip Bobbitt, *The Shield of Achilles: War, Peace, and the Course of History* (Knopf, 2002), pp. 496–500.

9. Quoted in Adam Watson, *The Evolution of International Society* (Routledge, 1992), p. 641.

10. As we have seen in our day with Oliver Stone's popular film *JFK*. In 2010 it was reported that 80 per cent of Americans believed that President Kennedy's assassination was the work of a conspiracy, despite the repeated and unequivocal repudiation of this idea by reputable historians. Stone's film is a kind of assassination of history itself.

11. Christopher Marlowe, *The Jew of Malta* (Dover, 2003); see also Joseph Khoury, 'Marlowe's Tamburlaine: Idealized Machiavellian Prince', in Patricia Vilches and Gerald Seaman (eds.), *Seeking Real Truths: Multidisciplinary Perspectives on Machiavelli* (Brill, 2007).

12. See Avery Plaw, 'Prince Harry: Shakespeare's Critique of Machiavelli', *Interpretation*, vol. 33, issue 1 (Fall/Winter 2005): 19. More generally, see also John Roe, 'Machiavelli and Shakespeare', in Patricia Vilches and Gerald Seaman (eds.), *Seeking Real Truths: Multidisciplinary Perspectives on Machiavelli* (Brill, 2007).

13. Barbara Riebling, 'Milton on Machiavelli: Representations of the State in *Paradise Lost*', *Renaissance Quarterly*, vol. 49, issue 3 (Autumn 1996): 573 (1996); Dilek Kececi, 'Satan as the Machiavellian Hero in "Paradise Lost"', *Ethos: Dialogues in Philosophy and Social Sciences*, vol. 2, issue 1 (Jan. 2009): 1.

14. See Guido Calabresi and Philip Bobbitt, *Tragic Choices* (Norton, 1978).

BOOK I: *ORDINI* – THE IMPORTANT STRUCTURE OF *THE PRINCE*

Chapter 1. The Emergence of the Modern State

1. Aldo Scaglione, essay on J. H. Whitfield's *Discourses on Machiavelli*, in *Modern Language Quarterly*, vol. 32, issue 2 (June 1971): 214, 217.

2. But see J. H. Whitfield, 'On Machiavelli's Use of *Ordini*', *Italian Studies*, vol. 10 (1955): 19, 38. 'It is only because his critics have persisted in seeking in the *Discorsi* (when they have troubled to look so far) the author of *The Prince*, instead of recognizing in *The Prince* the author of the *Discorsi*, that the vital elements of Machiavelli's political vocabulary . . . have not been recognized.' Whitfield notes that the term *ordini* occurs no fewer than 761 times in the *Discourses* and 65 times in *The Prince*, and that since Machiavelli explicitly asserts that it is incompatible with *imperio assoluto*, there is a statistical reason to doubt that either work proposes absolutism.

3. Scaglione, essay on Whitfield's *Discourses*, p. 217.

4. Adam Watson, *The Evolution of International Society* (Routledge, 1992), p. 96.

5. *Discourses*, book 2, chapter 17.

6. *The Shield of Achilles*, pp. 80–1. I have reproduced those passages drawn from *The Shield of Achilles*, and *Terror and Consent*, as closely as possible to the original texts, partly no doubt out of indolence, partly not to introduce any suggestion of elements not presented in the original, and partly because Machiavelli himself was in the habit of doing this, capturing paragraphs and pages from his dispatches or from his major works and inserting them in his later writings.

7. *Ibid.* p. 81.

8. *Ibid.*

9. For the origin of credit in the creation of bills and notes, see Niall Ferguson, *The Ascent of Money: A Financial History of the World* (Allen Lane, 2008); and also his *The Cash Nexus: Money and Power in the Modern World, 1700–2000* (Allen Lane, 2001).

10. Adam Watson, *The Evolution of International Society*, p. 164; see also the sources cited in *The Shield of Achilles*, p. 836, n. 22.

11. This debate is taken up in *The Shield of Achilles*, pp. 83–4.

12. *The Prince*, chapter 26.

13. *Ibid.*
14. *The Prince*, chapter 6.

Chapter 2. Can a Statesman Get into Heaven?

1. And see also Francesco Patrizi's *The Education of the King*; Giovanni Pontano's 'De Principe', in E. Garin (ed.), *Prosatori Latini del Quattrocentro* (Milan, 1952), p. 1024; and Bartolomeo Sacchi (Platina), *De Principe*.
2. On Cicero and his relationship to Machiavelli's work, see Curtis L. Hancock, 'Cicero Versus Machiavelli: Does the End Justify the Means?', *Contemporary Philosophy*, vol. 16, issue 6 (Nov.–Dec. 1994): 14–18; J. N. Stephens, 'Ciceronian Rhetoric and the Immorality of Machiavelli's Prince', *Renaissance Studies*, vol. 2, issue 2 (Oct. 1988): 258–67; Marcia L. Colish, 'Cicero's "De Officiis" and Machiavelli's "Prince"', *Sixteenth Century Journal*, vol. 9, issue 4 (Winter 1968): 80–93.
3. Marcus Tullius Cicero, *De officiis*, published as *On Duties* (Cambridge UP, 1991), book I, chapter 41.
4. On this famous passage, see Timothy J. Lukes, 'Lionizing Machiavelli', *American Political Science Review*, vol. 95, issue 3 (Sept. 2001): 561.
5. *The Prince*, chapter 18.
6. Cicero, *De officiis,* book II, chapters 58, 77.
7. There is a large literature on 'loss aversion', the idea that people tend to prefer avoiding losses to acquiring gains, even when it is irrational to do so. Among other implications of this human foible, it seems that one who loses $100 will suffer more than a person gains satisfaction from a $100 windfall; similarly, people would prefer to avoid a $5 surcharge rather than get a $5 discount. See D. Kahneman and A. Taversky, 'Choices, Values and Frames', *American Psychologist*, vol. 39, no. 4 (1984): 341.
8. Leo Strauss, *Thoughts on Machiavelli* (University of Chicago Press, 1958), pp. 9–10. Though one should note that Strauss also observes 'what is truly admirable in Machiavelli: the intrepidity of his thought, the grandeur of his vision, and the graceful subtlety of his speech'.
9. Cary J. Nederman, 'Niccolò Machiavelli', in *Stanford Encyclopedia of*

   Philosophy (Autumn 2009 edition), ed. Edward N. Zalta, accessible at
   http://plato.stanford.edu.

10. Letter to the author from Tom Schmidt.

11. But see Mark Hulliung, *Citizen Machiavelli* (Princeton UP, 1983), which
   seems to deprecate this distinction.

12. Thomas Nagel, 'War and Massacre', *Philosophy & Public Affairs*, vol. 1
   (1972): 123–44.

13. Michael Walzer, 'Political Action: The Problem of Dirty Hands', in
   Sanford Levinson (ed.), *Torture* (Oxford UP, 2004), pp. 61–2. This
   discussion is drawn from Philip Bobbitt, *Terror and Consent: The Wars
   for the Twenty-First Century* (Knopf, 2008), pp. 363–4.

14. Walzer, *op. cit.*, pp. 64–5.

15. Isaiah Berlin, 'The Originality of Machiavelli', in Myron P. Gilmore
   (ed.), *Studies on Machiavelli* (Florence: Sansoni, 1972), pp. 147–206.

16. *The Prince*, chapter 18 (emphasis supplied).

17. Isaiah Berlin, 'The Originality of Machiavelli', in *The Proper Study of
   Mankind: An Anthology of Essays* (Farrar, Straus & Giroux, 1997), pp.
   269–325; but see Maurizio Viroli and Antony Shugaar, *Machiavelli's
   God* (Princeton UP, 2010).

18. *Discourses*, book III, chapter 40.

19. Maurizio Viroli, *How to Read Machiavelli* (Granta UK, 2008), p. 34.

20. For a paper that puts this in psychological terms, see Cary J.
   Nederman, 'Machiavelli and Moral Character: Principality, Republic
   and the Psychology of "Virtù"', *History of Political Thought*, vol. 21, issue
   3 (Autumn 2000): 349.

21. Sebastian de Grazia, *Machiavelli in Hell* (Vintage, 1994), pp. 300–99.

22. *The Prince*, chapter 15.

23. *The Prince*, chapter 18.

24. *The Prince*, chapter 6.

25. See Erica Benner, *Machiavelli's Ethics* (Princeton UP, 2009), p. 427.

26. Paul E. Norton, 'Machiavelli's Road to Paradise: "The Exhortation to
   Penitence"', *History of Political Thought*, vol. 4 (Spring 1983): 31–2.

27. Machiavelli, 'Exhortation to Penitence'.

28. Machiavelli, *The Art of War*, book 7.

BOOK II: *LO STATO* – THE RELATION OF *THE PRINCE* TO THE *DISCOURSES ON LIVY*

1. *The Prince*, chapter 1.

Chapter 3. A Republic's Duty of Consequentialism

1. C. D. Broad, *Five Types of Ethical Theory* (Harcourt Brace, 1930), pp. 277–8 (emphasis supplied). Broad actually wrote 'teleological' or purposeful where I have used 'consequential' but here the distinction is the same.
2. The 'duty of consequentialism' is an idea found in my *Terror and Consent* and is associated with the obligations of officials in a twenty-first-century democracy. On consequentialism in Machiavelli, see Eugene Garver, 'After "Virtù": Rhetoric, Prudence and Moral Pluralism in Machiavelli', *History of Political Thought*, vol. 17, issue 2 (Summer 1996): 195–222; Eugene Garver, 'Machiavelli: Rhetoric and Prudence', in Patricia Vilches and Gerald Seaman (eds.), *Seeking Real Truths: Multidisciplinary Perspectives on Machiavelli* (Brill, 2007); G. H. R. Parkinson, 'Ethics and Politics in Machiavelli', *Philosophical Quarterly*, vol. 5 (Jan. 1955): 37–44; Raymond A. Belliotti, 'Machiavelli and Machiavellianism', *Journal of Thought*, vol. 13 (Nov. 1978): 293–300; Lee Thayer, 'Review: *Machiavelli and the History of Prudence*', *Clio*, vol. 17, issue 3 (Spring 1988): 309; see also Carlo Ginzburg, 'Pontano, Machiavelli and Prudence: Some Further Reflections', in Curto, Diogo Ramada et al. (eds.), *From Florence to the Mediterranean and Beyond: Essays in Honour of Anthony Molho* (Florence, 2009). For a contemporary example of this dilemma, see Paul Starobin, 'A Moral Flip-Flop? Defining a War', *New York Times Sunday Review*, 6 August 2011; see also Tara McKelvey, 'Interview with Harold Koh, Obama's Defender of Drone Strikes', *The Daily Beast*, 8 April 2012.
3. De Grazia, *Machiavelli in Hell*, pp. 54–5.
4. Savonarola ordered the burning of the elaborate frocks of Florentine women; some six centuries later, the Committee for the Propagation of Virtue and the Prevention of Vice simply allowed the women themselves to be burned when their garments were thought inappropriate. See the events of 11 March 2002, in which fifteen girls burned

to death after the Saudi religious police prevented them from exiting a burning school building because they were not properly dressed. 'Saudi police "stopped" fire rescue', BBC News, 15 March 2002, http://news.bbc.co.uk/2/hi/middle_east/1874471.stm.

5. Cicero, *De officiis*, book I, chapter 159.

6. *Discourses*, book III, chapter 41.

7. Cicero, *De officiis*, book III, chapter 41.

8. *Discourses*, book I, chapter 9.

9. Viroli, *How to Read Machiavelli*, p. 35.

10. De Grazia, *Machiavelli in Hell*, p. 311. Similarly, Sam Houston ruthlessly sought to preserve the Texas Revolution by refusing to reinforce the defenders of the Alamo in order to protect his main army; and George Washington followed a Fabian strategy – hateful to him – for the same reason.

11. *Discourses*, book II, chapter 21.

12. Sergio Bertelli, 'Machiavelli and Soderini', *Renaissance Quarterly*, vol. 28, issue 1 (Spring 1975): 1.

13. *Discourses,* book III, chapter 3.

14. See Maurizio Viroli, 'Books in Review', *Political Theory*, vol. 19, issue 2 (May 1991): 292–3. Viroli writes: 'The state attains perfection when the common good is best observed – that is, in a republic where the law rules, where women are honored, where public offices are open to all citizens on the grounds of virtue, where there is a moderate degree of social equality, and where everyone can safely attend to his business and enjoy his wealth and property. "This is the point of it all" [quoting de Grazia, *Machiavelli in Hell*, p. 173].'

15. See *Terror and Consent*, pp. 180–6.

16. Viroli, *How to Read Machiavelli*, p. 78.

17. *Discourses*, book I, chapter 16 (emphasis supplied). Machiavelli believed in the inevitability of war, but he had seen the conditions of war change in his lifetime, and they have continued to mutate throughout the life of the state. At present we are at war – though we cling to terminology that would relieve us of this awful fact – with global networks of terror. Since Machiavelli is thought to be the apostle of the rule 'the end justifies the means', does this suggest that he would have favoured a no-holds-barred approach to prosecuting that war? In the twenty-first century, when the democratic states are attacked by terrorists with far more significant weapons at their disposal than terror groups have

deployed in the past, such ethical questions, which hover over the issues of torture, targeted killings and the unavoidable civilian suffering attendant on warfare, will be even more insistent. Protecting people from fear – preserving 'the common utility which one draws from a free way of life . . . to be able to enjoy his things freely without any fear . . . to have no fear for himself' – and allowing the citizenry to do what they have a lawful right to do were important preoccupations of Machiavelli's. So one might actually conclude that he would have been more scrupulous than one might think when it comes to seeing that the state protects itself within the law and that the citizens of a state do not come to fear it more than the terror networks who would attack it.

18. On Machiavelli's republicanism, see Timothy J. Lukes, 'Descending to the Particulars: The Palazzo, The Piazza and Machiavelli's Republican Modes and Orders', *Journal of Politics*, vol. 71, issue 2 (April 2009): 520; Cary J. Nederman, 'The Renaissance of a Renaissance Man', *European Legacy*, vol. 4, issue 5 (Oct. 1999): 102; and for a more shaded view of Machiavelli's preference for republics, see Harvey C. Mansfield, *Machiavelli's Virtue* (University of Chicago Press, 1996), p. 302.

19. *Discourses*, book II, chapter 2.

20. *Ibid.*

21. *Discourses*, book I, chapter 58.

22. Abraham Lincoln, quoted in Mark E. Neely, Jr., *The Fate of Liberty: Abraham Lincoln and Civil Liberties* (Oxford UP, 1991), p. 12. Compare similar situations in which the letter of the law is neglected in order to avoid undermining the purposes of the law: A 'statute that prescribes criminal punishment for anyone who "shall, knowingly and willfully, obstruct . . . the passage of the mail" . . . could not have [been] intended to punish a police officer for arresting a homicidal postal carrier in the midst of his rounds . . . [A]n ordinance that provides "that whoever [draws] blood in the streets should be punished with utmost severity" . . . could [not have been] intended to condemn a doctor for performing emergency surgery on a person felled by a seizure in public.' John F. Manning, 'The Absurdity Doctrine', *Harvard Law Review*, vol. 116 (2003): 2387, 2402. The sign that says 'Keep off the grass' cannot be realistically applied to the groundskeeper whose efforts keep the turf alive (though it should be noted that Manning is critical of our ability to apply this doctrine).

23. Cicero, *De officiis*, book II, chapter 43.

24. Variously attributed to Lincoln, P. T. Barnum and Mark Twain.
25. De Grazia, *Machiavelli in Hell*, p. 296.
26. *The Prince*, chapter 18.
27. *Ibid.*
28 *The Prince*, chapter 7.
29. Adam Minter, 'Machiavelli, Violence and History', *Harvard Review of Philosophy*, vol. 2, issue 1 (Spring 1992): 25–33.
30. Victoria Kahn, '*Virtù* and the Example of Agathocles in Machiavelli's *Prince*', *Representations*, vol. 13 (Winter 1986): 63.
31. *Discourses*, book I, chapter 25.
32. Machiavelli, *History of Florence*, book II, chapter 8.
33. *Ibid.* (emphasis supplied).
34. *Ibid.*
35. See *Terror and Consent*, p. 470.
36. *The Prince*, chapter 17.
37. *Ibid.*

Chapter 4. Good Arms, Good Laws

1. Thomas Hobbes, *Leviathan* (Cambridge UP, 2009); Jean Bodin, *Six Books of the Commonwealth* (Basil Blackwell, 1955).
2. *The Prince*, chapter 3.
3. *The Art of War*, Preface.
4. On the coercive aspects of law, see Robert Cover, *Narrative, Violence and the Law: The Essays of Robert Cover* (University of Michigan Press, 1995). ('Legal interpretation takes place in a field of pain and death. This is true in several senses. Legal interpretive acts signal and occasion the imposition of violence upon others: A judge articulates her understanding of a text, and as a result, somebody loses his freedom, his property, his children, even his life. Interpretations in law also constitute justifications for violence which has already occurred or which is about to occur. When interpreters have finished their work, they frequently leave behind victims whose lives have been torn apart by these organized, social practices of violence. Neither legal interpretation nor the violence it occasions may be properly understood apart from one another.'). See also C. K. Y. Shaw, 'Quentin Skinner on the Proper Meaning of Republican Liberty', *Politics*, vol. 23, issue 1 (Feb. 2003): 46.

5. *The Prince*, chapter 12.
6. *The Art of War*, Preface.
7. *Discourses,* book I, chapter 3.
8. *The Prince,* chapter 7.
9. See Timothy J. Lukes, 'Martialing Machiavelli: Reassessing the Military Reflections', *Journal of Politics*, vol. 66, issue 4 (Nov. 2004): 1089.
10. Machiavelli, *I Primi Scritti Politici* 1499–1512, ed. Jean-Jacques Marchand (Padua: Antenore, 1975), p. 432.
11. *The Prince*, chapter 2.
12. Sean Erwin, 'A War of One's Own: Mercenaries and the Theme of Arma Aliena in Machiavelli's *Il Principe*', *British Journal for the History of Philosophy*, vol. 18, issue 4 (Sept. 2010): 541.
13. *The Prince*, chapter 12.
14. It has been suggested that Soderini was actually responsible for the appointment of Michelotto. See Roslyn Pesman Cooper, 'Machiavelli, Francesco Soderini and Don Michelotto', *Nuovo Rivista Storica*, vol. 66, issue 3/4 (Sept. 1982): 342.
15. See *The Shield of Achilles*, pp. 86–7. For more on Machiavelli's involvement in crafting the Florentine militia ordinance of 1506, see Mikael Hörnqvist, '*Perché non si usa allegare i Romani*: Machiavelli and the Florentine militia of 1506', *Renaissance Quarterly*, vol. 55, issue 1 (2002): 148–91.
16. Compare the current vogue for 'effects-based strategy'; see Thomas Kane, 'Building Thrones: Political Effect as an Emerging Principle of War', *Comparative Strategy*, vol. 24, issue 5 (Dec. 2005): 431.

BOOK III: *VIRTÙ E FORTUNA* – GOD DOES NOT WANT TO DO EVERYTHING

Chapter 5. *Virtù* is from Mars, *Fortuna* is from Venus

1. Felix Gilbert, 'Bernardo Rucellai and the Orti Oricellari: A Study on the Origin of Modern Political Thought', *Journal of the Warburg and Courtauld Institutes*, vol. 12 (1949): 101–2.
2. Maurizio Viroli, *Machiavelli* (Oxford UP, 1998), p. 20, quoting a poem by Machiavelli, 'Di fortuna', in *Il Teatro*.
3. Quoted in de Grazia, *Machiavelli in Hell*, p. 98.

4. *Discourses*, book III, chapter 9.

5. See Patricia Vilches, *Discourses on Livy* (reviewing the *Discourses* translated by Julia Conway and Peter Bondanella), *Sixteenth Century Journal*, vol. 36, issue 1 (Spring 2005): 265. See also Oded Balaban, 'The Human Origins of Fortuna in Machiavelli's Thought', *History of Political Thought*, vol. 11, issue 1 (1990): 21, arguing that because Fortune is the consequence of human activity, *virtù* is the ability to adopt means appropriate to the consequences of one's goal-directed actions; and see also the discussion of 'the duty of consequentialism' in chapter 3 of the present work.

6. Cf. Mansfield, *Machiavelli's Virtue*, p. 7.

7. Quentin Skinner observes that 'the idea ... is most clearly set out in Cicero's *Tusculan Disputations*, in which he lays down that the criterion for being a real man, a *vir*, is the possession of *virtus* in the highest degree. The implications of the argument are extensively explored in Livy's *History* in which the successes won by the Romans are almost always explained in terms of the fact that Fortune likes to follow and even wait upon *virtus* and even smiles on those who exhibit it.' Skinner, *Machiavelli: A Very Short Introduction*, p. 29. Compare the political philosopher John Gray's description of the entrepreneur's abilities as not a matter of learning but of 'serendipity and flair'. Lying 'beyond our powers of conscious control', the 'entrepreneurial perception' cannot be summed up in 'mechanical procedures'; its transformative power occurs spontaneously and upredictably. John Gray, *Hayek on Liberty*, 3rd edition (Routledge, 1998), p. 36.

8. *The Prince*, chapter 25.

9. *Discourses*, book II, chapter 29.

10. De Grazia, *Machiavelli in Hell*, p. 27.

11. Ross King, *Machiavelli: Philosopher of Power* (Atlas Books / HarperCollins, 2007), p. 212.

12. Machiavelli, *The Literary Works of Machiavelli: Mandragola, Clizia, A Dialogue on Language, and Belfagor, with Selections from the Private Correspondence*, ed. J. R. Hale (Greenwood, 1979).

13. *Discourses*, book III, chapter 31.

14. Quentin Skinner, *Machiavelli: A Very Short Introduction* (Oxford UP, 2000), p. 61.

15. *The Art of War*, book I.

16. *Discourses*, book III, chapter 41.
17. *The Prince*, chapter 25.
18. *Ibid.*
19. *The Prince*, chapter 26.
20. Kyung-Hee Kim, 'Machiavelli's Political Matrix of Virtù: His Theory of Humor and Mode of Proceeding'. This important paper has been put online as a draft, whose author does not wish to be cited. I have thus far been unable to contact him for permission to cite his work and have therefore chosen to defy his request rather than neglect to honour his work.
21. *Discourses*, book III, chapter 9.
22. Victoria Kahn, '*Virtù* and the Example of Agathocles in Machiavelli's *Prince*', *Representations*, vol. 13 (Winter 1986): 71.
23. Kyung-Hee Kim (see note 20 above).

Chapter 6. Machiavelli's View of History

1. Travis Pantin has made this interesting point that strikes a certain resonant chord with my larger argument about Machiavelli's relation to constitutional law. He writes: 'I often think that Machiavelli's use of history is, pedagogically speaking, quite similar to the case method one encounters in law school. Both pedagogical methods utilize concrete examples – often with seemingly conflicting underlying rules – in order to hone the reader's faculty of judgement. Machiavelli creates dissonance in the minds of his readers (especially by providing idiosyncratic characterizations of Biblical figures) in order to wake them up and to remind them that real politics requires making and breaking rules, not just following them. The case method similarly implies that the law is not entirely understandable as a rule-based system or a system of universal truths, but rather as an art relying on a sort of *phronesis*-like faculty that one can only gain through experience, and the study of good examples.' Letter to the author, 3 January 2013.
2. But see Margaret Leslie, 'In Defense of Anachronism', *Political Studies*, vol. 8, issue 4 (Dec. 1970): 433.
3. *Discourses*, book III, chapter 43.
4. As Viroli puts it, 'Machiavelli maintains that, through historical

examples, the orator can bring alive the horrors of corruption, ambi-tion, vainglory, avarice; he can touch the audience's feelings and imagination, not just their reason, and compel them to flee vice and follow virtue.' Viroli, *How to Read Machiavelli*, p. 54.

5. *Discourses*, book I, chapter 10.
6. On Machiavelli's use of history as rhetoric, see Peter Bondanella, *Machiavelli and the Art of Renaissance History* (Wayne State University Press, 1973); Desmond Fitzgerald, 'Machiavelli and History', *Proceedings of the American Catholic Philosophical Association*, vol. 43 (1969): 121; Eugene Garver, 'Machiavelli and the Politics of Rhetorical Invention', *Clio*, vol. 14, issue 2 (Winter 1985): 157; Mark Phillips, 'Representation and Argument in Florentine Historiography', *Storia della storiografia*, issue 10 (1986): 48; William E. Wiethoff, 'The Martial "Virtue" of Rhetoric in Machiavelli's *Art of War*', *Quarterly Journal of Speech*, vol. 64, issue 3 (Oct. 1978): 304.
7. *Institutio oratoria*, XIII.II, pp. 29–31.
8. *Discourses*, book I, Proem (emphasis added).
9. But see Viroli, who says that Machiavelli believed history was cyclical and not 'progressive'. Viroli, *How to Read Machiavelli*, p. 50.
10. Machiavelli, *The Golden Ass*, 5.103–4.
11. *Discourses*, book I, chapter 2.
12. *Ibid.*
13. See Harvey C. Mansfield, *Machiavelli's New Modes and Orders: A Study of the 'Discourses on Livy'* (Cornell UP, 1979). For a hostile review of Mansfield's (and Leo Strauss's) claims for Machiavelli's modernity, see Neal Wood, 'Mansfield on Machiavelli', *Philosophy of the Social Sciences*, vol. 15, issue 1 (1985): 45.
14. Anticipating Clausewitz by three centuries. Machiavelli is usually criticized for underestimating the significance of artillery; see Felix Gilbert, 'Machiavelli: The Renaissance in the Art of War', in Peter Paret (ed.), *Makers of Modern Strategy: From Machiavelli to the Nuclear Age* (Princeton UP, 1986), pp. 11–31; Azar Gat, 'Machiavelli and the Decline of the Classical Notion of the Lessons of History in the Study of War', *Military Affairs*, vol. 57 (Oct. 1988): 203–5. But he was well aware of the impact of developments in artillery on the vulnerability of fortresses. See Timothy R. W. Kubik, 'Is Machiavelli's Cannon Spiked?', *Journal of Military History*, vol. 61, issue 1 (Jan. 1997): 7; see also Ben Cassidy, 'Machiavelli and the Ideology of the Offensive:

Gunpowder Weapons in the *Art of War*', *Journal of Military History*, vol. 67, issue 2 (April 2003): 381; Timothy J. Lukes, 'Martialing Machiavelli: Reassessing the Military Reflections', *Journal of Politics*, vol. 66, issue 4 (Nov. 2004): 1089.

15. See *Terror and Consent*, pp. 183–4, 208–9; *The Shield of Achilles*, p. 10.

16. I note that my colleague Sanford Levinson, who has been an eloquent advocate for a more egalitarian Senate (see *Our Undemocratic Constitution: Where the Constitution Goes Wrong (And How We the People Can Correct It)* (Oxford, 2006), can be cleared of this fallacy in so far as he does not contend that the convention for which he calls could flout the requirement that the states unanimously agree to a reapportionment of the Senate as necessary to any amendment purporting to do so.

17. See Calabresi and Bobbitt, *Tragic Choices* (Norton, 1978), pp. 195–9.

18. Salvatore DiMaria, 'Machiavelli's Ironic View of History: The "Istorie Fiorentine"', *Renaissance Quarterly*, vol. 45, issue 2 (Summer 1992): 248.

19. See *Discourses*, book III, chapter 9 and *The Prince*, chapter 25. See also Tracy Goss, *The Last Word on Power* (Doubleday, 1996).

20. Ernst Cassirer, *The Myth of the State* (Yale UP, 1946), p. 130.

21. Najemy, *Between Friends*, p. 172.

22. But see Strauss, *Thoughts on Machiavelli*.

23. Viroli, *How to Read Machiavelli*, p. 4.

24. Henry Kissinger, *The White House Years* (Little, Brown, 1979), p. 54. This suggests supplementing strategic planning with scenario planning. Scenario planning creates alternative stories about the future that differ based on the decisions and individuals that drive each scenario; strategic planning is a formalized method of extrapolating from the present to the future in order to create a single, quantifiable, likeliest prediction about how things will turn out. That is, strategic planning assumes an answer to the question that scenario planning poses: what sort of future do we want? The time horizon for scenario planning is typically from five to more than twenty-five years; strategic plans usually go no further out than one to three years. Inputs to scenario planning are more qualitative – that is, they share certain factual estimates about the future but emphasize different possibilities that can be exploited by varying cultures, leaders and groups. Inputs to strategic planning tend to be more quantitative, looking to past performance, forecasts and probabilities. Thus scenario planning exploits

uncertainties, allowing the creation of alternative futures; strategic planning attempts to minimize uncertainty. The results of scenario planning are multiple, alternative outcomes versus the quantified single outcome based on the likeliest scenario that is the setting for strategic planning. Moreover, and perhaps most importantly, scenario planning can inspire by giving us a picture of a future that we wish to bring into being (or avoid) by actions we take in the present.

25. 'It has now become clear that most of the information from this "friend" did in fact come directly from one source and that this vital information was none other than Machiavelli's friend and fellow Florentine Leonardo da Vinci.' Paul Strathern, 'Machiavelli, Leonardo and Borgia: A Fateful Collusion', *History Today*, vol. 59, issue 3 (March 2009): 15–19.

26. On Leonardo and Machiavelli, see Paul Roazen, 'A Partnership of Geniuses?', *American Scholar*, vol. 67, issue 4 (Autumn 1998): 141; Roger D. Masters, *Fortune is a River: Leonardo da Vinci and Niccolò Machiavelli's Magnificent Dream to Change the Course of Florentine History* (Plume, 1999).

BOOK IV: *OCCASIONE* – THE INTERESTING TIMING OF *THE PRINCE*

1. 'These months – July to December [1513] – witness the birth of the treatise *De principatibus*, known to us as *The Prince*. The marginal notes on Livy are thrust aside.' Federico Chabod, *Machiavelli and the Renaissance,* trans. David Moore (Bowes & Bowes, 1958), p. 12.

Chapter 7. The Borgias and the Medici

1. Hans Baron, 'The *Principe* and the Puzzle of the Date of Chapter 26', *Journal of Medieval and Renaissance Studies*, vol. 21, issue 1 (1991): 83.

2. For a bizarre effort to integrate chapter 26 into the rest of *The Prince*, see Joseph M. Parent, 'Machiavelli's Missing Romulus and the Murderous Intent of "The Prince"', *History of Political Thought*, vol. 26, issue 4 (Winter 2005): 625.

3. 'Readers may be convinced that Spenser deployed his art to foster

ambitions for a sinecure at Elizabeth's court but few will find this attribute sufficient to accommodate their experience of *The Faerie Queene*, which like Machiavelli's *The Prince*, quickly overflows the provisions of an advocatory niche labelled "employment application".' M. F. N. Dixon, *The Polliticke Courtier: Spenser's* The Faerie Queene *as a Rhetoric of Justice* (McGill-Queen's UP, 1996), p. 19.

4. 'Bobbitt dwells with especial admiration on The Inquiry, the secret body of 126 experts assembled by House in the wake of the October Revolution, "to collect data that would provide the factual and analytical basis for an American-directed settlement" in Europe. What the United States needs today, he explains, is a comparable "Vision Team", also to be convened in secret, but now including not just lawyers and scientists as in Wilson's day, but also business executives, to offer true strategic guidance to the Presidency. The candidate for House's position is not hard to guess.' Gopal Balakrishnan, 'Algorithms of War', *New Left Review* 23 (Sept.–Oct. 2003). Actually the person I had in mind for this position was Dr Betty Sue Flowers.

5. Gennaro Sasso, *Machiavelli e Cesare Borgia: Storia di un giudizio* (Rome, 1966), p. 235.

6. James Reston, *Dogs of God* (Anchor, 2005), p. 287.

7. Daniel Pellerin, 'Machiavelli's Best Friend', *History of Political Thought*, vol. 27, issue 3 (Autumn 2006): 423.

8. See J. H. Whitfield, 'Machiavelli and the Problem of the Prince', in *Discourses on Machiavelli* (Cambridge, 1969).

9. See Herbert Butterfield, 'Professor Chabod and the Machiavelli Controversies', *Historical Journal*, vol. 2, issue 1 (March 1959): 78, who thinks accurate dating of the first section of the *Discourses* is impossible because 'the surviving historical data are too slight, too rough and too capricious'. J. H. Hexter (on the grounds that Machiavelli needed a translation of Polybius which did not appear before 1515) and Hans Baron (on the grounds that Machiavelli's famous letter to Vettori of 10 December 1513 would surely have mentioned his work before *The Prince* was commenced) both object to the dating of the early sections of the *Discourses* as prior to *The Prince*. My argument does not depend on this dating, though I am inclined to think it the right one as there is no other manuscript that would correspond to Machiavelli's statement in *The Prince* that he had already been working on an extended essay on republics.

10. Erasmus, Ep. 988.

11. Najemy, *Between Friends*.

12. Felix Gilbert, *Machiavelli and Guicciardini: Politics and History in Sixteenth Century Florence* (Princeton UP, 1956).

13. 'Machiavelli did not live to see in action the betrayer and torturer of the Florentine republicans, the counsellor and then defender of the tyrant Alessandro, finally the grey eminence who installed Duke Cosimo.' Scaglione, essay on J. H. Whitfield's *Discourses on Machiavelli*, p. 216; see also J. H. Whitfield, 'The Case of Guicciardini', in *Discourses on Machiavelli* (Cambridge, 1969).

14. [*E*]*stravagante di opinione . . . et inventore di cose nuove et insolite*, Guicciardini to Machiavelli, 18 May 1521, quoted in Erica Benner, *Machiavelli's Ethics*, p. 46.

Chapter 8. Machiavelli's Constitution

1. *The Prince*, chapter 25.

2. *Ibid.*

3. *Ibid.*

4. *Discourses,* book I, chapter 11.

5. *Discourses*, book I, chapter 3.

6. *Discourses*, book I, chapters 25, 37.

7. *Discourses*, book I, chapter 24.

8. *Discourses*, book I, chapter 16.

9. *Discourses*, book II, chapter 30.

10. This is the basis for Machiavelli's famous remark, otherwise puzzling, regarding Agathocles, the tyrant of Syracuse: 'He who reflects on the accomplishments of this man will find little that can be attributed to Fortune. Without the help of anyone, but rather by rising through the ranks, risking a thousand difficulties and dangers, he came to rule a principality which he then maintained by many courageous acts. Yet this cannot be called *virtù* to murder one's fellow citizens, to betray allies, to act without faith, pity or religion; such methods may gain power *but never glory.*' *The Prince*, chapter 8 (emphasis supplied). For Machiavelli, glory is a consequence of moral choice. See also Dan Eldar, 'Glory and the boundaries of public morality in Machiavelli's thought', *History of Political Thought*, vol. 7, issue 3 (Winter 1986): 419.

11. 'Words to speak on providing money, given a bit of proem and excuse', address written for Soderini in 1503 wherein Machiavelli asserts the necessity for arms if one is to have choice in foreign affairs and not forfeit the ability to choose to the will of invaders.

12. *Discourses*, book I, chapter 48. Thus John McCormick observes: 'Machiavelli suggests that writers who criticize the people hopelessly confuse popular opinon with popular judgement. The people may often claim that they want one thing or another in taverns, in their homes or in the street, but they often choose something quite different if they are formally empowered to deliberate and decide within the bounds of an assembly ... Machiavelli demonstrates how arrangements that formally empower the people to make decisions themselves actually allow the people to clarify their preferences when the latter are unclear and moderate their impulses when the latter tend toward excess.' 'Defending the people from the professors', available at www.artoftheory.com/mccormick-machiavellian-democracy (blog).

13. The important place of Machiavelli in the founding of the American state has been argued by J. G. A. Pocock in *The Machiavellian Moment* (Princeton UP, 1975), and Gisela Bock et al. in *Machiavelli and Republicanism* (Cambridge UP, 1990); cf. Paul Rahe (ed.), *Machiavelli's Liberal Republican Legacy* (Cambridge UP, 2006).

14. 'The key to solving the problem [of creating and sustaining collective *virtù*], he maintains, is to ensure that the citizens are "well ordered" – that they are organized in such a way as to compel them to acquire *virtù* and uphold their liberties ... If we wish to understand how it came about that "so much *virtù* was kept up" in Rome "for so many centuries", what we need to investigate is "how she was organized" ... To see how the city of Rome succeeded in reaching "the straight road" that led her "to a perfect and true end", we need above all to study her *ordini* – her institutions, her constitutional arrangements, her methods of ordering and organizing her citizens.' Quentin Skinner, *Machiavelli: A Very Short Introduction*, p. 69.

15. *Discourses,* book I, chapter 1.

16. Fortune does not 'wipe out our free will' (*The Prince*, chapter 25); God does not want to 'take from us our free will' (*The Prince*, chapter 26).

17. De Grazia, *Machiavelli in Hell*, p. 110.

18. I am indebted to Tom Schmidt for this arresting observation. See letter to author, 9 August 2011.

19. Philip Bobbitt, *Constitutional Fate: Theory of the Constitution* (Oxford UP, 1984), p. 182.
20. *Discourses*, book I, chapters 9.
21. See Mansfield, *Machiavelli's Virtue*, p. 302 (Chicago, 1996).
22. Filippo del Lucchese, 'Crisis and Power: Economics, Politics and Conflict in Machiavelli's Political Thought', *History of Political Thought*, vol. 30, issue 1 (Spring 2009): 75.
23. *Discourses*, book I, chapter 4.
24. Bondanella and Musa put this well: '[Human nature and economic scarcity are such that] political conflict is the inevitable result. Such conflict is not seen as an abnormal state of affairs, nor is the goal . . . a body politic which has abolished social struggle . . . But the mere recognition of the existence of conflict in society is insufficient grounds for establishing the originality of Machiavelli's views. The truly original conception, in this regard, was Machiavelli's belief that such conflict might, in fact, produce beneficial results in a properly organized government controlled by stable political institutions.' Bondanella and Musa, *The Portable Machiavelli*, pp. 28–9.
25. *Discourses*, book I, chapter 58.
26. *Ibid.*
27. *Ibid.*
28. *The Prince*, chapter 9.
29. *Discourses*, book I, chapter 2.
30. Although we use the term 'nation-building' to describe efforts to create viable political societies in impoverished and war-torn countries, in fact what we mean is 'state-building', and though the enthusiasm for such projects has dimmed after costly and painful expeditions in Iraq and Afghanistan, the problem of state-building is not going away. It is open to doubt whether the principal motive of the Bush administration in 2003, when it organized the invasion of Iraq, was to create a democratic regime to replace the autocracy of Saddam Hussein. But once American forces occupied Iraq, it was inconceivable that the old regime would be replaced with anything other than a democracy. And so, as the war began to proceed in earnest – despite American claims of victory – the war aim of a peaceful and benign democratic state took shape.

    As I write, democracy movements are under way in Egypt, Tunisia, Libya, Côte d'Ivoire, Yemen and Syria. The United States and its

Western allies have supported these movements, even to the extent of armed intervention in Libya. Yet it is acknowledged in many capitals that it is by no means certain that the outcome of these struggles will be a more pro-Western map than the one that existed before. The standard debate on this issue revolves around several poles: Can democracy be successfully imposed by an occupation force? Do democracies avoid armed conflict to a greater degree than other forms of government? Are they more solicitous of human rights? More economically dynamic? Are we sacrificing our strategic interests – in prosecuting the wars on terror, or decreasing narcotics exports to the US, or assuring regional stability – when we undermine old, but illiberal, allies? The intrepid author Robert Kaplan has written that

> [t]he bet in the West is that only democracy – precisely because it grants to each interest group a piece of the action – can instil the ethos of statehood that benign tyrannies such as [Côte d'Ivoire's] and unbenign ones such as [Libya's] failed to develop.
>
> Robert Kaplan, 'Beware the Void under Tyranny',
> *Financial Times*, 6 April 2011

Kaplan's concern is that post-colonial societies like Iraq, Libya, Yemen, Côte d'Ivoire and others have never developed stable states, and that their rulers in fact intensified some of the worst aspects of colonialism, setting favoured tribes and families to rule, mercilessly, over an agglomerate of peoples assembled within artificial borders.

31. Skinner, *Machiavelli: A Very Short Introduction*, p. 75; in a similar vein to this allusion to Adam Smith, see Roger D. Masters's suggestion in his *Machiavelli, Leonardo, and the Science of Power* (Notre Dame, IN, 1995) that Machiavelli was a 'proto-Darwinian' figure; see also Mary G. Winkler, 'Prophets of Modernity', *Hastings Center Report*, vol. 28, issue 2 (March/April 1998): 43.

32. *Discourses,* book I, chapter 4.

33. *The Shield of Achilles,* pp. 85–8.

34. Quentin Skinner, *The Foundations of Modern Political Thought, Volume 1: The Renaissance* (Cambridge UP, 1978).

35. Harvey C. Mansfield, *Machiavelli's Virtue.*

36. *The Shield of Achilles,* p. 91.

37. Which is not to disparage Pasquale Villari's *Life and Times of Niccolò Machiavelli,* trans. Linda Villari (1972), or the classic *Life of Niccolò*

Machiavelli by Roberto Ridolfi (Chicago, 1954; trans. Cecil Grayson, 1963), or the excellent *Machiavelli: Philosopher of Power* (Atlas Books/ HarperCollins, 2007) by Ross King. Each is worthwhile, but de Grazia's study has a literary quality that is reminiscent of Machiavelli's own style. Also illuminating is Niccolò Capponi's *An Unlikely Prince* (Da Capo, 2010), which has a uniquely Florentine flavour.

38. De Grazia, *Machiavelli in Hell*, p. 21.
39. *Discourses*, book I, chapter 2.
40. *Ibid.*
41. *Ibid.*
42. *Discourses,* book I, chapter 18.
43. *Discourses,* book II, chapter 2.
44. *Discourses,* book I, chapter 16.
45. *Discourses,* book I, chapter 58.
46. *Discourses,* book III, chapter 25.
47. *Summary of Lucchese Affairs;* see also J. R. Hale, *Machiavelli and Renaissance Italy* (English Universities Press, 1961), p. 198.
48. 'Our High and Magnificent Lords, considering that there can be nothing more praiseworthy than the ordering of a united and free republic, in which all private interests yield to the common welfare, and the cravings of vainglory are extinguished, being comforted and encouraged by our most Reverend Lord His Eminence Cardinal Giulio de' Medici, and invoking the name of the Almighty, do provide and decree . . .' There is some confusion over the titles of these two white papers by Machiavelli for the Medici. Viroli (see *Niccolò's Smile*, pp. 219–20) and Bernard (see *Why Machiavelli Matters*, pp. 14–15) style the first paper, written in 1520 for Leo, the *Discourse on Florentine Affairs after the Death of Lorenzo* (*Discorso delle cose fiorentine dopo la morte di Lorenzo*) in accordance with Judith A. Rawson, who translates it in *Machiavelli: The History of Florence and Other Selections*, ed. Myron P. Gilmore (New York, 1970). Viroli and Bernard entitle the second paper, written in 1522 for Giulio, *A Discourse on Remodelling the Government of Florence*, while Allan Gilbert in his translation for the *Chief Works* refers to the initial paper as *A Discourse on Remodelling the Government of Florence* (*Chief Works*, 1: 101). A good many commentators repeat Gilbert in this matter, doubtless because they – as well as I – have relied on his translations in so many other instances. In this case, I have chosen to go with Viroli et al. simply for clarity's sake. The important fact is that

there were two papers of significantly similar content, setting forth Machiavelli's constitutional designs for Florence, whatever we may title them.

49. To whom Machiavelli dedicated both the *Discourses* and *The Life of Castruccio Castracani*.

50. To whom Machiavelli dedicated *The Life of Castruccio Castracani*.

51. Lorenzo de' Medici, 'Letter to the Magistrates of Florence', 7 December 1479, reprinted in Christopher Hibbert, *The House of Medici: Its Rise and Fall* (William Morrow, 1999).

52. For an arresting and haunting essay, see Gopal Balakrishnan, 'Future Unknown: Machiavelli for the Twenty-First Century', *New Left Review* 32 (March–April 2005).

THE MACHIAVELLI PARADOX RESOLVED

1. Skinner, *Machiavelli: A Very Short Introduction*, p. 40.
2. Cicero, *De officiis*, book II, chapter 9.
3. Skinner, *Machiavelli: A Very Short Introduction*, p. 41.
4. *The Prince*, chapter 15.
5. *The Prince*, chapter 18.
6. *The Prince*, chapter 16.
7. Garrett Mattingly, 'Machiavelli's "Prince": Political Science or Political Satire?', *The American Scholar*, vol. 27 (1958): 482; see also Andrew Villalon, 'Machiavelli's "Prince": Political Science or Political Satire? Garrett Mattingly Revisited', *Mediterranean Studies*, vol. 12 (2003): 73.
8. Mary Dietz, 'Trapping the Prince: Machiavelli and the Politics of Deception', *American Political Science Review*, vol. 80, issue 3 (Sept. 1986): 777.
9. See Peter Donaldson, 'John Wolfe, Machiavelli, and the Republican Arcana in Sixteenth-Century England', in *Machiavelli and Mystery of State* (Cambridge UP, 1992), p. 86.
10. Letter from Machiavelli to Francesco Vettori, 10 December 1513.
11. 'Machiavelli was a proper man and a good citizen; but, being attached to the court of the Medici, he could not help veiling his love of liberty in the midst of his country's oppression. The choice of his detestable hero, Cesare Borgia, clearly enough shows his hidden aim; and the contradiction between the teaching of *The Prince* and that of the

Discourses on Livy and the *History of Florence* shows that this profound political thinker has so far been studied only by superficial or corrupt readers.' Jean-Jacques Rousseau, *The Social Contract*, book III.

12. Renzo Sereno, 'A Falsification by Machiavelli', *Renaissance News*, vol. 12, issue 3 (1959): 159–67.

13. See Mary Dietz, note 8 above.

14. On 'inconsistencies' among Machiavelli's works, see Heinrich Kuhn, 'Niccolò Machiavelli: A Good State for Bad People', in Paul Richard Blum (ed.), *Philosophers of the Renaissance* (Catholic UP, 2010), p. 116, n. 3.

15. Though, as will be seen, my argument does not depend on this dating. On the dating of *The Prince* and the *Discourses*, see Felix Gilbert, 'The Composition and Structure of Machiavelli's *Discorsi*', *Journal of the History of Ideas*, vol. 14, issue 1 (1953): 137–9; Federico Chabod, *Machiavelli and the Renaissance*, trans. David Moore (Bowes & Bowes, 1958), p. 12; Herbert Butterfield, 'Professor Chabod and the Machiavelli Controversies', *The Historical Journal*, vol. 2, issue 1 (1959): 81–3; Viroli, *Niccolò's Smile* (Hill & Wang, 2002), pp. 154–5.

16. Giovanni Sartori, 'What is "Politics"?', *Political Theory*, vol. 1, issue 5 (1973): 10. See Machiavelli, *Il Principe (De Principatibus)*, ed. Brian Richardson (Manchester UP, 1979).

17. See the compelling analysis by Heinrich Kuhn regarding the two references to *De principatibus* in the *Discourses*, in 'Niccolò Machiavelli: A Good State for Bad People', in Paul Richard Blum (ed.), *Philosophers of the Renaissance* (Catholic UP, 2010), p. 119. Although there is a single reference in the *Discourses* to 'De Principe', in book II, chapter 2, Kuhn concludes that this is likely to be an abbreviation. As far as I am aware, no text of Machiavelli's suggests that he ever called his work *Il Principe*.

18. Sayyid Hasan Islami, 'Ethics and Politics Relationship – (Part 1), *Rafed. net*, 16 October 2010, http://en.rafed.net/index.php?option=com_content&view=article&id=3685&catid=78&Itemid=843; see also William T. Bluhm, 'Machiavellian *Virtù* and the Emergence of Freedom Values: Machiavelli, the "Chicago School", and Theories of Group Process', in *Theories of the Political System: Classics of Political Thought and Modern Political Analysis*, 3rd edn (Prentice-Hall, 1978), p. 199. See also Jacques Maritain, 'The End of Machiavellianism', *Review of Politics*, vol. 4, issue 1 (Jan. 1942): 1–33, calling Machiavelli's

separation of ethics and metaphysics from politics 'the most violent mutation suffered by the human practical intellect'; Narayani Basu, 'Morality and the State', *Philological Quarterly*, vol. 25 (1958): 25.

19. '[A]ll these counsels are "hypothetical imperatives . . . there is no question whether the end is rational and good, but only what one must do in order to attain it. The precepts for the physician to make his patient thoroughly healthy, and for a poisoner to ensure certain death, are of equal value in this respect, that each serves to effect its purpose perfectly." These words [of Kant] describe exactly the attitude and method of Machiavelli. He never blames or praises political actions; he simply gives a descriptive analysis of them – in the same way in which a physician describes the symptoms of a certain illness . . . Machiavelli studied political actions in the same way as a chemist studies chemical reactions. Assuredly a chemist who prepares in his laboratory a strong poison is not responsible for its effects. In the hands of a skilled physician the poison may save the life of a man – in the hands of a murderer it may kill. In both cases we cannot praise or blame the chemist.' Ernst Cassirer, *The Myth of the State* (Yale UP, 1946), p. 154.

20. Augustin Renaudet, *Machiavel: Etude d'histoire des doctrines politiques* (Paris, 1942), who argues that a scientific approach was a distinct 'moment' in Machiavelli's thought.

21. Leonardo Olschki, *Machiavelli the Scientist* (Berkeley, CA, 1945); see also 'Machiavelli scienziato', *Pensiero politico*, vol. 2 (1969): 509–35.

22. See Arthur Applbaum, *Ethics for Adversaries: The Morality of Roles in Public and Professional Life* (Princeton UP, 1999); Arthur Applbaum, 'Professional Detachment: The Executioner of Paris', *Harvard Law Review*, vol. 109 (1995): 458–86.

23. Robin West, 'The Zealous Advocacy of Justice in a Less Than Ideal Legal World', *Stanford Law Review*, vol. 51 (1999): 973, 975.

24. Robin Radtke, 'Role Morality in the Accounting Profession: How Do We Compare to Physicians and Attorneys?', *Journal of Business Ethics*, vol. 79 (May 2008): 279.

25. For a persuasive critique see J. Andre, 'Role Morality as a Complex Instance of Ordinary Morality', *American Philosophical Quarterly*, vol. 28 (1991): 73–80.

26. See Daniel Markovits, *A Modern Legal Ethics: Adversary Advocacy in a Democratic Age* (Princeton UP, 2008). See also Gilbert Harman, *The Nature of Morality* (Oxford UP, 1977).

27. See Greg Russell, 'Machiavelli's Science of Statecraft: The Diplomacy and Politics of Disorder', *Diplomacy & Statecraft*, vol. 16, issue 2 (June 2005): 227. Russell casts doubt on the idea that role morality actually captures Machiavelli's understanding and practice of diplomacy.

28. See Leo Gross, 'The Criminality of Aggressive War', *American Political Science Review*, vol. 41, issue 2 (April 1947), distinguishing between illegality and criminality, but rejecting the ex post facto defence on the grounds that any such presumption under international law can be reversed by the international community.

29. Skinner, *Machiavelli: A Very Short Introduction*, p. 42.

30. Hillary Zamora argues that immortality could be earned through glory even if there were no afterlife and suggests that this is how Machiavelli looked at this problem. See 'A World without a Saving Grace: Glory and Immortality in Machiavelli', *History of Political Thought*, vol. 28, issue 3 (Autumn 2007): 449.

31. Cary J. Nederman, 'Amazing Grace: Fortune, God and Free Will in Machiavelli's Thought', *Journal of the History of Ideas*, vol. 60, issue 4 (Oct. 1999): 617; see also Viroli, *Machiavelli's God*.

32. *The Prince*, chapter 18 (emphasis supplied).

33. G. R. Berridge, 'Machiavelli: Human Nature, Good Faith, and Diplomacy', *Review of International Studies*, vol. 27, issue 4 (Oct. 2001): 539.

34. See Hersch Lauterpacht, 'Chapter XIII: The Judicial Application of the Doctrine "Rebus Sic Stantibus"', in *The Function of Law in the International Community* (Oxford UP, 1933). Compare the Vienna Convention on the Law of Treaties, Article 62 (adopted 1969, effective 1980), available at http://untreaty.un.org/ilc/texts/instruments/english/conventions/1_1_1969.pdf. And compare *Discourses*, book III, chapter 2 ('That Promises Extracted by Force Should not be Kept').

35. *Discourses*, book I, chapter 26.

36. United Nations Security Council Resolution 1973 (17 March 2011), available at http://daccess-dds-ny.un.org/doc/UNDOC/GEN/N11/268/39/PDF/N1126839.pdf, authorizing the use of force against Muammar Qaddafi's oppressive regime in Libya.

37. Najemy suggests that Machiavelli's correspondence with Vettori moved him from this position to a more sceptical stance about man's ability to master the 'uncontrollable mutability of events'. See Najemy,

Between Friends: Discourses of Power and Desire in the Machiavelli–Vettori Letters of 1513–1515 (Princeton UP, 1993).

38. I am encouraged in my interpretation by Najemy's persuasive reconstruction of the famous phrase s*i guarda al fine* in *Between Friends*, pp. 187–8.

39. *The Prince*, chapter 25.

40. Felix Gilbert, 'The Concept of Nationalism in Machiavelli's *Prince*', *Studies in the Renaissance*, vol. 1 (1954): 38–48.

41. Sheldon Wolin, *Politics and Vision* (Little, Brown, 1960), pp. 203–4.

42. Hugo Jaeckel, 'What is Machiavelli Exhorting in His Exhortatio? The Extraordinaries', in Jean-Jacques Marchand (ed.), *Niccolò Machiavelli: Politico, Storico, Letterato* (Rome, 1996), pp. 59–84; and Francesco Bausi, 'Petrarca, Machiavelli, *Il Principe*', in Marchand, *op. cit.*, pp. 41–58.

43. Leo Strauss, 'Machiavelli's Intention: *The Prince*', in *Thoughts on Machiavelli* (University of Chicago Press, 1958).

44. Cf. Thomas Berns, 'Knowing the Occasion: Rome and Fortune in Machiavelli', *Graduate Faculty Philosophy Journal*, vol. 28, issue 2 (2007): 89–102.

45. By early 1515 it had become obvious that Leo was determined to make Giuliano 'ruler of the Romagna, and since Paolo Vettori was a good friend of Giuliano, it seems certain that Paolo would be made governor of one of the cities in the new princedom . . . Paolo and Machiavelli began meeting for discussions in Florence, with Machiavelli passing on advice about how the new principality should be ruled. He advised Paolo to follow the example of Cesare Borgia . . . and concentrate on unifying the Romagna into a single state.' Ross King, *Machiavelli: Philosopher of Power*, p. 164.

46. See Machiavelli's letter to Vettori of 10 August 1513, *The Letters of Machiavelli*, ed. and trans. Allan Gilbert (University of Chicago Press, 1988), p. 124.

47. Strauss, 'Machiavelli's Intention: *The Prince*'.

EPILOGUE: SATAN'S THEOLOGIAN

1. Letter from F. Scott Fitzgerald to his daughter Frances Scott Fitzgerald, 1940, collected in Edmund Wilson (ed.), *The Crack-Up* (Scribners, 1945).

2. It is noteworthy that the Obama administration healthcare statute has fallen foul of just this phenomenon. By mandating that every person must purchase healthcare insurance in the market place – rather than setting up a national healthcare service or taxing the public to pay for the purchase of health services – the plan is a typical market-state device. Thus it has antagonized nation-state polities on both sides of the issue: liberals would have preferred a single-payer system (like Britain's NHS), while conservatives are outraged that the freedom to self-insure or not to be insured at all has been taken from them. The market state–nation state divide is thus by no means a left–right issue: when conservatives adopt anti-abortion statutes or anti-pornography laws, they are doing the same sort of thing that liberals do when they propose hate-speech crimes or advocate affirmative-action provisions. They are using the state to promote national values in defiance of the market.

3. In a remarkable body of work John McCormick has developed this point. See, for example, 'Machiavellian Democracy: Controlling Elites with Ferocious Populism', *American Political Science Review*, vol. 95, issue 2 (June 2001); *Machiavellian Democracy* (Cambridge UP, 2011); 'Machiavelli against Republicanism: On the Cambridge School's "Guicciardinian Moments"', *Political Theory*, vol. 31, issue 5 (Oct. 2003): 615.

4. *The Prince*, chapter 17.

5. *The Prince*, chapter 16.

6. *The Prince*, chapter 18.

7. Shunderson's speech to Professor Elwell. *People Will Talk* (1951).

8. See A. J. Parel, 'Machiavelli's Notions of Justice: Text and Analysis', *Political Theory*, vol. 18, issue 4 (Nov. 1990).

ACKNOWLEDGEMENTS

1. Machiavelli, *The Literary Works of Machiavelli: Mandragola, Clizia, A Dialogue on Language, and Belfagor, with Selections from the Private Correspondence*, ed. J. R. Hale (Greenwood, 1979).

2. Richard III is the most Machiavellian of all Shakespeare's characters, with his cynical asides to the audience; but even he has a disfiguring disability from which he unfairly suffers, and which wins him our sympathy.

3. Victoria Kahn, 'Greeks in Florence', in *Times Literary Supplement* (2010), reviewing Capponi's *An Unlikely Prince*, Viroli's *Machiavelli's God*, and Benner's *Machiavelli's Ethics*. In our day, an artful example of this might be found in Harold Pinter's play *Betrayal*, in which the playwright, by reversing the chronology of an adulterous love affair, begins with the man who had betrayed his best friend, confessing that he himself feels betrayed because the best friend never told him he knew about the affair; or perhaps in Tom Stoppard's witty masterpiece *Arcadia*, in which characters are given counterparts in an earlier century (portrayed by the same actors); or in Michael Frayn's *Copenhagen*, in which the same events are described differently by each protagonist some years later.
4. Though it has been argued that Bernardo welcomed exclusion from law practice as a way of maintaining a low, anti-Medici profile; see Robert Black, 'Debts, Dowries, Donkeys: The Diary of Niccolò Machiavelli's Father, Messer Bernardo', in *Quattrocentro Florence English Historical Review*, vol. 118, issue 479 (Nov. 2003): 1368.
5. Victoria Kahn, *Journal of Modern History*, vol. 67, issue 4 (Dec. 1995): 956 (reviewing Najemy's *Between Friends*).
6. Kahn, 'Greeks in Florence'. Again, Kahn renders this lucidly when she observes that 'agency for Machiavelli is always in response to existing necessities, and necessity is not so much an obstacle to action as an inducement for agents to order their own laws and legislate their own freedom'.

Select Bibliography

Machiavelli: The Prince (trans. Russell Price) (Cambridge UP, 2000).

The Prince (trans. Peter Bonadella) (Oxford UP, 2008).

The Prince (trans. Peter Constantine) (Modern Library, 2008).

The Prince (trans. Harvey C. Mansfield) (University of Chicago Press, 2nd edn, 1998).

The Prince (trans. David Wootton) (Hackett, 1995).

Discourses on Livy (trans. Harvey C. Mansfield and Nathan Tarcov) (University of Chicago Press, 1996).

Discourses on Livy (trans. Julia Conway Bonadella and Peter Bonadella) (Oxford UP, 2009).

Machiavelli: The Chief Works and Others (trans. and ed. Allan Gilbert), 3 vols (Duke UP, 1989).

The Essential Writings of Machiavelli (trans. Peter Constantine) (Modern Library, 2009).

Andre, J., 'Role Morality as a Complex Instance of Ordinary Morality', *American Philosophical Quarterly*, vol. 28 (1991): 73–80.

Applbaum, Arthur Isak, *Ethics for Adversaries: The Morality of Roles in Public and Professional Life* (Princeton: Princeton UP, 1999).

Applbaum, Arthur Isak, 'Professional Detachment: The Executioner of Paris', *Harvard Law Review*, vol. 109 (1995): 458–86.

Ascoli, Albert Russell, 'Review: *Between Friends: Discourses on Power and Desire in the Machiavelli–Vettori Letters of 1513–1515*', *Speculum*, vol. 70, issue 4 (Oct. 1995): 952–5.

Atkinson, James B., and David Sices, eds., *Machiavelli and His Friends: Their Personal Correspondence* (Dekalb, IL: Northern Illinois UP, 1996).

Austin, Kenneth, 'Review: *Well-Ordered License: On the Unity of Machiavelli's Thought'*, *Sixteenth Century Journal,* vol. 33, issue 2 (2002): 539–40.

Balaban, Oded, 'The Human Origins of Fortuna in Machiavelli's Thought', *History of Political Thought,* vol. 11, issue 1 (1990): 21–36.

Baron, Hans, 'The *Principe* and the Puzzle of the Date of Chapter 26', *Journal of Medieval and Renaissance Studies,* vol. 21, issue 1 (1991): 83–102.

Basu, Narayani, 'Morality and the State', *Philological Quarterly,* vol. 25 (1958): 25–8.

Bausi, Francesco, 'Petrarca, Machiavelli, *Il Principe*', in Jean-Jacques Marchand, ed., *Niccolò Machiavelli: Politico, Storico, Letterato* (Rome: Salerno Editrice, 1996): 41–58.

Bawcutt, N. W., 'The "Myth of Gentillet" Reconsidered: An Aspect of Elizabethan Machiavellianism', *Modern Language Review,* vol. 99, issue 4 (Oct. 2004): 863–74.

Belliotti, Raymond A., 'Machiavelli and Machiavellianism', *Journal of Thought,* vol. 13 (Nov. 1978): 293–300

Benner, Erica, *Machiavelli's Ethics* (Princeton: Princeton UP, 2009).

Berlin, Isaiah, *The Proper Study of Mankind: An Anthology of Essays* (New York: Farrar, Straus & Giroux, 1997): 269–325.

Berns, Thomas, 'Knowing the Occasion: Rome and Fortune in Machiavelli', *Graduate Faculty Philosophy Journal,* vol. 28, issue 2 (2007): 89–102.

Berridge, G. R., 'Machiavelli: Human Nature, Good Faith, and Diplomacy', *Review of International Studies,* vol. 27, issue 4 (Oct. 2001): 539–56.

Bertelli, Sergio, 'Machiavelli and Soderini', *Renaissance Quarterly,* vol. 28, issue 1 (Spring 1975): 1–16.

Black, Robert, 'Debts, Dowries, Donkeys: The Diary of Niccolò Machiavelli's Father, Messer Bernardo', in *Quattrocentro Florence English Historical Review,* vol. 118, issue 479 (Nov. 2003): 1368–70.

Bluhm, William T., *Theories of the Political System: Classics of Political Thought and Modern Political Analysis,* 3rd edn (New York: Prentice-Hall, 1978).

Bobbitt, Philip, *Constitutional Fate: Theory of the Constitution* (New York: Oxford UP, 1982).

Bobbitt, Philip, *Constitutional Interpretation* (Oxford: Blackwells, 1992).

Bobbitt, Philip, *Terror and Consent: The Wars for the Twenty-First Century* (New York: Knopf, 2008).

Bobbitt, Philip, *The Shield of Achilles: War, Peace, and the Course of History* (New York: Knopf, 2002).

Bock, Gisela et al., *Machiavelli and Republicanism* (Cambridge: Cambridge UP, 1990).

Bodin, Jean, *Six Books of the Commonwealth* (Oxford: Basil Blackwell, 1955).

Bondanella, Peter E., *Machiavelli and the Art of Renaissance History* (Detroit: Wayne State UP, 1971).

Bondanella, Peter E. and Mark Musa, eds. and trans., *The Portable Machiavelli* (New York: Penguin, 1971).

Bookman, John T., 'Machiavelli Scholarship: An Essay and List of Works in English', *Philosophy Research Archives* 9 (1537) (1983).

Broad, C. D., *Five Types of Ethical Theory* (New York: Harcourt & Brace, 1930).

Butterfield, Herbert, 'Professor Chabod and the Machiavelli Controversies', *Historical Journal*, vol. 2, issue 1 (March 1959): 78–83.

Calabresi, Guido, and Philip Bobbitt, *Tragic Choices* (New York: Norton, 1978).

Capponi, Niccolò, *An Unlikely Prince: The Life and Times of Machiavelli* (Cambridge, MA: Da Capo, 2010).

Cassidy, Ben, 'Machiavelli and the Ideology of the Offensive: Gunpowder Weapons in the *Art of War*', *Journal of Military History*, vol. 67, issue 2 (April 2003): 381–404.

Cassirer, Ernst, *The Myth of the State* (New Haven: Yale UP, 1946).

Chabod, Federico, *Machiavelli and the Renaissance*, trans. David Moore (Cambridge: Bowes & Bowes, 1958).

Cicero, Marcus Tullius, *On Duties*, ed. E. M. Atkins, trans. Miriam T. Griffin (Cambridge: Cambridge UP, 1991).

Colish, Marcia L., 'Cicero's "De Officiis" and Machiavelli's "Prince"', *Sixteenth Century Journal*, vol. 9, issue 4 (Winter 1968): 80–93.

Cooper, Robert, *The Breaking of Nations: Order and Chaos in the 21st Century* (New York: Atlantic, 2003).

Cooper, Roslyn Pesman, 'Machiavelli, Francesco Soderini and Don Michelotto', *Nuovo Rivista Storica*, vol. 66, issue 3/4 (Sept. 1982): 342–57.

Cover, Robert, *Narrative, Violence, and the Law: The Essays of Robert Corver* (Ann Arbor: University of Michigan Press, 1995).

Cover, Robert M., *Justice Accused* (New Haven: Yale UP, 1975).

D'Andrea, Antonio, 'The Political and Ideological Context of Innocent Gentillet's Anti-Machiavel', *Renaissance Quarterly*, vol. 23, issue 4 (Winter 1970): 397–411.

De Grazia, Sebastian, *Machiavelli in Hell* (New York: Vintage, 1994).

Del Lucchese, Filippo, 'Crisis and Power: Economics, Politics and Conflict in Machiavelli's Political Thought', *History of Political Thought*, vol. 30, issue 1 (Spring 2009): 75–96.

Dietz, Mary, 'Trapping the Prince: Machiavelli and the Politics of Deception', *American Political Science Review*, vol. 80, issue 3 (Sept. 1986): 777–99.

DiMaria, Salvatore, 'Machiavelli's Ironic View of History: The "Istorie Fiorentine"', *Renaissance Quarterly*, vol. 45, issue 2 (Summer 1992): 248–70.

Dixon, M. F. N., *The Polliticke Courtier: Spenser's* The Faerie Queene *as a Rhetoric of Justice* (Montreal: McGill-Queen's UP, 1996).

Donaldson, Peter, *Machiavelli and Mystery of State* (Cambridge: Cambridge UP, 1992).

Eldar, Dan, 'Glory and the boundaries of public morality in Machiavelli's thought', *History of Political Thought*, vol. 7, issue 3 (Winter 1986): 419–38.

Erwin, Sean, 'A War of One's Own: Mercenaries and the Theme of Arma Aliena in Machiavelli's *Il Principe*', *British Journal for the History of Philosophy*, vol. 18, issue 4 (Sept. 2010): 541–74.

Ferguson, Niall, *The Ascent of Money: A Financial History of the World* (London: Allen Lane, 2008).

Ferguson, Niall, *The Cash Nexus: Money and Power in the Modern World, 1700–2000* (London: Allen Lane, 2001).

Fitzgerald, Desmond, 'Machiavelli and History', *Proceedings of the American Catholic Philosophical Association*, vol. 43 (1969): 121–9.

Fitzgerald, F. Scott, *The Crack-Up*, ed. Edmund Wilson (New York: Scribners, 1945).

Garver, Eugene, 'After "Virtù": Rhetoric, Prudence and Moral Pluralism in Machiavelli', *History of Political Thought*, vol. 17, issue 2 (Summer 1996): 195–222.

Garver, Eugene, 'Machiavelli and the Politics of Rhetorical Invention', *Clio*, vol. 14, issue 2 (Winter 1985): 157–78.

Garver, Eugene, 'Machiavelli: Rhetoric and Prudence', in Patricia Vilches and Gerald Seaman, eds., *Seeking Real Truths: Multidisciplinary Perspectives on Machiavelli* (Leiden: Brill, 2007): 103–22.

Gat, Azar, 'Machiavelli and the Decline of the Classical Notion of the Lessons of History in the Study of War', *Military Affairs*, vol. 57 (Oct. 1988): 203–5.

Gilbert, Felix, 'Bernardo Rucellai and the Orti Oricellari: A Study on the Origin of Modern Political Thought', *Journal of the Warburg and Courtauld Institutes*, vol. 12 (1949): 101–31.

Gilbert, Felix, *Machiavelli and Guicciardini: Politics and History in Sixteenth-Century Florence* (Princeton: Princeton UP, 1965).

Gilbert, Felix, 'Machiavelli: The Renaissance in the Art of War', in Peter Paret, ed., *Makers of Modern Strategy: From Machiavelli to the Nuclear Age* (Princeton: Princeton UP, 1986): 11–31.

Gilbert, Felix, 'The Composition and Structure of Machiavelli's *Discorsi*', *Journal of the History of Ideas*, vol. 14, issue 1 (1953): 137–56.

Gilbert, Felix, 'The Concept of Nationalism in Machiavelli's *Prince*', *Studies in the Renaissance*, vol. 1 (1954): 38–48.

Ginzburg, Carlo, 'Pontano, Machiavelli and Prudence: Some Further Reflections', in Curto, Diogo Ramada et al., eds., *From Florence to the Mediterranean and Beyond: Essays in Honour of Anthony Molho* (Florence: Olschki, 2009): 117–26.

Goss, Tracy, *The Last Word on Power: Re-invention for Leaders and Anyone Who Must Make the Impossible Happen* (New York: Doubleday, 1996).

Gray, John, *Hayek on Liberty*, 3rd edn (London: Routledge, 1998).

Gross, Leo, 'The Criminality of Aggressive War', *American Political Science Review*, vol. 41, issue 2 (April 1947): 205–25.

Hale, J. R., *Machiavelli and Renaissance Italy* (London: English Universities Press, 1961).

Hancock, Curtis L., 'Cicero Versus Machiavelli: Does the End Justify the Means?', *Contemporary Philosophy*, vol. 16, issue 6 (Nov.–Dec. 1994): 14–18.

Harman, Gilbert, *The Nature of Morality* (New York: Oxford UP, 1977).

Haywood, Eric, 'Touring the Hall of Fame', *Review of Politics*, vol. 62, issue 4 (Autumn 2000): 833–5.

Hibbert, Christopher, *The House of Medici: Its Rise and Fall* (New York: Morrow, 1999).

Hobbes, Thomas, *Leviathan* (Cambridge: Cambridge UP, 2009).

Hörnqvist, Mikael, '*Perché non si usa allegare i Romani*: Machiavelli and the Florentine militia of 1506', *Renaissance Quarterly*, vol. 55, issue 1 (2002): 148–91.

Hulliung, Mark, *Citizen Machiavelli* (Princeton: Princeton UP, 1983).

Islami, Sayyid Hasan, 'Ethics and Politics Relationship – Part 1', *Rafed.net*,

16 October 2010, http://en.rafed.net/index.php?option=com_content &view=article&id=3685&catid=78&Itemid=843.

Jaeckel, Hugo, 'What is Machiavelli Exhorting in His Exhortatio? The Extraordinaries', in Jean-Jacques Marchand, ed., *Niccolò Machiavelli: Politico, Storico, Letterato* (Rome: Salerno Editrice, 1996): 59–84.

Kahn, Victoria, 'Greeks in Florence', in *Times Literary Supplement*, 19 Dec. 2010.

Kahn, Victoria, 'Reading Machiavelli: Innocent Gentillet's Discourse on Method', *Political Theory*, vol. 22, issue 4 (Nov. 1994): 539–60.

Kahn, Victoria, 'Review: *Between Friends: Discourses of Power and Desire in the Machiavelli–Vettori Letters of 1513–1515*', *Journal of Modern History*, vol. 67, issue 4 (Dec. 1995): 956–7.

Kahn, Victoria, '*Virtù* and the Example of Agathocles in Machiavelli's *Prince*', *Representations*, vol. 13 (Winter 1986): 63–83.

Kane, Thomas, 'Building Thrones: Political Effect as an Emerging Principle of War', *Comparative Strategy*, vol. 24, issue 5 (Dec. 2005): 431–8.

Kaplan, Robert, 'Beware the Void under Tyranny', *Financial Times*, 6 April 2011.

Kececi, Dilek, 'Satan as the Machiavellian Hero in "Paradise Lost"', *Ethos: Dialogues in Philosophy and Social Sciences*, vol. 2, issue 1 (Jan. 2009): 1–7.

Khoury, Joseph, 'Marlowe's Tamburlaine: Idealized Machiavellian Prince', in Patricia Vilches and Gerald Seaman, eds., *Seeking Real Truths: Multidisciplinary Perspectives on Machiavelli* (Leiden: Brill, 2007): 329–56.

King, Ross, *Machiavelli: Philosopher of Power* (New York: Atlas Books/ HarperCollins, 2007).

Kissinger, Henry, *The White House Years* (New York: Little, Brown, 1979).

Kubik, Timothy R. W., 'Is Machiavelli's Cannon Spiked?', *Journal of Military History*, vol. 61, issue 1 (Jan. 1997): 7–30.

Kuhn, Heinrich, 'Niccolò Machiavelli: A Good State for Bad People', in Paul Richard Blum, ed., *Philosophers of the Renaissance* (Washington: Catholic UP, 2010): 116–23.

Lauterpacht, Hersch, *The Function of Law in the International Community* (Oxford: Oxford UP, 1933).

Leslie, Margaret, 'In Defense of Anachronism', *Political Studies*, vol. 8, issue 4 (Dec. 1970): 433–47.

Levinson, Sanford, *Our Undemocratic Constitution: Where the Constitution Goes Wrong (And How We the People Can Correct It)* (New York: Oxford, 2006).

Lukes, Timothy J., 'Descending to the Particulars: The Piazza and Machiavelli's Republican Modes and Orders', *Journal of Politics*, vol. 71, issue 2 (April 2009): 520–32.

Lukes, Timothy J., 'Martialing Machiavelli: Reassessing the Military Reflections', *Journal of Politics*, vol. 66, issue 4 (Nov. 2004): 1089–1108.

Lukes, Timothy J., 'Lionizing Machiavelli', *American Political Science Review*, vol. 95, issue 3 (Sept. 2001): 561–75.

McCormick, John P., 'Machiavelli against Republicanism: On the Cambridge School's "Guicciardinian Moments"', *Political Theory*, vol. 31, issue 5 (Oct. 2003): 615–43.

McCormick, John P., *Machiavellian Democracy* (Cambridge: Cambridge UP, 2011).

McCormick, John, 'Machiavellian Democracy: Controlling Elites with Ferocious Populism', *American Political Science Review*, vol. 95, issue 2 (June 2001): 297–313.

Machiavelli, Niccolò, *I Primi Scritti Politici*, ed. Jean-Jacques Marchand (Padua: Antenore, 1975).

Machiavelli, Niccolò, *Il Principe (De Principatibus)*, ed. Brian Richardson (Manchester: Manchester UP, 1979).

Machiavelli, Niccolò, *The Literary Works of Machiavelli: Mandragola, Clizia, A Dialogue on Language, and Belfagor, with Selections from the Private Correspondence*, ed. J. R. Hale (Westport, CT: Greenwood, 1979).

Manning, John F., 'The Absurdity Doctrine', *Harvard Law Review*, vol. 116 (2003): 2387–486.

Mansfield, Harvey C., *Machiavelli's New Modes and Orders: A Study of the 'Discourses on Livy'* (Ithaca: Cornell UP, 1979).

Mansfield, Harvey C., *Machiavelli's Virtue* (Chicago: University of Chicago Press, 1996).

Mansfield, Harvey C., 'Review: *Machiavelli*', *American Political Science Review*, vol. 93, issue 4 (1999): 964–5.

Maritain, Jacques, 'The End of Machiavellianism', *Review of Politics*, vol. 4, issue 1 (Jan. 1942): 1–33.

Markovits, Daniel, *A Modern Legal Ethics: Adversary Advocacy in a Democratic Age* (Princeton: Princeton UP, 2008).

Marlowe, Christopher, *The Jew of Malta* (New York: Dover, 2003).

Masters, Roger D., *Fortune Is a River: Leonardo Da Vinci and Niccolò*

Machiavelli's Magnificent Dream to Change the Course of Florentine History (New York: Plume, 1999).

Masters, Roger D., *Machiavelli, Leonardo, and the Science of Power* (Notre Dame, IN: Notre Dame Press, 1995).

Mattingly, Garrett, 'Machiavelli's "Prince": Political Science or Political Satire?', *The American Scholar*, vol. 27 (1958): 482–91.

Minter, Adam, 'Machiavelli, Violence and History', *Harvard Review of Philosophy*, vol. 2, issue 1 (Spring 1992): 25–33.

Nagel, Thomas, 'War and Massacre', *Philosophy & Public Affairs*, vol. 1 (1972): 123–44.

Najemy, John M., *Between Friends: Discourses of Power and Desire in the Machiavelli–Vettori Letters of 1513–1515* (Princeton: Princeton UP, 1993).

Najemy, John M., ed., *The Cambridge Companion to Machiavelli* (Cambridge: Cambridge UP, 2010).

Nederman, Cary J., 'Amazing Grace: Fortune, God and Free Will in Machiavelli's Thought', *Journal of the History of Ideas*, vol. 60, issue 4 (Oct. 1999): 617–38.

Nederman, Cary J., 'Machiavelli and Moral Character: Principality, Republic and the Psychology of "Virtù"', *History of Political Thought*, vol. 21, issue 3 (Autumn 2000): 349–64.

Nederman, Cary J., 'Niccolò Machiavelli', in *Stanford Encyclopedia of Philosophy* (Autumn 2009 edition), ed. Edward N. Zalta, accessible at http://plato.stanford.edu.

Nederman, Cary J., 'The Renaissance of a Renaissance Man', *European Legacy*, vol. 4, issue 5 (Oct. 1999): 102–5.

Neely, Jr., Mark E., *The Fate of Liberty: Abraham Lincoln and Civil Liberties* (Oxford: Oxford UP, 1991).

Norton, Paul E., 'Machiavelli's Road to Paradise: "The Exhortation to Penitence"', *History of Political Thought*, vol. 4 (Spring 1983): 31–42.

Olschki, Leonardo, 'Machiavelli scienziato', *Pensiero politico*, vol. 2 (1969): 509–35.

Olschki, Leonardo, *Machiavelli the Scientist* (Berkeley, CA: Gillick, 1945).

Oppenheimer, Paul, *Machiavelli: A Life Beyond Ideology* (London: Continuum, 2011).

Parel, A. J., 'Machiavelli's Notions of Justice: Text and Analysis', *Political Theory*, vol. 18, issue 4 (Nov. 1990): 528–44.

Parent, Joseph M., 'Machiavelli's Missing Romulus and the Murderous Intent of "The Prince"', *History of Political Thought*, vol. 26, issue 4 (Winter 2005): 625–45.

Parkinson, G. H. R., 'Ethics and Politics in Machiavelli', *Philosophical Quarterly*, vol. 5 (Jan. 1955): 37–44.

Pellerin, Daniel, 'Machiavelli's Best Friend', *History of Political Thought*, vol. 27, issue 3 (Autumn 2006): 423–53.

Phillips, Mark, 'Representation and Argument in Florentine Historiography', *Storia della storiografia*, issue 10 (1986): 48–63.

Plaw, Avery, 'Prince Harry: Shakespeare's Critique of Machiavelli', *Interpretation*, vol. 33, issue 1 (Fall/Winter 2005): 19–44.

Pocock, J. G. A., *The Machiavellian Moment: Florentine Political Thought and the Atlantic Republican Tradition* (Princeton: Princeton UP, 1975).

Pontano, Giovanni, 'De Principe', in E. Garin, ed., *Prosatori Latini del Quattrocento* (Milan: Riccardo Ricciardi, 1952): 1021–67.

Quintilian, *Institutio Oratoria*, trans. H. E. Butler (Cambridge, MA: Harvard UP, 1920).

Radtke, Robin, 'Role Morality in the Accounting Profession: How Do We Compare to Physicians and Attorneys?', *Journal of Business Ethics*, vol. 79 (May 2008): 279–97.

Rahe, Paul A., ed., *Machiavelli's Liberal Republican Legacy* (New York: Cambridge UP, 2006).

Renaudet, Augustin, *Machiavel; Étude d'histoire des doctrines politiques* (Paris: Gallimard, 1942).

Reston, James, *Dogs of God* (New York: Anchor, 2006).

Ridolfi, Roberto, *Life of Niccolò Machiavelli*, trans. Cecil Grayson (Chicago: University of Chicago Press, 1963).

Riebling, Barbara, 'Milton on Machiavelli: Representations of the State in *Paradise Lost*', *Renaissance Quarterly*, vol. 49, issue 3 (Autumn 1996): 573–97.

Roazen, Paul, 'A Partnership of Geniuses?', *American Scholar*, vol. 67, issue 4 (Autumn 1998): 141–3.

Russell, Greg, 'Machiavelli's Science of Statecraft: The Diplomacy and Politics of Disorder', *Diplomacy & Statecraft*, vol. 16, issue 2 (June 2005): 227–50.

Salter, F. M., 'Skelton's *Speculum Principis*', *Speculum*, vol. 9 (1934): 25–37.

Sartori, Giovanni, 'What is "Politics"?', *Political Theory*, vol. 1, issue 1 (1973): 5–26.

Sasso, Gennaro, *Machiavelli e Cesare Borgia* (Rome: Edizioni Dell'Ateneo, 1966).

Scaglione, Aldo, 'Review: *Discourses on Machiavelli*', *Modern Language Quarterly*, vol. 32, issue 2 (June 1971): 214–18

Sereno, Renzo, 'A Falsification by Machiavelli', *Renaissance News*, vol. 12, issue 3 (1959): 159–67.

Shaw, C. K. Y., 'Quentin Skinner on the Proper Meaning of Republican Liberty', *Politics*, vol. 23, issue 1 (Feb. 2003): 46–56.

Shell International Ltd., *Shell Global Scenarios to 2025: Trends, Trade-Offs, and Choices* (London: Shell, 2005).

Skinner, Quentin, *Machiavelli: A Very Short Introduction* (Oxford: Oxford UP, 2000).

Skinner, Quentin, *The Foundations of Modern Political Thought, Volume 1: The Renaissance* (Cambridge: Cambridge UP, 1978).

Stephens, J. N., 'Ciceronian Rhetoric and the Immorality of Machiavelli's Prince', *Renaissance Studies*, vol. 2, issue 2 (Oct. 1988): 258–67.

Strathern, Paul, 'Machiavelli, Leonardo and Borgia: A Fateful Collusion', *History Today*, vol. 59, issue 3 (March 2009): 15–19.

Strauss, Leo, *Thoughts on Machiavelli* (Chicago: University of Chicago Press, 1958).

Thayer, Lee, 'Review: *Machiavelli and the History of Prudence*', *Clio*, vol. 17, issue 3 (Spring 1988): 309.

Unger, Miles, *Machiavelli: A Biography* (New York: Simon & Schuster, 2011).

Vilches, Patricia, 'Review: *Discourses on Livy by Niccolò Machiavelli*', *Sixteenth Century Journal*, vol. 36, issue 1 (Spring 2005): 265–7.

Villalon, Andrew, 'Machiavelli's "Prince": Political Science or Political Satire? Garrett Mattingly Revisited', *Mediterranean Studies*, vol. 12 (2003): 73–101.

Villari, Pasquale, *Life and Times of Niccolò Machiavelli*, trans. Linda Villari (London: Scholarly Press, 1972)

Viroli, Maurizio, 'Books in Review', *Political Theory*, vol. 19, issue 2 (May 1991): 292–3.

Viroli, Maurizio, *How to Read Machiavelli* (London: Granta UK, 2008).

Viroli, Maurizio, *Machiavelli* (Oxford: Oxford UP, 1998).

Viroli, Maurizio, *Niccolò's Smile* (New York: Hill & Wang, 2002).

Viroli, Maurizio, and Antony Shugaar, *Machiavelli's God* (Princeton: Princeton UP, 2010).

Walzer, Michael, 'Political Action: The Problem of Dirty Hands', in Sanford Levinson, ed., *Torture* (Oxford: Oxford UP, 2004): 61–77.

Watson, Adam, *The Evolution of International Society: A Comparative Historical Analysis* (London: Routledge, 1992).

Weissberger, L. Arnold, 'Machiavelli and Tudor England', *Political Science Quarterly* 42 (1927): 589–607.

West, Robin, 'The Zealous Advocacy of Justice in a Less than Ideal Legal World', *Stanford Law Review*, vol. 51 (1999): 973–89.

Whitfield, J. H., *Discourses on Machiavelli* (Cambridge: Heffer, 1969).

Whitfield, J. H., 'On Machiavelli's Use of *Ordini*', *Italian Studies*, vol. 10 (1955): 19–39.

William E. Wiethoff, 'The Martial "Virtue" of Rhetoric in Machiavelli's *Art of War*', *Quarterly Journal of Speech*, vol. 64, issue 3 (Oct. 1978): 304–12.

Winkler, Mary G., 'Prophets of Modernity', *Hastings Center Report*, vol. 28, issue 2 (March/April 1998): 43–4.

Wolin, Sheldon, *Politics and Vision* (New York: Little, Brown, 1960).

Wood, Neal, 'Mansfield on Machiavelli', *Philosophy of the Social Sciences*, vol. 15, issue 1 (1985): 45–52.

Zamora, Hillary, 'A World without a Saving Grace: Glory and Immortality in Machiavelli', *History of Political Thought*, vol. 28, issue 3 (Autumn 2007): 449–68.

A Note on the Author

PHILIP BOBBITT IS the Herbert Wechsler Professor of Federal Jurisprudence at Columbia University and Distinguished Senior Lecturer at the University of Texas at Austin. He has served as a senior official at the White House, the State Department and the National Security Council, in both Republican and Democratis administrations. He is a fellow of the American Academy for Arts and Sciences and has written seminal works in constitutional theory, diplomatic history and social choice. *Terror and Consent*, published in 2008, was a *New York Times* and *Evening Standard* bestseller. He lives in New York, Austin and London.

Index